The Art of Discussion

How to have better conversations

James Wyatt

Clink Street

Published by Clink Street Publishing 2021

Copyright © 2021

First edition.

ISBN:
978-1-913568-98-6 - paperback
978-1-913568-99-3 - ebook

Dear Stephane

Many thanks
for buying the
book and the
many fascinating
discussions at
the Crick.

James

This book is dedicated to my dear husband, who has taught me so much.

He inspires me with his hunger to learn and his unconstrained ambition to achieve his dreams; and

then he educates me with his extraordinary brain and unique perspective.

He motivates me with his endless love and support and his constant encouragement; and

then he challenges me with his critical insight and eye for perfection.

Without these great qualities, this book would never have taken shape; and

I am incredibly grateful for all he has done and all he continues to do to enhance my life.

Contents

CHAPTER 1

The Opinions that Prevent Progress

It's mind-blowing how things have changed in my lifetime. Thinking back to my childhood in the 1980s, who could possibly have imagined the world we are now living in? We used to watch cardboard sci-fi films, where we would laugh at the incredulity of video phones, and now we have them in our pockets! And whilst it is easy to focus on the technological advancement, I am more amazed how the developments have shifted our perspectives. Growing up in a small middle-class town in the pre-internet era, I was blind to the big world out there; but now the digital age and the resulting globalisation has connected us directly with it. This has opened our minds to a multitude of different ideas, cultures and concepts, and as Western culture has become increasingly liberal and diverse, our freedom of expression has transformed. There is still plenty to be done to eliminate discrimination, as preference for our "own kind" is still prevalent and cultural expectations continue to reinforce the "normal" path. However, as a rule, there is much increased tolerance of the differences between people and considerably greater freedom to live our lives in the way we choose. We have certainly come a long way.

If you had told me this was going to happen and I had actually believed you, then I would have guessed that this broadened understanding and greater tolerance would have helped us to get on better with each other. I would have presumed that increased appreciation of our differing perspectives would lead to improvements in the quality of our interactions and enable deeper and more empathetic conversations. This is what I would have anticipated, but sadly, this is not what we see. Strong opinions and our stubborn, defensive mindsets result in a failure to listen to what others have to say. As a result, we simply do not learn from the diverse perspectives and invaluable insight that surrounds us. Our connected world should be bringing us closer together, but the sad reality is that our polarised opinions and dysfunctional conversations are keeping us apart, as debates become increasingly confrontational. *The Art of Discussion* has never been more important.

In the past, sparring between exaggerated characters used to be the preserve of light entertainment. Whilst we were laughing at the hilarious squabbles in Laurel & Hardy or Tom & Jerry or the bullying fighting in Punch & Judy or *Fawlty Towers*, the corresponding news programmes were a model of factual seriousness. We brought in experts to inform us, and we actually listened to them! Nowadays, the lines between entertainment and news reporting have blurred. The growth in channels and 24-hour news has driven increasing competition for audiences, such that serious journalism has evolved into infotainment. The media seem to seek the most extreme and intransigent views in the belief that this will deliver the slapstick fights and comedic jousting that will maximise the entertainment value. This may attract more viewers, but shouldn't we discuss serious topics with a bit more intelligence? Shooting down the other person's perspective is easy, and if done charismatically can be both funny and scarily effective. But beyond establishing that two parties are not in agreement, it gets us nowhere in terms of understanding. As a result, in a world where we should have all the information at our fingertips, discussions are leaving us dangerously uninformed.

The perfect example of this was provided by the backdrop to the UK's momentous decision to leave the European Union

(EU). Once the decision was handed to the voting public, the information at our disposal became all important as we faced the unenviable dilemma of picking between two opposing choices. We may have been pro-European but feeling uncomfortable about the direction or accountability of the EU, or anti-Europe but wary of the economic risks that leaving may bring. We may have held other views that meant we were sympathetic to both sides, but there was no "best of both worlds" option to represent us. All these people in the middle needed some insight to help them decide which way to step. These were the critical people, the swing voters who would sway the result, so you would have hoped for sensible discussions that focused on them, understanding their predicament, and empathising with their conflicting opinions. You would have thought that the leaders on both sides would have relished the opportunity to inform those in the middle to help push them in their direction and achieve the result they wanted. Sadly not!

The politicians decided to give extreme opinions at either end of the spectrum. The "Remainers" chose the path of an apocalyptic economic forecast, claimed that everything that was good around social policy and international cooperation came purely from the EU and accused anyone who did not agree of being isolationist and xenophobic. These were not exactly arguments to resonate with those in the middle. On the other hand, the "Brexiteers" encouraged us to stem the terrifying wave of immigration, produced spuriously dodgy financial calculations and economic projections containing holes the size of a bus and just dismissed the pro-Europe arguments as "Project Fear". These statements were equally implausible to the uncertain floating voters. The extreme and oversimplified arguments managed only to reinforce the opinions of those who had already decided to vote a certain way, and helped to stir up bitterness and antagonism between people who had lived together happily with their quietly contrary opinions for so long. Outside this increasing nastiness, those in the middle were left in a factual vacuum and had to make a judgement based purely on emotion and gut feeling. It's just lucky that it wasn't an important decision!!!!!

The Brexit debate may have been a particularly clear example of our failings in discussing important subjects, but in the world of politics, this is certainly not an isolated case. Most campaigning is based on oversimplified messaging as if it is a battle between good and evil. Viewpoints are not based on fact and logical argument, but slogan and emotion. In fact, things have got so bad that the 2016 Oxford English Word of the Year was post-truth, the definition of which is:

> relating to or denoting circumstances in which objective facts are less influential in shaping public opinion than appeals to emotion and personal belief

... with Brexit and the election of Donald Trump highlighted as clear examples of this concept. It is true that both campaigns were dominated by fact-free arguments from both sides, but I do wonder whether this is a particularly new phenomenon. Throughout my adult life, politicians have been evading questions, employing spin doctors to help present things in a misleading but favourable light and taking full advantage of "lies, damned lies and statistics". The only real difference is that our current digital age has brought greater transparency and we are increasingly aware of what is happening in the murky corridors of power. Putting it simply, we have a lot more information, and in theory, this should leave us more informed and aware of what is going on in the world.

It should, but it hasn't! Whilst the digital age has opened our eyes, it has also created more opportunities for emotive messaging and slick presentations to influence us. In other words, a good sales job is increasingly powerful! And it is this dichotomy that is the real travesty. As the facts have increasingly extended into the public domain, we have allowed the power of media, celebrity and image to take centre stage, such that the facts have become a complete sideshow in the way we communicate, and as a result, in the way we make decisions.

So why do I find this quite so infuriating? I suspect it's largely because a much more balanced approach was drilled into me through some key elements of my upbringing. The first main influence was my father who pretty much managed his life using the concept of "pros and cons". Faced with any difficult or important decision, he would literally draw a line down a page and list out the reasons for and against something to help choose his course of action. Granted, this can be a bit of a crude approach in some circumstances. However, it planted a critically important concept in my mind, and that was the importance and benefit of evaluating both sides of the argument with an open mind. Rather than rely on instincts or gut feeling that may be based on erroneous preconceptions, it encouraged me to consider the facts and competing arguments and to properly think things through. To this very day, whilst I may not use a physical piece of paper, I mentally apply this approach all the time.

The second main influence was the time I spent listening to late-night talk shows on BBC Radio 5, when I had difficulties falling asleep as a young adult. The shows would regularly have guests in the studio but devoted a huge amount of time to listeners calling in and sharing their views. As a result, I would get to hear a vast range of contrasting opinions on various issues. Tucked up in bed, with the sleep mode on and the remote control far away, I would listen to the views, whether I agreed with them or not. I found it absolutely fascinating to hear their thoughts, under the guidance of an impartial presenter, who focused on making sure that the listeners had the chance to get their views across, irrespective of whether he agreed with them or not. Whilst in a conversation, I would probably have interrupted and shared my opinion, I did not have this option. Rather than being irritating, this felt hugely empowering as it forced me to listen, and as a result, it enabled me to learn – well until I fell asleep! As well as helping me to realise how much

I could learn from the remarkable diversity of opinions in the world, the fascinating discussions taught me one other thing. They taught me that a poorly constructed argument in support of my own opinion was far more exasperating than anything an opponent could say.

Ultimately, these facets of my upbringing planted the seeds in my mind that I should get the facts on the table, evaluate both sides of the argument with an open mind and be willing to listen to and learn from people with different views. Thinking about this now, these are excellent foundations for a constructive discussion! But as we all know, this is not as easy as it sounds. Away from the radio, I didn't manage to get the same diversity of opinion or put the same effort into listening. Moreover, with my background in mathematics, my geekish mind couldn't quite comprehend why everyone else wasn't as excited by the facts and the numbers as I was. Failing to connect with others, I often felt like the embattled man in a Monty Python sketch who pays to have an argument. We can all feel his frustration as it descends into the mindless contradiction that we see so much nowadays. In valiantly trying to elevate the quality of the discussion, he points out that contradiction is just "the automatic gainsaying of anything the other person says", while an argument is "an intellectual process" that involves "a connected series of statements intended to establish a proposition". He paid for an argument, and that is what he wants! Unfortunately, our poor hero can't elevate things out of pantomime world, and he doesn't manage to induce a response that is any more intelligent than, "No it isn't!" I know how he feels!

Fortunately, I have learned a lot over the years, and managed to escape from the Monty Python blueprint. The steady broadening in the diversity of my circle of friends has been a key factor in this, as I have learned so much from them and it has really helped me to appreciate the different ways people think, and the different ideas that they have. This has not only helped me personally but has also had a huge impact professionally as it has helped me navigate the complex world of business. Whilst I certainly have not lost my enthusiasm for a bit of number-crunching, I have realised that my complicated spreadsheets and detailed analysis are only of interest to me and my fellow bean counters. What matters is not the numbers themselves, but how I can bring them to life in the subsequent discussions and use them to guide and inform the decisions that are taken. I know I do not always have the operational expertise, the strategic knowledge or the market understanding that the business experts may hold, so I can't make the decisions for them. But I can bring insight and information that empowers them to make the right choices, and the conversations that we have make both of us stronger. Ultimately, my passion for numbers has therefore evolved into a passion for intellectual, engaging and insightful discussions that share information, transform understanding and combine the powers of the people involved.

The other big learning over the years is a better understanding of the importance of emotion. Whilst emotion can often kill a discussion as it tends to curtail any sense of objectivity, it would be totally wrong to underestimate its value. The first job in any discussion or debate is to get people interested, and a vision with a creative and inspiring story to back it up is the best way of stimulating that interest. Focus purely on hard facts, whatever they tell us, and people will probably glaze over and switch off, rather than be persuaded. A bit of emotion is essential, but as with most things in life, it needs to come with a sense of moderation. If we lose this sense of balance or lack the factual basis underpinning our emotion, then we are in the dysfunctional conversations of the modern world. But if we can keep things in check and show a desire to engage in the intelligent exchange of views and ideas that is described by our Monty Python hero, then we have a chance. And when we have open minds constructively discussing the facts, with both parties clearly articulating their point of view and allowing the space for rational thought, then we create the environment for the participants to share and combine their knowledge and ideas. By combining powers, they are wiser than any of them as individuals, and this can only help to get to the best solutions and the right decisions on complex subjects.

So how do we get there? Well... first of all, we all need to admit that we are part of the problem. It's easy to point the finger of blame at our out-of-touch politicians and the drift towards infotainment. But if we are honest, this is a deep-seated behaviour that pervades across all of society from top to bottom. Social media is overwhelmed by people sharing their fervent opinions, without a care for the facts, because they have no responsibility for the consequences, but it would be wrong to dismiss it as an online problem. Conversations with families, friends or work colleagues are also weighed down by the same failings. We constantly massage the truth to influence the perspectives of others and to protect ourselves. We make assumptions, exaggerate our strengths, hide our weaknesses and make it sound like we know it all. We are all part of the problem!

As a result, we need to focus on ourselves. Most of us are blissfully unaware of our unconscious biases and blind to some of the well-intentioned weaknesses that we display in many of the discussions and conversations we have on a daily basis. I certainly realised this as I started writing this book as it opened my eyes to my own shortcomings. And this is why we all need to take the personal responsibility to change things. If we are not prepared to listen to both sides of the story, or to challenge our own preconceptions, or to gain the full insight to make difficult decisions, then we cannot expect that of others. If we allow people to spin a story, avoid challenge and scrutiny, or engage in factless arguments, then we are implying that this is acceptable. If we get frustrated and confrontational to these behaviours and push the discussion into an emotional slanging match, then we are contributing to the problem, even if we may think the other person started it! We may not be the people in power or with the greatest influence, but if each and every one of us changes our approach to discussions, we can start to change the tide.

This pursuit of self-improvement is at the heart of this book. One-by-one, the chapters explore some clear and major examples of contentious debates where views are the most polarised and discussions are the most fractious. These are the hot topics where the problems are greatest as we hold strong emotional opinions and therefore find it incredibly difficult to remain objective. You included! But in this book, it doesn't matter what you think, what matters is how you came to your current way of thinking and how you share that in discussions. When we avoid the temptation of assuming we are right or that we know better, we start to appreciate that other people's experiences are different, their knowledge is different, their taste and personality is different, and as a result, quite validly, their opinions might be different. So, as you are reading, hold your views in the background. Allow me to discuss both sides of the argument without being distracted by the right and wrong. When I say something that you fundamentally disagree with, or which irritates or even angers you, then bite your tongue. Keep calm and reflect on why you want to shout at the book! Stay focused on the balance of discussion and the approach that both sides are taking, and in particular, think about the hurdles that we all encounter as we try to discuss these delicate subjects. By opening our eyes to some of the behaviours we exhibit, we can start to realise the changes we all personally need to make.

Moving from one subject to another, the book helps us build a set of principles that should enable us all to have more empowering discussions. We will start to listen more actively and become more informed. We will be drawn to others with different experiences and approach them with a genuine openness to learn why they think the way they do, and to question why they don't think the same as us. We will learn to reflect and self-analyse and come to our own authentic conclusions, not something driven by our surroundings, but the truth that the real version of us actually believes. We will learn to challenge others openly, but with no presumptions of superiority, so that we maintain a good discussion until we really understand their views. We will learn how to have much better discussions that can provide a catalyst for change, both personally and in the world around us.

This book is just the start of the journey and we will need to work hard to change our own mindsets. But if more and more of us manage to do this, we can start to encourage others to do the same. And if more and more people start to listen and think, and the world starts to operate with frank discussions involving a diverse range of open minds, then maybe, step-by-step, we can start to solve some of the key issues that we face in our society. It's a big change from the post-truth, anti-establishment world we are currently living in, but I believe it can happen!

CHAPTER 2

Arguing with your ear plugs in

It takes effort and energy to actually pay attention to someone, but if you can't do that, you're not in a conversation. You're just two people shouting out barely related sentences in the same place.

CELESTE HEADLEE

The United Kingdom is a wonderful country and the welfare system is a long-established and admirable part of its fabric, involving a broad range of measures and expenditure to improve the health, education, employment and social security of our inhabitants. Its development rose out of the extreme poverty in Victorian times, as we may recognise from the books of Charles Dickens. At this time, the poor and less privileged were largely left to fend for themselves. Initial measures were introduced by the Liberal Party between 1906 and 1911, and included free school meals, a "Children's Charter" to protect children from neglect and exploitation, pensions, labour exchanges to help the unemployed find work and a precursor to the NHS through the provision of a national insurance scheme providing free healthcare to some 13 million workers.

This was just the start, however, and the development accelerated following the impact of the First World War and the ensuing slump through The Great Depression of the 1930s. During this time, the Government became increasingly involved in people's lives and started to extend the state's responsibility for looking after its people. This culminated in the Beveridge Report of 1942, written by the Liberal economist, William Beveridge, which suggested far-reaching reforms to the system that was in operation at the time. Within the report, he identified the five "Giant Evils" in society (squalor, ignorance, want, idleness and disease) and effectively recommended an insurance scheme (like the National Insurance scheme that we would recognise today) to help eradicate these. This would be via a single scheme that consolidated healthcare with support in both unemployment and retirement. Following their success at the next election, at the end of the Second World War in 1945, the incoming Labour party promised to eradicate the "Giant Evils" and introduced a range of policies to care and provide for the people of the country throughout their lives.

A comprehensive set of policies were therefore in place long before I was born, and ever since I have been sufficiently grown-up to understand and care about the system, it has been a topic of hot debate. This is mainly because the level of spend on social security has become so significant, increasing steadily from just 4% of GDP at the time of its introduction in 1948 up to 12% by the mid-1980s. This was driven by increases in individual payments, but also increased levels of claimants, particularly as a result of the ageing population. At current levels, the expenditure represents about 30% of total government spending, and as a result, decisions around the level of this expenditure are critical in defining taxation policy and discussions as to where it is distributed are a major subject of political debate.

In fact, saying that it is a major topic of debate is probably a gross understatement. Until Brexit came along, it was perhaps accurate to say that there were few things that could quite polarise opinion such as benefits. Despite this, I believe it is fair to say that all sides are united behind the concept that we should be providing government support for people in need.

The disagreement comes because there are some very different definitions of what constitutes "in need" and some very different perspectives as to whether we should increase taxes to fund our increasing requirements or make tough decisions around where the available funds are allocated.

These discussions have become even more toxic in recent years following austerity measures introduced by the Conservative Government in the 2010s in order to reduce the levels of borrowing to a manageable level. Moreover, as the Government chose to redistribute some benefits towards the ageing population, this led to a real and evident reduction of support to working-age families. Whilst the Government chose to focus on fiscal responsibility and the difficult choices that need to be made at times of economic weakness, the Opposition view was that the social impact meant these decisions were coming at an unacceptable cost. This was not just a policy difference but a fundamental distinction in ideological principles. As such, it was a touchpaper to escalate the intensity and hostility of the conflicting left-wing and right-wing opinions on this subject. The ideological backgrounds generated a hugely emotional response and pushed this well beyond a rational discussion.

Standing back without the emotional intensity, what underpins the differences of opinions between the left and right on this topic? Without getting too deeply into the subject, there are some key gaps between their viewpoints:

Left-wing perspective:
Government-provided services and support
As a general rule, the left wing is in favour of government responsibility for the welfare of the people, with the core services all therefore being provided from within the public sector. Although not suppressing an individual's freedom, they would want laws, structure and regulations in place that ensure the protection of individuals within an equal society, prioritising this over and above the economic freedom of individuals and business. Where needed, they would therefore lean on the side

of increased taxes to fund these services, with higher-income earners paying a much higher percentage of their income in the form of taxation to help look after those needing support.

With this in mind, when considering people that are on benefits, the left-wing see decent and deserving people that are getting the support that is only fair and right. As a result, they tend to have a positive perception of the money spent on benefit, with a high percentage being a good story and reflective of a supportive and caring society. As part of managing the overall budget, they tend to have a generous perspective of who is "in need", erring on the side of paying someone who is not really deserving rather than risking the chance of missing a worthy recipient. At times of economic strife where tough decisions are required to balance the books, they would prioritise raising taxes or borrowing to ensure that all the needy were supported, rather than burden them with a reduction in support at a critical time.

Right-wing perspective:
Individual responsibility and economic freedom

In contrast, the right wing is generally in favour of minimal government intervention, with the belief that competition in the private sector leads to improved service and efficiency. They want minimal laws and regulations, ensuring that the basic and fundamental protections are in place, but encouraging personal economic responsibility. In effect, this means rewarding individual success and entrepreneurship, on the basis that a successful economy is better for everybody. They would lean on the side of maintaining low taxes to encourage positive action from those who are able to stimulate the economy and the overall wealth of the nation, seeing this as the path to success.

Consequently, whilst acknowledging that there are many who are genuinely needy and deserving support from the society, they also see many wastrels sitting comfortably in a safety net that the system provides. As such, they tend to have a negative perception of the money spent on benefit, because it is a huge financial burden that protects the needy but also discourages self-sufficiency and personal responsibility. As part of managing the overall budget, they would tend to have a restricted perspective of who is "in need", therefore erring on the side of avoiding payments to fraudsters, wrongful claimants and lazy people, even if this creates a risk of missing a worthy recipient. At times of economic strife where tough decisions are needed to balance the books, they would prioritise cuts in expenditure for those they perceive as least deserving, rather than raise taxes or make economic decisions that will stifle growth and investment.

If we consider welfare expenditure as a percentage of national income (per the graph below), but focus on the more recent history, we can see there is an element of truth in both arguments with benefit generosity and economic prosperity both driving fluctuations in the level of expenditure.

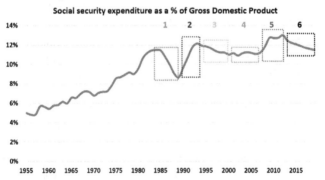

Social security expenditure as a % of Gross Domestic Product

During the late-1980s (1), the percentage of income directed to social security dropped for the first time under the Thatcher government. This was partly driven by a deliberate policy of pegging benefit increases to inflation, a lower level than in previous years, but was primarily caused by strong economic growth and therefore significant reductions in unemployment. The percentage grew again in the early-1990s (2) as an economic downturn had the dual effect of reduced national income and increased levels of unemployment and therefore the number of claimants for income support, but this reversed as the economy started to grow again in the second half of that decade (3). The economy stayed strong into the start of the new millennium (4) but the trajectory flattened as the continued strengthening of the economy was matched by increased generosity of benefits aimed at lower-income families and pensions. However, the banking crisis and global recession at the end of that decade (5) resulted in significant increases in the social security burden which peaked at well over 13% in 2012–2013. With the economy proving slow to recover (6), the austerity measures were introduced to reduce the expenditure to more "affordable" levels, and this combined with some economic recovery has driven the percentage reduction since the all-time peak.

The reality of this up-and-down story over the last 35 years is that whilst some of the fluctuations were driven by changes in benefit policy and the level of generosity of the governments at that time, the economic performance was also a key factor. In essence, both sides are right and both sides are wrong. The arguments to maintain benefits during an economic downturn is compelling, particularly as the low-income families on benefit are the ones most exposed. It is the low-income groups who are usually quickest to lose their jobs, who are not spending on luxuries that they can temporarily sacrifice, and who are lacking in savings, which means that they are completely dependent on welfare and charity to help them through the difficult times. But we all know from our personal situations that however difficult things are, running unacceptable levels of borrowing is a vicious circle that will rapidly spiral out of control. One glance at the horrific interest rates on payday loans demonstrate that ignoring this, even if the consequences are hugely undesirable, is not the answer. For the country, just as for individuals, the most likely routes to a sustainable solution involve taking difficult decisions to minimise our expenditure, whilst we find ways of boosting our income. However, this needs to be done with great compassion, empathy and care or we are going to hurt people at the times they are most vulnerable.

Ultimately, this is therefore an immensely delicate balance of the two arguments. Different people will approach it in different ways, and nobody will get it 100% right. Some will err too much on the side of those needing the payments, failing to make difficult decisions around cuts because of the human impact, and therefore prolonging our economic woes. Others will err too much on the side of the economic recovery, pushing too far with the austerity measures and causing real harm to those in need. Moreover, because the economic recovery is uncertain and dependent on a multitude of factors both within and outside of our control, there is no right answer and we will have good reason to criticise whoever is making the decision and whatever decisions they are taking. Some decisions will be more popular than others, but they are not necessarily more accurate than others.

So are we able to appreciate this complexity and balance the competing arguments to make the best decision? Unfortunately, not! As is often the case, we tend to create exaggerated caricatures of the two arguments. On one side, we have the ideological do-gooders with no grasp on economic reality, and on the other side we have the heartless capitalists who are out of touch with the general public. This polarisation does nobody any favours, and generally leads to oversimplified arguments that seek to highlight the victims of cuts who have been forced into poverty, or the fraudulent scroungers who are getting more than they need. This focus on individuals triggers an intense emotional reaction, either about the harsh realities of tough decisions or about the money being wasted on people who don't need it. However, beyond the sides repeatedly emphasising that they are right, we achieve nothing. We start with a large gap between the combatants and we end with one, as nobody is able or willing to bring any insight on the economic or political complexities that underpin the differing perspectives.

A great example of this polarisation was seen in relation to the so-called "Bedroom Tax", an informal name for one of many measures introduced by the UK government as part of the Welfare Reform Act 2012. This nickname was given because benefits were reduced for social tenants if they had a spare bedroom. The rules said that if you had more bedrooms than you need, then you would not receive housing benefit to cover the full cost of the rent. In effect, the government would pay the cost of what is "needed" and the tenant should pay for the cost for the "perk" of a spare room.

To many people who are privately renting or buying their properties and would love to have an extra room or a bit more space, this may seem a pretty sensible proposal. I have personal experience of having to sell and move out of our "dream" home when our income dropped below expectations, and suddenly the spare bedroom was a luxury we could not afford. Considering the context leading up to the decision and the struggling economy, then funding people to have spare rooms would have seemed a sensible and obvious target for savings. The local authority or social housing provider was paying more for a three-bedroom house than a one-bedroom house, so we were wasting money if we funded a single person living in a larger property. Moreover, given examples of whole families in one-bedroom properties, because we did not have any larger houses in the area, while we simultaneously have people "blocking" those properties with more space than they need, then surely we should try to resolve the situation. Remove any emotion and temporarily ignore any imperfections in the way the policy was implemented, and then in the world of limited resources, there was good logic for exploring this potential saving.

Adding a personal example, I know someone who lived with his mother in a three-bed property, so two of them in a three-bed property. For lengthy periods, the third bedroom was sublet, giving them additional income when the cost of providing that room was being provided by the local authority. They were effectively making a profit on the social housing investment. After his mother passed away, the boy then continued living on his own in a three-bedroom property. He spent long periods living abroad, rejected all efforts to take on any work as he was receiving benefits, and as he was letting out both spare rooms, his existence was very comfortable. As a family, they even built a four-bedroom property overseas on some family land (where he now lives) that was entirely funded by this money from the UK government. A unique set of circumstances, but the unchallenged system meant that a single person was blocking a three-bedroom house and making a profit out of the additional rooms. He therefore represented a case study of what they were trying to prevent.

Take another personal example of a couple, both individually given two-bedroom properties, one in London and one in the New Forest. They have been together for many years, but intentionally avoided getting married as they knew they would then be assessed together. Being assessed separately, they were both able to keep their individual properties, basically living as a couple in their property in London, letting out the second room, and having a lovely holiday cottage in the New Forest. Another different and unique set of circumstances, but another clear example where limited social housing was being given to people who were thoroughly deserving of support, but who were collectively benefiting from significantly more space than they needed. Another perfect case study of what the policy was trying to prevent.

Following the announcement of the Bedroom Tax, however, the proposals were met with forceful criticism. The Opposition condemned the fact that it would have a swathing impact on the most vulnerable in society and pledged to scrap the policy when they came into power. Both them and the media accurately highlighted some clear examples where people would be dramatically and unfairly impacted by the proposals. This included foster parents who may have a room spare between placements or the parents of military personnel who were away on service, two deserving cases whereby rooms would only be temporarily unoccupied. They also highlighted the example of disabled people who had a room for a carer, which was therefore not permanently occupied, but used and needed from time-to-time.

Going beyond these cases, this measure was also a direct cut in income for many individuals and families. As mentioned before, these are cuts for people without savings and a support network, who are not spending on luxuries. Irrespective of any potential justification, reductions in the benefits and income they are being provided therefore has a direct and uncompromising impact on the necessities of life, such as food and heating. These are sometimes the only options for efficiencies and therefore leads to people skipping meals and turning to food banks. These concerns were flagged at the time and have been the harsh reality in the years since the implementation of the policy. A formal evaluation of the policy in 2015 by the Department of Work and Pensions estimated that about three-quarters of people had cut back on food and nearly a half had cut back on heating since the law was introduced. This demonstrated that there had been a clear and direct impact for people who were on the receiving end of the new rules, reinforcing that the concerns of the Opposition were fully justified.

With strong arguments on both sides, there was every need for a robust debate to help evaluate the best approach. However, this was invisible when the polarised furore descended. Listening to one of the main exchanges in the House of Commons, the leader of the Opposition, Ed Miliband, challenged the Prime Minister, David Cameron, by saying that:

> the only people he listens to are a small group of
> rich people and powerful people at the top …
> that's why he has come up with a policy that is
> unworkable and unfair.

The Prime Minister responded by saying that:

> If you think that we are spending too much on
> housing benefit, you just said the bill is going up,
> why do you oppose each and every attempt we
> make to get the welfare bill under control?

These polarised and point-scoring opinions are the inevitable consequence when people have decided their position before they enter the discussion. When people have entrenched themselves into opposite camps where one believes it is a rational solution and the other believes that it is cruel and heartless, then there is little room to manoeuvre. Rightly or wrongly, the Government had reached a conclusion that savings needed to be made in social security, and those savings were going to happen. Complete dismissal of their proposal was only ever going to lead to the sort of reaction outlined by the Prime Minister, followed by a stubborn refusal to budge because the criticism was deemed irrational. We created a situation of stubbornness and intransigence when we really needed:

- An Opposition to listen, pick through the detail, engage and influence the course of a policy; and
- A Government to listen, evaluate the feedback, engage and steer a path that avoided the pitfalls.

Knowing the strength of opinion on this topic, some of you may be raging as you are reading this, wondering how I can justify saying there are strong arguments for both sides. Even by doing so, you may think I am suggesting that a policy that is cruel, unfair and causing immense hardship could be justified. And being honest, I would fully understand this perspective! However, even if you find it uncomfortable to admit it, there is rationality behind the proposal. Even if we believe that this is cold, emotionless, spreadsheet-based rationality, there is a justification. Not only is there a justification, but a justification that many people truly believe is the best course of action, having put a lot of thought into both the problem, the possible solutions, and the public roasting that they were going to get for introducing this proposal. Despite all of this, they still went ahead on the basis that they believed this difficult decision was the best decision. With this in mind, however unjustified we believe is the counter-opinion, completely dismissing it is a bad error of judgement.

This rigidity and refusal to listen does not help anyone. The Opposition failed to stop or significantly influence the implementation of the policy, and the Government failed to win over the public and convince them of the justifications. Ultimately, rather than the win–win situation we are aiming for, we ended up in the lose–lose scenario that is so common in the modern world. Poor attitudes and ineffective discussions meant we did not reach the best conclusion. So why does this happen? It is probably because hammering our own point across in the most colourful and imaginative way is fun and crowd-pleasing and gets us in the headlines. Getting into a more challenging, intellectual conversation that tries to analyse, problem solve and determine the best path or the win–win situation is difficult and challenging and not newsworthy in our impatient world. In addition, it may involve compromise and that has become an ugly word. Rather than being perceived as a positive outcome to derive a better solution that draws the benefits from both sides, it is perceived as a retreat from an ideological soapbox.

This is exceptionally unhealthy. Dr Frank Crane, a Presbyterian minister, speaker, and columnist from the late-nineteenth/early-twentieth century once said that:

> In discussion you are searching for the truth, and
> in argument you want to prove that you are right.

The furore over the "Bedroom Tax" is a classic example where we have strayed from discussion to argument. But I think we all know that this malaise is not restricted to conversations on social security. The world is becoming increasingly polarised and we tend to have quite strong opinions on most things. As a result, Celeste Headlee, the radio presenter, was very accurate when she said that:

> Every conversation has the potential to devolve
> into an argument.

Sadly, we probably all know from interactions with our loved ones, exactly what happens when a discussion becomes an argument! Rationality is lost and emotion takes over. We have already decided that we know the truth. Any arguments made by our opponents just enrage us further, and so we do not listen to a word that they are saying. We are right, and their refusal or failure to see that is just a further indictment of their wrongness! As a result, we end up making cheap shots that are completely irrelevant, but very satisfying in the short term, as they give us a sense of victory. In reality, the only sure thing is that we will probably both say things that we would wish we could take back; and that we will be no nearer to the truth at the end of the slanging match.

We see the same with debates and discussions. As soon as emotion seeps in, we stop listening to the other side, and resort to win-at-all-costs tactics that achieve nothing, except making us feel a bit better in the moment. The distorting effect of emotion is well understood and is exactly why there is the concept of mediation in extreme situations such as divorce proceedings. This involves the introduction of a neutral third party to try and facilitate more positive discussions. But we don't have that in our everyday conversations. We don't have the counsellor to calm us down when we are getting emotional. We don't have the neutral diplomat to capture the good arguments from both sides and to look for the middle ground. And we don't have the referee to remind us to listen and directly hear those good arguments.

This means that we need to find our own way of controlling ourselves, and probably the start of this is to follow the guidance of Will Rogers, the American silent movie star from the 1920s and 1930s, who suggested that we should:

> Never miss a good chance to shut up.

This advice is priceless as the ability to listen and genuinely give the other party the time of day to make their point is where we are lacking. As Celeste Headlee pointed out:

> A conversation requires a balance between talking and listening, and somewhere along the way we lost that balance.

Putting this plainly, we talk too much and we do not listen enough! As it was nicely put by an unknown author:

A wise old owl lived in an oak,
The more he saw the less he spoke
The less he spoke the more he heard.
Why can't we all be like that wise old bird?

Whilst there is a lot to be gained from listening, the reality is we are not very good at it! And there are many reasons for this. First and foremost, our brain is subconsciously selective in what we listen to. With so many stimuli around us, our brain needs to prioritise to pick through the sea of noise and avoid sensory overload. Julian Treasure (a sound and communication expert) describes how the brain achieves this by basically applying "filters" to help "define what we pay attention to". This explains, for example, how we may block out background noise or switch off when someone is speaking a language we don't understand or is talking about something we consider irrelevant. But the filter can also kick-in for less positive reasons such as prejudice, bias, jealousy, boredom or stress. Effectively, the brain is simply deciding that we will find this information inaccurate, irrelevant or irritating, or simply too much for us to handle. Good filtering is invaluable, but bad filtering will mean we miss things.

Secondly, Julian Treasure observes how the modern world is not helping. The world is becoming "noisier" with ever-increasing levels of visual and auditory distractions that makes it harder to concentrate, whilst increasing the likelihood that we filter out the wrong things. The immediacy of the modern world, with everything always in reach, means that we are becoming impatient and oratory is being replaced by soundbite and headline. We don't feel the need to listen to the full story, and this issue is exacerbated by the way we use sensationalism and drama to make the headlines grab our attention. The outcome of this is that we are out of the habit of concentrating through a longer explanation, and that we become blind to the "quiet, subtle and understated", even if they may be critical elements of the story. This was perhaps best demonstrated to me by a work colleague who was extolling the virtues of an app that had summarised versions of self-help books so that you could quickly get the point whilst commuting. Getting the answer quickly can be hugely appealing, but sometimes we only get the value with the slow, thoughtful, reflective interpretation of nuanced narrative that allows us to draw our own emotional relevance. This is often lost in the modern world.

Thirdly and finally, and this is probably the most painful admission, is that we are actually a bit selfish. We tend to enjoy bringing ourselves into the conversation and sharing our nuggets of wisdom or making ourselves look good. We do this all the time, even at the times we most need to shut up and listen, something that Celeste Headlee describes perfectly:

> Don't equate your experience with theirs. If they're talking about having lost a family member, don't start talking about the time you lost a family member. If they're talking about the trouble they're having at work, don't tell them about how much you hate your job. It's not the same. All experiences are individual. And more importantly, it is not about you.

When I first heard her say this, I actually felt really guilty, as I know I do this. I didn't think I was being selfish, as in my mind, I was sharing my experience with good intentions. But the reality is that I stopped to listen and at least temporarily, I switched the spotlight to myself. Being honest, I still do it. The only difference is that I now feel guilty the moment I open my mouth; but sometimes it is then too late. Once we stop someone in their flow, it is sometimes hard to get it back; especially if they are on a difficult, personal topic that has been hard for them to start talking about. If we are listening, we need to fully invest our focus and attention on the person who is talking. As it was put so beautifully by the author and motivational speaker, Simon Sinek:

> We may believe that we are good listeners, but listening
> is more than waiting for your turn to interrupt.

To really understand how well we are listening, it can be useful to assess ourselves against a scale that measures the quality of listening, a concept that is introduced in *7 Habits of Highly Successful People*, the wonderful book by Stephen R. Covey. His five-point scale ranges from Level 1 when we are not actually listening at all, to a Level 5 where we are properly engaged and invested in what the other person is saying. Reflecting on these levels gives invaluable insight on the ways we are behaving in discussions.

Level 1: Ignoring the Speaker

There are lots of ways that we effectively ignore the speaker, but this is usually when we take over a conversation. At the extreme end, this can be a domineering person who just monopolises the conversation and prevents people from speaking, or completely steers the conversation where they want it to go. However, it also includes interrupting people, because although it may be with a different intent, we are retaking control of the conversation from the speaker to ourselves and their perspective is getting lost.

The problem with interrupting is not just that we intervene and stop the other person talking, but that we have usually stopped listening quite some time before we make our point. We may have been listening until the other person said something that triggered a thought in our head, and then all the focus is on turning our thought into the comment or point or question that we want to make. Once we're ready, we will either blurt it out straight away (literally interrupting the speaker in full flow), or in an effort to be polite, we will hold it until a lull in the conversation. But while we are waiting to share our great wisdom or humour, our focus is on remembering what we are going to say, and any focus on the speaker has been completely derailed. And moreover, by the time we make our point, the context is often completely wrong and the moment has passed.

I genuinely thought that I was a good listener until reading this list and thinking how much time I really spend in Level 1. Just because my interventions are thoughtful and focused on the other person doesn't hide the fact that I drift in and out of the conversation as I focus on things I am going to say. And it doesn't hide the fact that while I'm thinking of what I am going to say, I'm not listening to what the other person is saying. I have since tried to follow Celeste Headlee's advice, which is:

> Go with the flow. That means thoughts will come into your mind and you need to let them go out of your mind.

But this is hard! When we think of something that we think is brilliant, the temptation to interrupt is so strong, and like many of you, I'm sure, I remain a long way from mastering this skill!

Level 2: Pretending to Listen

This is also a remarkably common failing in our busy lives. In the modern world, multitasking is considered a positive quality, but if one of those tasks is listening then this is definitely not the case. If we do not focus our attention on the person and what they are saying, we are not going to hear everything they are saying. Sometimes, our multitasking is an active choice, such as when we are talking on the phone, whilst typing an email or watching television. Sometimes, it is a bit more subconscious, for example when we are a bit stressed and our mind is somewhere else; or where our mobile is vibrating and it has distracted our attention. In either case, however good we think we are at multitasking, listening is something that requires our full attention. Otherwise we won't pick up anything more than the basic facts that we probably knew anyway!

One of my biggest failings in this respect is when I meet new people. Yet again, even though I am fighting to change my ways, I am still a complete disaster at remembering their names. Because so many people admit to this weakness, I used to just accept it as something that I'm not very good at. However, having realised what I am doing, I am now not so accepting! The reality is that during the first ten seconds or so, I'm making the criminal mistake of getting distracted by their appearance and behaviour. For a short period, I'm therefore not listening to what they are saying, and you can be fairly sure that their name will be shared at some point during that first ten seconds. I did vaguely hear their name, but as I wasn't paying attention, I can't remember it! In theory, I'm now ready to start listening. However, I'm now distracted by desperate efforts to trawl my memory and dredge out the name that I can't remember or am willing the third person in the conversation to say the person's name again. As a result, I am still not listening!!!! Ultimately, this is not an acceptable weakness, but just a lack of focus on what the person is saying.

To try and fix these problems, many workplace training sessions teach us tips about how to focus on the conversation. They suggest things like nodding, maintaining eye contact, showing an open receptive body language, or repeating what has been said to us. Rather than being skills to help us listen, these are really skills to help us pretend. Staring into the speaker's eyes may fool them that we are focused, even though we are actually thinking about what we are going to have for dinner. As Celeste Headlee quite rightly pointed out:

> There is no reason to learn how to show you're
> paying attention if you are in fact paying attention.

Level 3: Selective Listening

This is another common failing, where we pay some attention, but are drifting in and out of the conversation. We are heavily using the filters that I discussed earlier to ignore vast swathes of what is being said, but periodically switching on as we hear something that we think may be of interest. This can be unintentional, such as when we are a bit bored or tired and therefore our attention is drifting until something is said that catches our attention and we manage to summon the efforts to focus for a short while. However, usually there is a conscious decision to selectively listen, and it is for one of two reasons.

Firstly, it is where we are knowledgeable on a subject but have a bit of a gap that we want to fill. We walk into the one-hour presentation with no intention of listening to the whole thing and are simply waiting and looking out for the part we want to hear. This either means just following the agenda, and switching on at the relevant point, or in many cases, listening out for some key words that trigger our attention. For the rest of the presentation, we are in our own world, and if there was new information or a different perspective that would have been useful for us, we would completely miss it.

The other scenario is where we have strong opinions. Our natural tendency is to apply something called confirmation bias that will be discussed further in Chapter 8. In simple terms, however, this means we selectively hear all the information that reaffirms our opinions and gloss over those points that contradict us. We will pay much more attention to a like-minded person than an adversary, and where someone is more balanced, we will tend to concentrate and remember their supportive points and tend to drift as we dismiss their counter-arguments. As with the politicians discussing the Bedroom Tax, if we are actually giving our opponents any time, then we are almost certainly applying selective listening. We are waiting for their slip-up, their inappropriate comment or their erroneous overgeneralisation. Basically, we are not listening to what they are saying, but searching for the mistake that will help us win the argument!

Level 4: Attentive Listening

If you are honestly reflecting as you are reading through, then like me, you are probably getting to this stage and realising what a sizeable majority of your "listening" time is at Levels 1–3. Sadly, for many of us, it is rare that we make it to the heady heights of Level 4! This is when we are giving the speaker our undivided attention. We are hanging on every word and listening intently to what they are saying. We will ask them to repeat things if we miss anything, ask for clarifications or examples if we are not clear, ask follow-up questions to help with our understanding. We are focused on what they are saying and for the first time, we are applying some good listening skills.

This is good listening, and you may be wondering why this is not the top level. And the reason is that we are listening but very much from our own standpoint. I have heard an expression saying that "Your perception of me is a reflection of you" and this is the problem in this instance. We are hearing what the person is saying, we are understanding all their words, but we are putting our own lens on what they are saying. As a result, we are not truly feeling what they are saying.

If we are with like-minded people from the same background, we may just about get away with it, although we will carry a grave risk of making erroneous preconceptions. However, for someone that is very different, then this can cause us real problems as their views can appear incomprehensible. Where their underlying personality is very different, then it is a challenge to relate to what they are saying. I remember the early days of my relationship with my husband, when my analytical mindset truly struggled to understand the way he would make decisions on gut feelings. I was irritated if he could not articulate exactly why he was doing something. It's similar to the way we may struggle to comprehend someone who may self-harm or consider suicide, as we are trying to understand their irrational state from our rational perspective. Without truly "walking in their shoes", we cannot fully understand; and therefore although we are listening, our listening is not complete.

Level 5: Empathic Listening

This is where Level 5 comes in, as true listening requires us to transcend these limitations and to listen with empathy. As per the dictionary definition, this means truly "sharing someone else's feelings or experiences by imagining what it would be like to be in that person's situation". Many of us naively think we are good at this, but few of us actually are. This is because our understanding of individual difference is imperfect, and we therefore struggle to truly relate to the experiences of others. Successfully listening with true empathy is therefore extremely challenging, but it has two major benefits. Firstly, it has the obvious impact that we get that greater depth of understanding, hearing not just the words, but feeling the emotion and sensing the underlying meaning. Secondly, however, it tends to bring more out of the speaker. Weger, Castle & Emmett wrote a psychological paper in 2010 where they observed that if we "attempt to demonstrate unconditional acceptance and unbiased reflection", the speaker will respond to this acceptance by being more open. As a speaker, we all know how we tend to open up when we sense that someone is really listening and understanding what we are saying. We feel encouraged to talk!

Now Level 5 is clearly something needed by a counsellor or therapist when they are working with a patient, when misjudgements or preconceptions are particularly critical. However, the reality is that we all need to hit this level if we are trying to guide, mentor or advise someone. We cannot possibly understand what is best for them if we do not take the time to properly understand them and their full story, or if we fail to empathise with the situation they are facing. Sadly, we are frequently ready to dish out advice without having gained this insight. But in other situations, we don't need to be at this level. When we are debating a topic or making a decision where it is less about the emotional connection, then Level 4 is often enough. We do need to listen to what the other person is saying and understand the arguments that they are making. However, as the information they are sharing is probably much less personal, we don't necessarily lead to feel that emotion quite so much. Capturing the information and the details with a calm, open and objective mind is probably quite enough.

But being honest with ourselves, how often do we hit the heady heights of Level 4? How often do we devote our full attention to what is being said? How often have we cleared our mind of preconceptions and are we actively listening with an open mind to learn and understand? How often do we keep doing that the whole way through the discussion and not get distracted or irritated or side-tracked? How often do we keep the open and questioning mind until we have got the full understanding, without getting 80% of the way and then just assuming the final piece? If you're anything like me, I would suggest it is very rare! Sometimes we start with the intention of listening and understanding but lose our focus on the way. But in many cases, we don't even get that far, as we are multitasking or half-listening from the very start.

If we reflect on our earlier examples about discussions around benefits, then we're probably being generous to say they reach Level 3. There may be times when they are doing some selective listening to try and pick holes in the opponent's arguments (Level 3), but more often than not, they are just rolling out their predetermined arguments and then pretending to listen in between (Level 2). As the animosity starts to escalate, they struggle to even apply the common courtesy of pretending to listen, interrupting when they can and demonstrating with their responses that they have been ignoring what has just been said (Level 1). When our listening skills have slid to such a low level, we are not in a discussion at all.

As Julian Treasure says:

Conscious listening creates understanding.

… and without that we have our impasse. An impasse where one side lacks empathy and understanding of the plight of the most vulnerable, and the other side lacks awareness and understanding of the economic reality. No wonder we think our politicians are "out of touch".

Now don't get me wrong, I'm not expecting that we will necessarily make a fundamental change in our thinking as a result of listening. When we are discussing something with people who are ideologically opposed to us, then this is almost certainly not going to happen. I'm also not expecting us to be wallflowers who quietly listen and let everyone talk over us. Conversations need challenge and debate. When it is our time to talk, we should be expected to argue our side with oomph and passion and a desire to influence and persuade. But as it is part of a conversation, we should have the intelligence and courtesy to say things that are connected to what our counterpart has just said, and this requires us to have listened. And when I say listened, I mean properly listened. We shouldn't respond to a judgemental, summarised version of what we think our opponent would say, because that is easy to knock down and we have got our clever argument pre-prepared. We should respond to the real and truthful argument that our counterpart has just shared, by thinking on our feet.

This is so much harder. It requires us to put energy and effort into listening and understanding. It requires us to think quickly to analyse their points, process them against our views and opinions, and then build a strong and convincing response. It requires us to react to the situation and not just use all the clever soundbites and cheap one-liners that some clever scriptwriter came up with, but which are irrelevant and completely unrelated to what has just been said. It really is much harder, but it results in a much better conversation where we get to the truth. It guides the discussion away from the extremes that excite our blinkered supporters and allows it to focus on the middle ground in a way that attracts the neutrals and the floating voters. Ultimately, we successfully engage the people who are waiting to be convinced.

It is so important to remember that a good discussion involves the participation of at least two people, and each participant therefore needs to get the right balance of talking and listening. Conversations are so much better when both sides approach them with the intention of listening to what the other party has to say, recognising that this is just as important as the opportunity to share their own insight. This involves a true appreciation of the opportunity that listening gives us to gather information on the subject and to gain an educated awareness of why others disagree. But starting with that intention is not enough. To truly master the art of communication, we must find a way of keeping that balance throughout. At some stage, if we have a strong opinion, we will want to get our message across in a firm, clear and decisive manner. But even when we are doing this, we must try to keep listening, arguing with passion and energy without allowing our blinkers to stop us listening to the responses. When both parties share their knowledge and insight with clear, structured and passionate articulation, but also listen with the same energy and enthusiasm, then we have the foundations of a successful discussion.

FIRST PRINCIPLE

Maintain an open mind and a preparedness to listen all the way to the finish line

CHAPTER 3

The Indecisive Politician is not all Bad!

I may be wrong in regard to any or all of them; but holding it a sound maxim, that it is better to be only sometimes right, than at all times wrong, so soon as I discover my opinions to be erroneous, I shall be ready to renounce them.

ABRAHAM LINCOLN

When we are young, we learn from everything. Whether at home, at school, or as we explore our surroundings, we go around trying things and asking questions, with a natural curiosity to help us learn and understand the many things that we do not understand. From such a blank canvas, we really take the time to listen and observe. We notice and absorb details because they are so fresh and interesting. We make the effort to understand them and to build knowledge that we did not have before. We are seeing and experiencing things for the first time and are therefore captivated by them and approach every interaction with an openness and willingness to discover.

These early learning journeys can be completely different for different people. The most obvious differentiator is the schooling that we receive. In countries such as the UK, however much standards may vary between individual schools, we are blessed with high-quality education that gives us so many opportunities for the future. On a global stage, however, it is a different situation altogether, with UNESCO suggesting that 10% of children get no formal education. Conflict zones, poverty and gender discrimination are particularly key factors, leaving these children hugely disadvantaged. As a consequence, it is no wonder that so many charities are focused on trying to give educational opportunity to youngsters in the third world, because this is something that not only helps them in the here and now but can be transformational for the rest of their lives.

But it goes beyond the quality of schooling. I grew up in a settled and loving family that encouraged and supported me, and there is no doubt that this was a considerable factor in helping me to achieve my academic potential. My cousin was diagnosed as dyslexic at school, and was therefore given additional teaching, guidance and support that helped him to truly overcome the resulting challenges at an early age. This helped lift him onto a level playing field and to achieve great success. Conversely, my dyslexic husband grew up in a country with good schools but no understanding of dyslexia, and in a family that gave him no support or encouragement. His learning experience was a real challenge, he was constantly called "stupid" and was left with a real lack of confidence about his ability. When I met him, he may not have had the academic polish or confidence, but I could instantly spot his intelligence, curiosity and talent. However, it is rare for recruitment to focus on potential, and he lacked the academic qualifications that are a passport into the sort of jobs he wanted to pursue.

Fortunately, my husband is the most determined dreamer I have ever met, and despite the negative comments he had dealt with for much of his life, he had ambitions to pursue and he was definitely not ready to admit defeat. So, he embarked on a degree course in Psychology, and an early module on dyslexia led to a friend quickly realising that the case study was a perfect description of him! Before being fully diagnosed, he had to deal with an unprofessional educational psychologist who told him to switch to an easier, manual course which would be more suited to his capabilities – "something like gardening"! This was not exactly the confidence boost he needed, but undeterred, he was prepared to fight hard to achieve success and the diagnosis fundamentally changed things. Alongside the love and stability of a new family, he had student support, extra teaching and guidance on how to overcome the problems he had faced his whole life. With this structured assistance, suddenly things were a bit different!

However, there is so much more than academic knowledge that we gain as we go through our early life. We learn from our parents and upbringing and the culture that surrounds us. We learn from the things that we see as we walk around. We learn from the way we feel when things happen. We pretty much learn from everything. As youngsters, we are like a sponge, constantly absorbing information and experiences and emotions, which in a good or bad way, will help guide the way we think, the opinions we hold and the decisions that we take.

As an adult, are things any different? We say that we "can't teach an old dog new tricks", reflecting our belief that it is much harder to learn when we are older, but is this true? There is no doubt that the metaphorical sponge is already holding a lot of information, and there is now some research suggesting the challenges behind adult learning are more due to the interference from existing information, than any reduced capability of the brain. In other words, reprogramming something we already think and believe is harder than taking on something new and fresh. However, in addition, I believe there is a contribution from the fact that we do not create the same environment for learning:

- When we are young, we are studying at school full time, and therefore totally focused on our learning and education – at least when we are paying attention and not messing around! How often can we say we do that as an adult, with the pressures of work and relationships and children tending to get in the way? If we choose to learn a language as an adult, we are probably listening to an audiobook while we are commuting on a packed train carriage, hardly the same environment as a formal lesson with a teacher in a classroom. Is it the adult brain or the environment?

- When we are young, we are constantly facing new experiences and readily absorbing that new and exciting information. How often can we say we do that as an adult, with our commitments and our established routines? We become creatures of habit, spending time with the same people and doing the same things. We get comfortable in our lives and are wary of pushing ourselves out of that comfort zone. Hardly the same level of opportunity to gain new experiences. Is it the adult brain or the restricted access?

- When we are young, and particularly when we are very young, we have that natural curiosity that means we want to try things. We have not created those preconceptions that says we do not like something, or that we are too cool for something; or in the adult mind, that we are too old for something! When my husband and I went to a gymnastics class in our early 40s, which led to me doing my first ever cartwheel, you would not believe how many people said, "Aren't you too old for that?" Hardly the same environment as when we want to see and touch and taste everything that is in front of us, and we are encouraged to do it! Is it the adult mind, or simply that we have closed ourselves to properly experiencing new things?

When we are adults, there is no doubt we are older and wiser. We have learned, experienced, enjoyed and suffered, and we have gained much from all this. But however much we do know, there is even more that we don't know. If we make the same commitment to learning as we did as a child, there is so much that we can achieve, and it's the winners at the top who continue to do that.

This is exemplified by somebody like Roger Federer, the much-loved tennis superstar. He has excelled at tennis for an incredibly long time, continuously ranked in the world's top ten from October 2002 to November 2016, and after a short blip following injury, he was back in the top ten in early 2017 and was still there when the tour joined the rest of the world in COVID lockdown. It is easy to believe that this has happened through work done in the past, which took the innate talent, added skill, fitness and mental strength, and created the superstar tennis player that we look on and admire. But this would be underselling the constant efforts from him as a champion to stay at the top for such a long time. The game is progressing and changing, opponents are learning from the best to both improve their own abilities, but also to identify the ways of overcoming the champion. Staying at the top therefore requires a constant desire to learn, practice and improve; as well as an ability to keep inspired and motivated when so much has already been achieved. There may be so much flair, elegance, class and skill in the way that he plays; but it is this relentless desire to learn and improve, when he is already so talented, which is the real inspiration for me.

This desire for continuous improvement is something to which we should all aspire. There is a Japanese word, KAIZEN, which basically means "change for better", but which was applied in a business context following the introduction of US management techniques into Japanese industry after the Second World War. These approaches became a critical element of the successful rebuilding and development of businesses (particularly in technology and manufacturing), with Toyota being an especially well understood example. The concept encourages employees at every level to constantly look for small manageable changes, creating an almost experimental mindset of trying things, monitoring the outcome and then implementing changes. This is engaging for the employees, but in addition, although each of the changes may be small, they quickly multiply up if this methodology is applied on a consistent basis. This can generate significant and sustained improvements in both engagement and productivity, without the top-down focus on targets and process transformation, which can feel daunting, threatening, imposed from above and hugely disruptive. This is a great outcome, but the real beauty of this approach is it is never-ending. Targets, by nature, imply that we aim for a certain standard, and we can be content once we achieve them. Continuous improvement suggests that however good we are, we can always be a bit better!

This is a mindset that I believe we can and should apply to ourselves, although we do need to be a little bit careful with this. A desire to improve should never suggest that we should be discontented with the way we currently are. Thinking that we can do better does not mean that we cannot be proud of our present selves or what we have already achieved. Reflecting again on Roger Federer, I am sure he is hugely proud of his 20 grand slam titles, but this does not stop him from making the small improvements or changes that will help him to win his 21st title! Vishen Lakhiani refers to this balancing act as "Bending Reality" in his wonderful book called *The Code of the Extraordinary Mind*. He advocates that one of the main keys to success is our ability to "Be happy in the now" whilst simultaneously being able to "Develop an exciting vision for your future".

This balance is not always easy to achieve but is hugely empowering. As such, we should apply it to our knowledge, experience, behaviour and character, injecting a sense of kaizen that enables us to get the most out of the amazing people that we are, and all the things we can do and achieve. Whatever our sphere of knowledge or expertise, however broad or impressive that may be, or however much we have already achieved, we should look at the future with the excitement about the opportunity to evolve and learn.

My husband is the greatest inspiration for me in this respect. In his mid-40s, he travelled across to the other side of the world to try and kick-start a change in career that was just not possible in the UK. It is hard for us both to be apart, but he is chasing his dreams, and I could not be prouder of him. This is just the latest example in a never-ending stream of examples where he has challenged himself to get the most out of life, and to be the best person that he can be; and all of this has come later in his life. I met him when he was 28, and since then, he has done a degree and a Masters, he has set up a business, he has travelled to Peru to volunteer with underprivileged children, he has learned the violin, and Japanese, and how to overcome his dyslexia; and he has developed patience and resilience and a strength of character that I love and admire. He is an unbelievable person who I truly cherish.

There is no doubt our strengths have complemented each other. My husband's dreaming has pushed me to think big and challenge myself, while my pragmatism has helped him put some structure in place to guide him forwards. We have combined powers to make each other stronger. However, his hunger to learn has also inspired me to learn. Some people have said about people they love that they make them "want to be a better person". I've never specifically thought that, but there is no doubt that he has helped to make me a better person. This is not because he has actively tried to change me – I think he was very happy with the person he first met! However, he has got a very different perspective to me, which he has constantly shared in a very nonconfrontational way. I've been interested in his views as I cared about them and wanted to understand. I've reflected on those perspectives and challenged my own way of thinking, and I've had an openness and willingness to learn and change. I wouldn't even be writing this book if it wasn't for my husband!

And what is better than all of this, is that I see no end to this learning process. Now that I'm in my mid-40s, my partner and some of my friends continue to inspire me with their desire to learn, evolve, change, and to try new things. And this gives me the motivation to keep changing as well. Too many give up on their personal development when they hit adulthood; and in addition, too many people put a dampener on others that want to change. When my husband told people he was planning to go back to square one and train for a new career, so many people made comments along the lines of "Are you crazy?" or "Aren't you too old for that?" Now my parents are in their 70s, people just assume they will be useless with technology, whereas in fact my father is much more interested in learning about new technology than I am. Just like the man who recently celebrated his 100th birthday by skydiving, you are never too old. The real question, however old someone is, should be "Aren't you too young to say you can't do it?"

Learning and growing should be a lifelong adventure. What's more, we don't need to go anywhere for most of this. Of course, we can see some amazing things when we travel, but we don't need to travel the world to learn – there's a wonderfully multicultural, cosmopolitan and diverse community on our doorstep. We just need to want to see it, and want to understand it, and be prepared to step into it. Uncomfortable maybe, but it's there!

I have focused mostly on personal development, as I have reflected on the desire for lifelong learning, but the reality is that there is no reason for it to be any different in relation to our opinions and beliefs. If we are walking through the world with our eyes and ears open, we will constantly be picking up new information and new experiences that should continue to inform the way we think and the opinions that we hold. In many cases, where we have faced similar situations before, then probably the new experiences will reinforce the opinion that we already hold. But this will not always be the case. Sometimes it will challenge our current thinking, and we need to realise when our previous path was wrong and have the confidence to admit that.

This need to change opinion is demonstrated by a small but specific example concerning a good friend of mine, who stayed with me for a few weeks shortly after he finished university.

At that time, I still hadn't admitted to anyone that I was gay and was consciously hiding the truth. During the stay, my friend did not help my internal battle, because of some very discriminatory comments he made while we were watching television together. It was probably a year later when I started to come out, and I was absolutely terrified to tell this one friend. Based on the comments he had made, I thought he would react badly, and it would be the end of our friendship. You're probably wondering why I would want to be friends with someone who had homophobic views? The truth is that when you're struggling to find your place in the world and lacking self-confidence, then losing any friend seems like a big deal and a potential reinforcement that you're making wrong "choices". Anyway, I plucked up the courage to tell him, he reacted well, showed great empathy and interest, and over the years since, has proved himself to be pretty much the most open-minded of all my friends. He is someone who truly goes beyond tolerance, continually demonstrating he cares for me and my partner. My husband truly sees and appreciates that, and considers him a true friend, just as much as I do.

Before I told him that I was gay, I had an opinion or belief that he was homophobic. His comments had great significance to me at a time when I was feeling vulnerable, even though to him, his comments were just stupid, throwaway remarks in response to a brainless TV programme. Whether throwaway or not, his comments were offensive, so should I just bank that fact as conclusive proof and never change my mind? Or should I stand bank and take account of his subsequent behaviour? Since then, he has shown his genuine warmth and friendship to both me and my husband, he has supported us with the life decisions we had to make, he has openly welcomed us as a couple to his growing family and he has demonstrated his open-minded lack of judgement about us and given us freedom to talk. I have focused on the way he is now, allowing his current behaviour to change my opinion. Maybe his comments were simply not representative of what he truly thought. Maybe he held those opinions at the time but has since learned the error of his ways. Who cares! Ultimately, his actions and behaviour have spoken much more powerfully than his words, and I have changed my opinion.

Focusing on a little example like this, then it may seem obvious that we should take on the new information and change our perspectives. However, we often fail to do this. Firstly, I could have reacted to his comment and made the decision that he was not the right person to have as a friend. If I had done that, I would never have given him the chance to change my view. Secondly, I could have spent time with him, but approached him on a defensive footing with a deep underlying suspicion and established bias, which never gave him the chance to change my mind. As a general rule, one of these two responses is probably more common. When someone upsets us, or says something controversial, we will often immediately react by spending less time with them. Outside of our extremely close and deep relationships, we often tend to avoid fighting through the conflict, and therefore do not give people the chance to change our minds. Alternatively, we approach them with a closed mind and a completely fixed viewpoint that probably won't change, irrespective of the amount of contradicting evidence. We not only do this with the people we know, but they do it to us.

Have you ever had someone hold a false opinion of you? It can be the most frustratingly debilitating situation, as you know it is wrong, but whatever you do, you seem powerless to change their mind. I've had it in my family, when we turned up late to one family Christmas (because we were delivering presents at a care home!) and have been questioned about our punctuality ever since. This is exasperating, especially when others can be repeatedly late without any repercussions! The same has happened in the workplace, where it has directly impacted my progression. I remember a time where huge amounts of good work were counteracted in a performance review by one mistake that I had made in a meeting about three years before!

Another time, I missed a promotion because someone with whom I had very little interaction had overridden the views of those who worked closely with me. Unfair, and maddening, but very difficult to overcome once a perception has been formed.

The reasons these situations are so infuriating is because we know the views are unfounded. In many cases, this is because people are forming opinions based on little snippets of information. This is particularly a problem in the workplace, as my boss and my staff may see very closely the work that I do on a daily basis, but those are not the people who are going to give me my next job! Those who can influence my next step are likely to have incomplete information (from their occasional interactions with me) or information that is second-hand (and therefore actually just the opinion of someone else). It is no surprise that they therefore draw a different conclusion!

But we need to realise, we are all doing that, particularly when we are relying on information from others. When we get information from a third party, there is a danger that it is distorted by their opinions and the "fact" may not be so much of a fact! But even when receiving the information directly, it can also be distorted by our perspective. Gandhi described this perfectly in a parable by explaining how there were two types of truth, absolute truth and relative truth:

> Put your left-hand in a bowl of ice-cold water,
> then in a bowl of lukewarm water. The lukewarm
> water feels hot. Then put the right had in a bowl
> of hot water, and then into the same bowl of
> lukewarm water. Now the lukewarm water feels
> cold. The ABSOLUTE TRUTH is the water's
> constant temperature, but the RELATIVE
> TRUTH perceived by the hand, changed in the
> two scenarios.

In nearly all occasions, we experience relative truth. In other words, the "truth" is coloured by our judgement, which is why the same facts can be interpreted by two people in different ways. Absolute truth is something that is very rarely experienced, as we would need to develop that ability to view the situation with complete impartiality.

With this knowledge that our beliefs are based on facts that may be incomplete or distorted by the perspectives of others or even ourselves, it becomes even more important to be able to accept that these opinions may need to change as new information is received. First and foremost, thinking of ourselves, we should never accept that our views and personalities are fixed because that is the way things have always been. We should be ready to allow them to change and evolve with new knowledge, new experience and new perspectives. Secondly, we need to allow others to do the same. We need to give them the benefit of the doubt that they can change and support them by showing our appreciation when they make that change happen. This means forgetting past indiscretions, like my friend's homophobic comment, or my lateness to one Christmas, or my bad error in a meeting, and focusing on what is currently happening.

This can be hard enough when it is just a matter of opinion, but it can be even harder when there are structures in place. Let me reflect on the example of my husband going back to university at the age of 32 to do a degree in Psychology. Earlier in the chapter, I outlined how the support and guidance that followed his diagnosis as dyslexic was incredibly empowering; but he did not have this from the first day. The start was tough, as he battled with the volume of reading and his ability to retain the details of academic references and complex terminologies. After his diagnosis, he started to understand why he was facing so many challenges, learn how to deal with them, build the confidence to believe he was not "stupid" and to learn how to learn! But this was not an overnight transformation and the degree was quite a journey for him. This meant that after struggling in the first year, he improved during the second year, and was flying by the third year. To me, this sounds like a true advert for university education, someone who started with a lot of difficulties and challenges, learned hugely during the time he was there, and emerged as a different person. You might think therefore that he would be rewarded for the progress he had made and be congratulated on being a top student at the culmination of the course?

Sadly not. His degree score was built up from his performance across the whole three years. This therefore meant that rather than being rewarded for the strong improvement he had made, he was penalised by the poor marks that he got in the first year before being diagnosed as dyslexic. Do we really expect our students to be experts from day one? Rather than marking him down for struggling at the start, shouldn't we have celebrated and rewarded his learning, progress and positive development? When I was at university, my whole mark was based on my final exams i.e. the culmination of three years of study. This was questioned heavily as it allowed people to cram at the end, but also placed huge pressure on a few exams right at the end. However, it did measure purely my knowledge at the end of the course. Unfortunately, my husband did not benefit from this approach, and despite a subsequent Masters degree, these first year grades have haunted him ever since. Our tendency to remind people of former limitations, weaknesses or failings can have a long-lasting effect.

Now this may seem a bit unfair that he was penalised for past performance, but this is what we are all doing when we keep remembering or reminding people of past mistakes. Sometimes past form is a good indication of the way someone truly is; but only if that person has not changed. By placing so much weight on the past, rather than focusing on the person in front of us now, we remove any credit or incentive for learning. This is particularly relevant for people who may have been to prison, or battled addictions, whose attempts to rehabilitate are only worthwhile if we give them the credit for their efforts. While we remain distracted by their past, how can we blame them for losing the motivation to improve and change their course?

Being honest, this is something that we are all doing every day on a personal level. However, this issue becomes much more pronounced in the world of politics. In politics, changing your mind is almost always seen in a negative light, with the culprit castigated for their U-turn. The reason why it is seen in this light is normally for one of two reasons. Firstly, changing our view is often perceived as a sign of weakness. If we have conviction in our principles, then standing firm against the disagreement and challenge that is coming our way is considered a sign of strength. The alternative criticism of a U-turn is normally around hypocrisy and inconsistency. Saying one thing in one speech, and then saying something contradictory on another occasion would suggest we are either completely lacking in those principles or varying our message to suit the audience; neither of which are likely to paint us in a positive light.

I am not sure if there is a point when changing direction started to be perceived as a sign of weakness, but the view that standing firm is a sign of strength was encapsulated by Margaret Thatcher. In a speech at the Conservative Party Conference in 1980, she famously said:

> You turn if you want to. The lady's NOT
> for turning.

This was a real demonstration of her determination and persistence under great pressure and opposition to her policies. It also showed her real conviction in the path she was taking and was therefore considered to be a show of great strength and strong leadership. Now there is no doubt, that there is an element of real strength in this. When we are getting huge amounts of flak and criticism, and yet we stand strong to lead people towards our ultimate objective, then there is no doubt that is a sign of great strength. However, suppose we are boldly leading on that chosen path, and we get new information that changes our perspective. What should we do? Stay "strong" and keep going or show "weakness" and change course?

As with most things in life, there is not a simple answer to this question as it depends on the situation and circumstances.

I would argue that changing our mind because we're easily swayed by the opinion of others is weak. We should have challenged our viewpoint more strongly in the first place before we voiced any strong opinions, and we should therefore be able to stand firm to quite considerable challenge. However, a blind conviction that our path is right, irrespective of the challenge and the opinions of others is more stupid than strong. Putting our head in the sand and just ignoring what other people are saying is just a stubborn denial of reality. We need to remember that the world is fluid. Even if we were right in the first place, which may or may not be the case, then things can change, and we need to react to that. Ignoring new information is wrong and a sign of weak leadership.

Using a simple analogy, suppose we're driving the car, and we hear on the radio that there is a major accident just after the next junction and that it will take a few hours for the emergency services to sort everything out. We now have two options. Continue the route we had chosen at the start of the journey, even if that means sitting there for hours, or turning off at the next junction and finding a way around the problem. Hopefully, we would all agree what is the better decision! Now political leadership may be more complicated, with a lot more consequences to our decisions, but the principle is no different. We need to learn and react. Putting it more bluntly in the language of Mike Tyson, "Everyone has a plan until they get a punch in the face". The plan that we started with, however perfectly it was formed, needs to change when something happens.

For me, these qualities were demonstrated by two very different leaders. As they are historical figures, I never had the chance to see them in action, and it is quite possible that some of this praise is more perception than fact. However, the mental image I have formed reflects personality traits and qualities that I believe we should all aspire towards.

The first of the two individuals is probably a bit controversial, as he is not universally admired. Richard the Lionheart was

King of England for just ten years between 1189 and 1199 and spent precious little of his reign within his Kingdom. Much of this period was on a Crusade, trying to recapture Jerusalem on behalf of the Church, while spending other periods in captivity and defending his lands in France, as he made many political enemies. He was widely considered to be cruel, unforgiving, brutal and rather terse, and he is certainly not revered for his ability as a king. However, he was almost universally admired and respected as a military leader, with his own troops having the utmost belief he would lead them to success, and his enemies acknowledging his bravery and subtlety and leadership.

It is easy to jump to easy reasons why he was admired from a military perspective. He was immensely courageous, leading from the front and expecting others to follow him into the danger of battle, never expecting others to take risks without him being at the heart of it. He had great skill from a personal combat perspective, but also superb military nous, and he was therefore a great tactician. On top, he had the looks, charisma and sense of confidence (or arrogance for his detractors) that meant he stood above the crowd, and you would instantly know he was king just by that air of authority that he carried with him. But these are not the reasons I look to him as inspiring. I admire him for his ability to think and listen and learn.

This was a time of religious conflict with Christian warriors fighting in the name of the Church to reclaim lands that had been "captured" by the Muslim warriors under Saladin. Nearly everyone on the Christian side completely dismissed the Muslim Saracens as infidels, believing that the views of those who did not believe in the Christian God were worthless and deluded. However, despite criticism and challenge, Richard did not follow this line. He greatly admired the Muslim warriors and wanted to learn from them. He knew, rightly or wrongly, that they were equally inspired by their God as he was by his own, and he wanted to understand this in order to learn about their motivations and their passions. He knew this was key to understanding his enemy. He also greatly admired their military skill, wanting to learn from their techniques and weapons, knowing that everything he could glean from their ideas would make his own army more successful. He also understood that he knew little about the lands where he was fighting, and therefore wanted to listen and learn from people who lived there and who understood the challenges of the tough and uncompromising climate and terrain. And ultimately, he was also prepared to negotiate with the Saracens, knowing that a final conflict for Jerusalem would lead to an almighty slaughter on both sides, probably for precious little gain. By negotiating, he may be able to gain advantages that could not be achieved through military conquest, even with him at the front! He was criticised for all of this, with many believing that he should pursue the end goal of the Church to the bitter end and that his engagement and admiration for the Muslims was heresy. But to me, this was his greatest quality. Despite his immense skill and great confidence, he embraced the importance of observing, listening and learning, and there is no doubt that his military success was greatly enhanced by what he learned from his enemies.

My second role model is hopefully less disputed, and that is Mahatma Gandhi, one of the key leaders of the Indian independence movement. This was a man of tremendous principles, who galvanised the mood of a nation. His unbending commitment to nonviolent protest, despite everything that was thrown at him, is truly inspiring. His preparedness for self-sacrifice, combined with his demand for the truth, his ambition and ideology, and his powerful writings and oratory, were a combination that provided him with great influence and enabled him to achieve so much in his extraordinary life. However, underneath this, there were two core elements about Gandhi, without which, I do not believe he would have achieved so much.

Firstly, he engaged with the people and genuinely listened to them. He rejected the trappings of wealth and success, living modestly, wearing traditional clothing and eating simple vegetarian food. But more importantly, he would talk and listen to the people when travelling around. This meant that he could generally represent them from a base of understanding. Secondly, and more importantly, he assimilated this information in order to formulate his own views. Despite our accurate perception of him as someone who was steadfast and stood his ground in defending and living to his principles, underneath these unbending values, he was consistently prepared to change his mind and learn from others. This was perfectly captured in the book, *Freedom at Midnight* by Larry Collins and Dominique Lapierre when they described an exchange between Gandhi and one of his disciples who asked him:

> "Gandhi ji, I don't understand you. How can
> you say one thing last week, and something quite
> different this week?"

> "Ah," replied Gandhi, "because I have learned
> something since last week."

This made Gandhi flexible, but incredibly difficult to negotiate with, as his opinion would change as his perspective changed. This is a quality that I hugely admire. A great man, with great ideas, leading and inspiring the transformation of a nation, and yet consistently ready to listen and change his view.

Personally, I find the qualities of both these individuals incredibly inspiring, and the very definition of strong leadership. Holding principles, but an open readiness to listen, learn and change your mind; whether that is from your enemies (in the case of King Richard) or from the wider society (in the case of Gandhi). But how would these be perceived in the world of modern-day politics? Sadly, there is a true danger that they would have both been vilified for admirable behaviours that are not considered acceptable in the current day and age:

1. Learning from or admiring our enemies

Richard the Lionheart learned a huge amount from his opponents, and greatly admired their faith, as well as their military prowess. We often see this in sport, with great rivalries characterised by a huge respect for their adversaries. But move into the political field, and it is a whole different story. Discussions between our main political parties normally involve a complete disdain for the other side, who are portrayed as incompetent or as a pantomime villain. This is understandable in the context of winning votes but is a disaster for constructive discussion. In truth, it means that ideas are not judged on their merit, as political point-scoring leads to opponents just looking for what is bad, rather than ever focusing on what is good.

A great leader, like Richard, would latch onto the ideas, the suggestions, the proposals, and not worry about where they came from. It is true that Richard was King and did not therefore have to fight for votes. However, he did show a confidence that people believed in him, and therefore showed no fear in learning from a good idea thrown his way, just because it came from the opposition. He was criticised by many for admiring and learning from the Saracens, but he did it anyway, as he knew when they were good and right. This is the attitude that made him successful. Do you think many of our current political leaders could manage to do that?

2. Changing our mind as we gain new information

Gandhi was always on the lookout to learn and showed no fear in changing his mind from what he said previously, where he now had new information or a new perspective. He was not a flip-flopper, and nothing shifted his deep-rooted principles, but he listened, learned and if persuaded, he changed his mind on some of the elements of this. Nowadays, I wince every time someone raids social media and finds a snippet showing that a politician once said something different to what they are saying now, particularly when they have trawled the archives to find some contradictory comment from 20 years ago. Just like my friend who made a homophobic remark, people change. Why do we treat people like they must still believe what they believed or may have stupidly said many years ago?

Rather than dwell on the past, we should encourage everyone, politicians included, to listen, learn and to use the new information to revise their views. Normally, we would expect that this will just refine an opinion, but occasionally new knowledge may take us over a tipping point that completely changes our mind. This must be a good thing! We criticise our politicians for being "out of touch", but if they make the slightest effort to learn and change their view, we dismiss it as U-turn, and castigate them for being weak and hypocritical. The best of us learn from our mistakes, we therefore need to appreciate it when others do that. I would agree that constant or repeated mistakes would be a sign of weakness, but not someone who occasionally has the confidence to admit that they have changed their mind on something. It makes you wonder what would have happened to Gandhi if he lived in the modern world. Would we have just pulled him apart every time he changed his mind, completely undermining the great man for one of his greatest qualities?

If these great leaders would potentially be criticised for their approach in the modern world, then maybe it is time to change our definition of strong leadership. Maybe we should shift away from the pure emphasis on strong opinions that are inflexibly applied with a rigid determination. Maybe it is time to admire leaders who have a real strength of character but combine these qualities with a certain humility and the ability to listen and learn. Nobody is perfect, particularly politicians, and we all know that, so it does them no favours to try and pretend that they are!

A great font of thoughts on this topic is the American pastor, Andy Stanley, who said that:

> Admitting a weakness is a sign of strength.
> Acknowledging weakness doesn't make a leader
> less effective.

He also suggested:

> Don't strive to be a well-rounded leader. Instead,
> discover your zone and stay there. Then delegate
> everything else.

What this is really saying is that a great leader is fully aware of their weaknesses and failings, but sufficiently confident in their capabilities in their area of strength. Rather than vie for personal perfection, they should engage the right people to fill any gaps. I talked earlier about Gandhi, but one of the greatest examples of this quality is another key figure in the battle for Indian independence, Jawaharlal Nehru. He became the first prime minister of India after they successfully gained independence from Britain in 1947 and remained prime minister until his death in 1964. Having fought for so many years to get independence, and to help India escape from the clutches of British rule, he was now given that opportunity to help India set its own path. However, in the immediate aftermath of independence in mid-August, the country descended into a chaos of bloody religious violence following the segregation of the sub-continent into India, West Pakistan and East Pakistan (now Bangladesh). During this time, hundreds of thousands of people were killed. Following this, according to the book *Freedom at Midnight*, Nehru did something extraordinary. Acknowledging that "our experience is in the art of agitation, not administration", he approached Lord Mountbatten, the last Viceroy of India who had worked with them in negotiating the freedom of India and asked:

> While you were exercising the highest command
> in war, we were in a British prison. You are a
> professional high-level administrator. You've
> commanded millions of men. You have the
> experience and knowledge colonialism has denied
> us. You English can't just turn this country over

to us after being here all our lives and simply walk
away. We're in an emergency and we need help.
Will you run the country?

As a result of this, Lord Mountbatten remained in India
for another ten months after independence, acting as the first
Governor-General of the independent India, and ultimately,
he continued to lead the country. Nobody knew of this
conversation and the precise terms of their arrangement. It was
kept a closely guarded secret, as it would have been political
suicide, if the wider population had known. But it should not
be considered suicide. Nehru had the belief in his capabilities,
and the conviction of what was right and best for the country,
and knew he needed to ask for help. I understand why some
would argue this as a weakness; asking for help as soon as he
obtained the power that he had been seeking his whole life.
But for me, the opposite is true. He had the confidence to do
the right thing. Clearly, they all considered it best to keep the
arrangement a secret, but ultimately Nehru knew that it was
the right thing to do, irrespective of how it may be perceived.

This is a big example, but you see this in action on a day-
to-day basis in the workplace, and the irony is that it is always
the good managers who feel no shame in asking for help. Their
greatest skill is not their knowledge or expertise, but their
ability to identify the talent in the organisation, nurturing that
talent and getting the most out of them. They are therefore
surrounding themselves with the brightest and the best,
without any concerns about being outshone. They are prepared
to be consultative, to delegate and to let their subordinates
shine and get the credit, because they are benefiting from the
ideas, experience and knowledge of all the best people in the
company and this is helping them make the best and most
informed decisions. Open discussions with their staff and open
minds to listen and learn have built a team that is stronger than
its individual parts. As leaders, they are more bothered about
collective achievement than individual power, and so they will

gain power and influence, but this is a by-product of their success rather than ever being the goal itself.

On the other hand, the weaker leaders are the ones who need that help, but they do the opposite! They fear being outshone by those around them, so they try to impose their authority by being directive and desperately trying to show they are in charge. They surround themselves with like-minded or submissive "yes-men" who agree with everything they say. This may make them look good compared to those around them, but it does not lead to the best outcome as they do not have the sharp thinkers that they could learn from. They therefore make mistakes, lead the team in the wrong direction, alienate the talented individuals around them, and ultimately get a bit isolated. Quoting Andy Stanley once again:

> Leaders who don't listen will eventually be
> surrounded by people who have nothing to say.

This approach may result in some short-term victories, but it doesn't help them achieve great success. In reverse, it normally leads to them becoming increasingly dictatorial to try and keep maintaining that impression of power and authority. In public, it is good to have a team that appears loyal and supportive, but in private, it is critical that any team gives their leader the honest truth, helping them to learn and change. Without this, you have bad leaders who focus on getting respect purely based on status, rather than on their accomplishments. Fortunately, they are generally found out in the end.

Whilst the self-confidence and capability of individuals is probably the main influence as to which type of leader they become, we should not underestimate the impact of our response to them. When people get up to a position of power and authority, we tend to pick holes and shoot them down. With most leaders or politicians, we are much better at spotting their weaknesses than their strengths, to the extent that for leaders that we don't like or would vote against, we become almost incapable of seeing any of their qualities. This behaviour on the part of ourselves and the media helps to reinforce the shortcomings of the leaders. If an admission of weakness is jumped on with an adverse and judgemental reaction, then it is no surprise that these leaders will try to cover them up. This creates a lack of honesty and openness, which drives a lack of trust and connection; but we are complicit in creating this dishonest environment.

Politicians will stay out of touch if we don't let them admit their weakness, make mistakes, learn from those around them, and change their mind. Clearly it is not good if they don't have any informed opinions of their own, or if they are constantly changing their mind without demonstrating any clear convictions or principles or vision. But if they learn and change their path, whether it was an idea from them, their colleagues, the opposition or even the general public, then we should celebrate their readiness to change their course. Whatever they may have said or done in the past, if they have genuinely changed their view and it's not just an act to capture votes, then we should admire their readiness to listen and act in our best interests. I see strength as a firm conviction that we pursue with determination and intensity, but with an openness to listen and to learn, a desire to value the help and input from others, and a confidence to admit when we are wrong.

These attributes are important in our politicians and leaders, but they are relevant to all of us in the discussions we have. Creating an environment with an emphasis on learning and an appreciation of the ability to change and develop would be transformational. But that transformation only comes when we are listening to and learning from a range of diverse and challenging opinions. We are always stronger if we can capture the full spectrum of thoughts and ideas, and therefore make a decision based on the full spectrum of knowledge at our disposal. That is why diversity in the workplace is not just about fairness, it is genuinely about getting the very best outcome. This is not achieved if the concept of diversity is a "tick-box" exercise of getting people into the room, but we then don't listen to what they have to say. Or even worse, if we blindly dismiss everything that we disagree with!

However much we disagree with someone, we can learn from them, as long as we choose to listen! And it will make us all the stronger for it. As a bit of an odd analogy, let me take you back to the 1936 Olympics in Berlin, which is mainly remembered for two things – the fact that Hitler turned the event into a Nazi propaganda show and the fact that Jesse Owens, the African-American athlete proved a bit of an embarrassment by winning four gold medals! However, few are probably aware that the Olympic "tradition" of the torch relay was borne out of these games and was part of the Nazi propaganda show. This has been a wonderful part of every Summer Games since and should not be condemned because of its origins. It should be celebrated for the great idea that it is.

Rest assured, I am not suggesting we invite someone who is evil into our group, in order to get a diversity of opinion! However, what I am saying is that however much we dislike or disapprove of someone, we should continue to judge what they are saying or doing on its merits. If we detest someone, but they are talking sense, we should be prepared to admit that. If we disagree with 99% of what somebody says, we should not dismiss the 1% where they hit the nail on the head. And even more importantly, we should not close our ears to them or completely ignore them, just because we have a different view. Receiving that alternative perspective is invaluable, even if we do not agree with it, as it teaches us about the views of other people.

The problem is not only that our preconceptions tend to close our mind to giving the other party the benefit of the doubt, but that we also approach most interactions with the wrong goal. Stephen R. Covey, author of *7 Habits of Highly Successful People* put this beautifully when he said:

> Most of us don't listen with the intent to
> understand. We listen with the intent to reply.

As soon as we hear something that we disagree with, we are desperate to get our opinion across. Instead of rushing, we should try to take the time to properly understand. Only then should we choose to give our opinion, as otherwise, we lose the chance to gain that understanding.

This makes me think of an amazing story I read about a prison visitor. She was a black woman and one of the prisoners was a violent white supremacist. While all her colleagues avoided him, she decided she wanted to talk to him to understand why he thought the way he did, and so she started visiting him as part of her rounds. The initial conversations were, unsurprisingly, incredibly difficult and awkward, but she was not seeking to change him, more to learn and understand, and so they persisted. Gradually, the conversations became easier and easier. As they talked, she got to understand the circumstances and upbringing that had created his set of beliefs, and he got to understand her and realised the errors in the way he had been thinking. As the prejudices fell away, they were able to see the people underneath, developed a strong bond and connection, and ultimately fell in love. It just shows that when two people enter a situation where they really seek to understand the other person's perspective, then anything is possible!

This reinforces the point that we need to have a readiness to learn. This should apply to skills and capabilities, where we should constantly embrace the spirit of kaizen, and strive to improve until the very end of our lives. But more importantly, in the context of discussions, it should happen with our opinions and views. Bill Nye (an American science communicator and TV presenter) once said that:

> Everyone you will ever meet knows something
> you don't.

It is rare for us to appreciate that, as we are usually too excited to give our own opinion than to draw out the new knowledge from the person we are talking to. We need to flip this, and follow the guidance of the Dalai Lama, who said:

> When you talk, you are only repeating what you already know. But if you listen, you may learn something new.

If we recognise the opportunity that every interaction gives us to gain new knowledge and insight, and truly embrace the chance to learn from those around us, then we can genuinely get the best of our diversity. We should value this, always striving to learn, however old we are and however much we know. Moreover, we should encourage those around us to do the same. People who evolve and improve deserve our admiration and appreciation about how they have learned and changed, rather than being slapped down and reminded of their past failings. In the same way, we should encourage our politicians to learn and to make better decisions in the future than they did in the past, and then give them the credit for making that shift. This just needs an open mind to constantly learn new things, a preparedness to change our views and the mindset that learning should never stop. And if we're ever in doubt how to do this, then we should just copy the approach of Celeste Headlee who said:

> I keep my mouth shut as often as I possibly can. I keep my mind open. And I'm always prepared to be amazed.

SECOND PRINCIPLE

Never stop learning and have the courage to change your mind

CHAPTER 4

Change the way you Think and you can Change the way you are

The most significant visions are not cast by great orators from a stage. They are cast at the bedsides of our children. The greatest vision casting opportunities happen between the hours of 7:30 and 9:30 PM Monday through Sunday. In these closing hours of the day we have a unique opportunity to plant the seeds of what could be and what should be. Take every opportunity you get.

ANDY STANLEY

When we are born into this world, we are small and fragile and completely dependent on our parents. We may have support measures in place in the developed world, but even so, we rely on our parents for our very existence in the early days of our lives. They provide us with the food and drink that keeps us alive and helps us grow, and they protect us from the many dangers of the world that are too much for us while our skeleton is delicate and our biology is developing. Over time, we become increasingly self-sufficient, but this is a long and slow process over many years of growth, as we slowly become the adults that will make our own way in the world.

This physical development is the easiest to observe, but there is an equally important psychological development that is happening at the same time. Alongside becoming bigger and stronger, we start to develop a personality, a way of thinking and a perspective on life. These have a huge impact on our later life as they will shape what we do, who we meet, and potentially how successful we are. There has always been debate whether these more psychological elements are shaped by nature or nurture. In other words, is it driven by genetics and we are largely predestined to behave in a certain way or is it more caused by the influences and experiences that we face as we journey through our formative years? Most likely, it is a bit of both, and our parents or primary care-givers, as the people with the most permanent recurring impact on our lives, have a critically important role in this psychological development.

The evidence for the nurturing impact is particularly clear if we focus on some extreme negative cases, as I think it is hard to disagree that there must be an impact when a child is a victim of abusive or neglectful parenting. Reading the wonderfully thought-provoking *A Road Less Travelled*, you'll see numerous references to the link between the quality of parenting and the mental health and wellbeing of a child. This is backed up by plenty of psychology research that reinforces this causal link. It's obviously no guarantee – children of woeful parents can emerge remarkably unscathed, while similarly, children from a loving and secure background can have problems – but the chances of mental health issues are significantly increased when the parenting is poor, with proven connections including the facts that:

a. Children from broken homes are more likely to get in trouble when they are older;
b. Children who get no encouragement or support in their academic work or sporting pursuits are less likely to be successful; and

c. Children who are constantly told lies or let down will grow up with a natural suspicion of what they are told and therefore find it difficult to trust people.

We all know these extreme examples are bad for the child, and fortunately, the vast majority of parents can quite rightly demonstrate that they are not providing this sort of toxic environment for their children. But what is the impact of less serious or malicious actions that a child probably experiences on a daily basis? Let us imagine a few different scenarios:

1. Parents are busy and at times of the day, they just need to do their own thing, whether it's to cook the dinner, do the household chores or just get a bit of time to themselves after a stressful day. The child wants company and to spend some time with their parent so is snapping at their heels, craving attention. So, the parent puts on the TV or iPad, chooses the child's favourite film or TV programme or video game, and as if by magic, there is silence! The child is engrossed, and the parent has the time and space to get things done. Is this a sensible use of a modern tool to help us be productive? Or is this a mild example of being neglectful towards our child?

2. Due to the financial pressures of life and particularly the cost of bringing up a child, both parents may be forced to work in order to provide for their children. This may ensure their children have food, comfort and a secure home, but this may come at the expense of quality family time. In the developing world, we see extreme examples of this with fathers travelling overseas to seek work and send money back to their families. But we also see this compromise in the United Kingdom, and in some cases, either the work itself or the associated stresses can interfere with the time spent as a family. But is this right? Does the income and financial security provide the best opportunity for the children's future, or are we better just having time as a family?

3. For many, relaxing and socialising may often involve a drink or two, and there is nothing wrong with that. This is an integral part of the world we live in, and there is not necessarily any reason why we should stop as parents. Or is there? Society has accepted that drinking and driving should not be permitted, because we have less focus and attention when we have drunk even limited amounts of alcohol. But surely there is nothing more important than parenting our child, so shouldn't we consider the same logic, abstain from drinking and make sure our child is getting the best care and attention? Or should we just relax with a glass or two, safe in the knowledge that providing our child a relaxed and loving home is all that matters?

There is no right or wrong to any of these scenarios. Different people could quite reasonably reach different conclusions as to how they want to approach the upbringing of their child. Some actively decide to make financial sacrifices to keep one parent full-time at home with their child, while others believe that going out and doing a day's work makes them more engaged parents when they are then back at home with their child. Someone who is risk averse may always want to be sober so they are conscious of their surroundings and could jump in the car if anything went wrong, while others may consider that this overanxious and pessimistic mindset is unhelpful for their family. And it's not just people that vary, circumstances may change the way we should behave. If we are concerned about a child being very shy and withdrawn, then leaving them to themselves or fobbing them off with an iPad is probably inappropriate, but when a child is doing well at school or happily engaged in activities or hobbies, then these actions may be fine. If a child is suffering from health problems, then working too late or drinking alcohol may seem wrong as our presence and full ability to care is critical, but when they're bouncing round with great energy and have plenty of friends, then this may not be a problem. What really matters is therefore our awareness of what we are doing and the impact that this is having on our child, so we know if we are getting things right or if we need to make a change.

I could go and dig out psychology research that demonstrates this, but a TV programme called *The House of Tiny Tearaways* captured this beautifully. It was a simple concept whereby some parents who were really struggling to cope with their errant young children (with the most common issues being children throwing tantrums, refusing to eat or proving impossible to get to sleep) would stay in a house under constant surveillance from a clinical psychologist. This gave the psychologist the chance to observe the situation, study the behaviours of all the family, and to understand what was causing the problems. Without fail, what we saw was some kind, loving parents, wishing the very best for their child, and turning to the psychologist to ask why their child was behaving in that way.

The parents were turning their full attention to the behaviour of the child, when 99% of the time, the problem was their own behaviour. Nothing was malicious or intentional, but small behaviours, for whatever reason, were having major consequences. This included things like arguing in front of the children, undermining each other when one gives instructions to the child, different perspectives on the best parenting approach, lack of structure or discipline and particularly a lack of consequences for negative actions. The parents would never have realised without being told, partly because their behaviours did not necessarily appear that major, but moreover because they were focused on the child. They were asking "Why is the child doing this?" rather than "What am I doing to cause it?" Had they focused on their own behaviours, challenged themselves and thought through the consequences of what they were doing, then maybe they would have worked it out. However, in the absence of this, it was left to the psychologist to tell them, teach the parents to correct their behaviours and issues they had battled with for months were solved in a matter of days.

These parent-child interactions are incredibly common, and the only thing that is unusual about the above situation (other than it being televised!) is that a psychologist was given the chance to intervene. Most parents having similar issues with their children will just battle through, considering it to be the luck of the draw as to whether they got a happy, calm, good sleeper with a healthy appetite, or a bit of a troublemaker! As we are acting with such good intentions, we fail to notice the warning signs that these behaviours are giving to us. We probably therefore exacerbate the situation, by getting frustrated and tired as a result of the child's behaviour. Ultimately, the child's behaviour starts to feel like a trial and a challenge, when the symptoms we are seeing are actually a real blessing as they are flagging a problem. What we really need to fear are the hidden issues that may be building up slowly over time without any external representation. These festering issues may not surface until much later in a child's life, maybe when they're struggling to make their own way in the world, or to start a relationship of their own. By this time, they have probably been reinforced for many, many years and rooted themselves deep into their psychology. Fixing things is going to take a lot more than a couple of days behavioural change from the parents!!!! Just like a more physical illness like cancer, catching problems early, makes them easier to cure.

So, the warning signs from our children are actually a good thing, but we tend not to see them this way, and we fail to respond to these small bumps in the road. We usually need a bigger jolt to initiate a sense of self-reflection. A great example of this is the very sad case of Maddie, the small girl who went missing from the Portuguese resort of Praia da Luz in Portugal on a family holiday. Few people in the UK could have missed the story, but the parents were eating nearby their accommodation and popping back periodically to check on their sleeping children. Who cannot imagine the sinking feeling one time they popped back to their rooms and discovered that their daughter was no longer there? We can only imagine the horror and sheer panic that must have induced, a feeling that resonated with the whole country to the extent that many years later, the case remains fresh in everyone's minds.

I don't propose to consider whether the actions of the parents were right or wrong – thousands or even millions of parents have done the same without any negative consequences. The risk was therefore negligible, and this family were just appallingly unlucky. There is no right or wrong here, and it is very much up to individual parents to decide what they thought was right or wrong. However, what struck me with this situation was the reaction of other parents. This represented a jolt! My friends who were parents changed their behaviour. Suddenly the negligible risk seemed a risk not worth taking. Friends who would have gone to a hotel, tucked their children in bed and then gone downstairs for dinner were now not prepared to do this. In essence, nothing had changed. The risk was negligible, and it remained negligible, but the parents' perception of it had shifted, and so they changed their behaviour.

And this is important, because in all aspects of our lives, a change in our perception tends to lead to a change in our behaviour. But wouldn't it be great if we didn't need the seismic jolt from something going horribly wrong, and just noticed the small, but almost imperceptible red flags? Working at British Gas, the dangerous nature of the business (involving not just gas and electricity in the domestic and business environment, but offshore gas rigs and large power stations) meant the importance of keeping staff safe was paramount. A culture of Health & Safety was therefore instilled into the workforce, whether in a high-risk job or more office-based role. Health & Safety gets a lot of bad press, because of some of the extreme practices, but there is a key underlying principle that is hugely valuable, and that involved reporting on incidents, analysing them, and therefore taking the necessary precautions to make sure the same incidents don't happen again.

We all do this to a certain extent, learning from our mistakes as we go, and this often involves the hurt or harm that we may want to avoid. However, what was particularly interesting about the Health & Safety monitoring was that we were required not just to report the accidents, but the near misses. Deep to the core, this felt very weird. Having to file a report to say that "I picked up a solar panel, it caught the wind and I nearly dropped it" or "the carpet tile in the office was a bit loose and I stumbled" felt so strange. What a palaver over something that didn't go wrong! However, it's a great concept. Learning from our mistakes means things go wrong only once, while learning from our "near misses" means that it never goes wrong at all. We don't need someone to smash a solar panel and break their toe, or someone to fall over carrying a full cup of scalding coffee, before we insist that two people lift a solar panel, or we fix the carpet! This does not mean we have to put a rule around everything – this is when Health & Safety gets its bad reputation. But it does make us aware of the risk and then we can decide if we need to do something about it. A risk that is unknown becomes a known risk that we consciously decide to take, just as after the Maddie abduction.

Reflecting on my own childhood, I was incredibly lucky with the parenting I received. I was given the opportunity to try everything, particularly a sport like rugby which became my passion, even though my father had never played. I was supported and encouraged completely in study, sport and play and one of my parents attended pretty much everything I ever did. They devoted time to me and my siblings and I have incredibly fond memories of Sunday lunch and Sunday tea as a family, amazing family holidays in Sandbanks, as well as hours spent playing in the garden and being helped with my homework. But they also gave me the time and space that I wanted, and I spent hours and hours playing games by myself, which my introverted nature hugely enjoyed. They showed me so much love that I was incredibly close to my family, and being honest, as I was growing up, they were all that mattered to me.

As amazing as they were there though, there were some well-intentioned things that had a negative impact on me while

I was a child or as I grew older and made my own way in the big wide world:

1. Pride means pressure

First and foremost, I did pretty well at school, and I'm glad to say that this made my parents feel very proud of my achievements, to the extent that they would tell family, friends and anyone they spoke to about what I had done! This sounds wonderful, and clearly a complete lack of pride from my parents would have been far worse. However, the problem was that it made me feel under pressure, with an ever-growing shadow of fear that it wasn't going to last. The better I did, the greater the burden of pressure, and the more anxious I felt. It didn't cross my parents' mind that they were doing anything wrong, as their actions were fuelled by overwhelmingly positive sentiments of pride and goodwill and I never said anything about the growing fear that I didn't know how to control. Fortunately, this anxiety never led to anything more serious than long, sleepless nights and a lack of self-confidence, but the impact lingered long into my adult life and I was really in my mid-twenties before developing a sense of self-belief. It was only as part of writing this book that I told my parents how I had felt, and they were mortified that their actions had unintentionally ended up with me feeling incredibly stressed. I never did and still don't blame them, as in reality, I put the pressure on myself, but there is no doubting that they would have behaved differently if they knew how I was feeling.

2. Good advice with the wrong outcome

Another well-intentioned but impactful habit of theirs was a tendency to guide me to the path of least resistance, rather than necessarily the right one. A small but personally significant example of this took place shortly after I had learned to drive. At this time, I had reached the conclusion I didn't want to drink alcohol, and this was proving difficult in social situations, and at the rugby club with its drinking culture. I spoke to my parents about how to deal with this situation, and they suggested at the time what appeared to be the great idea of driving and using this as a bit of an excuse for why I was not drinking. It worked a few times, but then there was an occasion when I did not have the car, and everyone knew I did not have the car, and suddenly the pressure to drink was multiplied. The coping strategy was not fixing the problem, I was merely shifting it and finding a way to reduce its frequency.

When I finally had the guts to admit that I did not want to drink, it became quite a life-changing moment for me. It was nothing do with alcohol, but more a matter of self-confidence. This was probably the first time that I had gone against the flow and stood up for what I wanted without the fear of impressing others. The overwhelmingly positive reaction was empowering and spread into other areas of my life. This was the trigger that ultimately liberated me from the fear of failure I described above. Was the advice of my parents wrong? Not necessarily. Their advice was with the best of intentions and aimed to protect me from any negative reaction. However, they focused on keeping me safe and we both underestimated the importance of confronting my fears.

3. A wonderful place but not for me

A final element of my upbringing that had a profound impact is where they chose to live. As a very young child, we moved to a small town, just outside London. This was before "the start of my memory" so is the only home I remember as a child. There are so many positives about where they chose. We had a nice house that was full of love where we could flourish as a family. We were close to their parents so I could spend plenty of time with my grandparents and develop close bonds. It was wonderfully safe affording me great security in everything I did and there were fantastic schools that maximised my potential. In fact, it was such a wonderful home-life that in the first year after I left, when heading back on Christmas Eve singing along to 'Driving Home for Christmas' by Chris Rea, I had to stop by the roadside as I was so overwhelmed by tears of happiness.

However, it did have one downside, which was that it was an affluent town, lacking diversity, where everyone carried that middle-class expectation of the path you should follow – university, good job, wife, children. My parents never imposed that pressure and were much more open-minded than their friends, but this sense of expectation was there, and became quite a burden as I realised Steps 3 and 4 were not going to be for me! The consequence was a lot of mental anguish in my late teens and early twenties as I tried to battle between my feelings and the path I felt "obligated" to follow. It also led to a tendency to avoid social interaction as it was easier to keep secrets away from the crowd, and ultimately, a failure to admit the truth to myself until I was 25! Once again, there is no wrong from my parents. Firstly, the positives of where we lived massively outweighed any negatives, and they made the decision to move there when I was about two, when even I didn't know I was gay! However, later in my life, it did become very difficult as I felt incredibly safe and loved inside my family unit, but a real outcast as a gay, teetotal rugby player in a straight world. They did not know this, and I could not tell you what they should have done if they were armed with this knowledge, but I was hugely impacted by the surroundings that my parents chose.

I am not writing this in any way to criticise my parents. I love them passionately, as they are (still to this very day) incredibly loving, making every decision with the right intentions to always put their children first and to make whatever sacrifices are needed to help us on the way. Many people probably read these examples and think they are trivial compared to the challenges they have faced, and I know I am blessed and lucky to have had the wonderful, secure, loving childhood that I had, filled with opportunity, laughter and happiness. I will never stop being grateful for having two such amazing people in my life. Even in the above examples, I know exactly why they did what they did, and the loving motivations behind them, so it is very difficult to criticise. However, they did feel significant to me at the time, and they did have a major impact on many years of my life.

What this emphasises is what an impossible job it is being a parent, and the fact that we cannot expect any parent to get everything right all the time. Every single day, in fact every single moment with a child, is a balancing act of:

- The need to impose some sense of control and structure into the family life, but without being excessive and preventing the child from making any choices or decisions;
- The need to allow children the freedom to try things, make mistakes and learn in the process, but without being reckless and letting the children get hurt;
- The need to encourage and support children to achieve things, but without doing it for them and stopping them learning or stressing them with pressure.

This would be hard enough anyway, if it were a job, where we were on duty from 9–5 and had evenings, weekends and four weeks of holiday, where we could rest and recover. But there is no break, it is full time and relentless with the challenge of our own issues, pressures, stresses and temptations at the same time! Add to this that the consequences of our actions are often not physical but locked away in the minds of our children. This means we can only see and understand them if our child is open to share their feelings with full transparency and honesty and that we listen, understand and interpret every word. With the best will in the world, this is not going to happen!

When the job is so hard, the ability to reflect on the impact of our behaviour and to learn from our mistakes is so critical. Just as the clinical psychologist in *The House of Tiny Tearaways* could shed a light, this is where opinions from others can be so valuable, especially if they have a different perspective on what we are doing. This may be because they are not so immersed in the situation, and just get a bit more time and space to stand back and observe. It may be because they are a bit more impartial and can see things without the cloud of emotion. It may be because they have been through similar experiences in their life or have a different understanding to us. Or it may be because they have heard something through the child or one of their friends, which has not been shared with the parents. For whatever reason, this input is invaluable as a chance to self-reflect and realise what we are doing.

But do we all see it that way? When we're doing an incredibly challenging job to a great standard with so much love, it's not nice to receive criticism and someone telling us what to do! We may be thinking, "What do they know anyway? They don't know half the story. They don't know what's really happening! I'm doing a good job as a parent!" This reaction is wholly understandable as all of this may be true – an independent observer probably doesn't know all the facts, and probably hasn't got it 100% right. However, irrespective of this, it is invaluable information, and the best thing is to use that information and reflect. We should not be too defensive, but be confident that we're doing our best, such that comments from others do not feel like criticism but feel like an opportunity to learn. It allows us to question ourselves and reassure us of our path. This self-reflection will either reinforce that we were doing the right thing and allow us to continue with greater confidence or will allow us to fix the small mistakes or avoid the undesired impacts. Ultimately, however good a parent we are, this will make us even better! Parents normally say they "would do anything" to give their child "the best chance in life", but sometimes being defensive and resistant to challenge can get in the way of delivering on that. We can be just a bit too proud to admit the truth, and the only person who then suffers is the child that we want to cherish.

This last point is why our approach to parenting is such a good representation of some of the problems we have in discussions. When we believe our opinions are right, fair or well-intentioned, we tend to show the same defensiveness. We put up the barriers to criticism, and defend our corner, with the consequence that we fail to see the weaknesses in our argument. Just like parents focusing on their children rather than themselves, we tend to focus on why other people are wrong, rather than valuing the chance to self-reflect and determine whether we are really right. And to reinforce this, we become blind to the smaller warning signs that we may have got things slightly wrong, and so only realise when our errors get properly exposed. Our perspective on our opinions becomes blinkered, one-dimensional and defensive, and this is hugely limiting when we are trying to discuss those opinions with others.

So, there is much to learn from our parenting, but just as there are two people in a discussion, the parent is just one side of that interaction. While adult figures are influencing their development (whether positively or negatively), children are the recipients of all this, and at one point in time, we were all that child. Both the treatment we were receiving and perhaps more importantly the way we perceived and reacted to that treatment, was shaping the people we are and our state of mind. This makes it even more important for parents to self-reflect as, just like in my personal examples, it is not always what the parents are doing, but the personal reactions of their children. Well-intentioned acts do not always have the well-intentioned impact! But whilst our childhood experiences are hugely significant, this behavioural learning does not stop as we grow up. Our experiences, our relationships, our friendships, our ups and our downs, and the way we react to everything is constantly developing the people that we are. It gives us experience that may help us to deal with similar situations in the future, it may help us learn and broaden our minds and understand, but most importantly, it will shape the way we feel and our outlook on life.

As briefly mentioned earlier, whilst we often talk of experiences, it is really our perception on what happens that drives our "truth", and it is therefore our perception of events that drives our development. A great example of this is outlined in the much-lauded book, *Awaken the Giant Within* by Anthony Robbins. In one section, the author describes two sons of an alcoholic and drug-addicted father, who was constantly in trouble with the police and ultimately ended up with life imprisonment for murder. One of the sons followed the path of his father, and his life rapidly skidded off the rails until he wound up in prison; while the other son worked hard, went to university, and then had a successful marriage and career. It's interesting that two boys with the same upbringing could take their lives in such different paths, but there are probably many examples of this. What made this example intriguing is that both boys gave exactly the same reason for why their life had turned out the way it did.

> What else could I have become, having grown up
> with a father like that?

Two people with the same horrible experience, but one was dragged down by the experience, while the other used it as an inspiration for everything he shouldn't be. This shows that it is our perspective on experiences that shapes things, rather than the experiences themselves; which is why such an honest self-reflection on the inner workings of our mind can be so invaluable.

Looking back, this is not something we have been very good at, but there are some signs of change. We are starting to challenge the "stiff upper lip" so famed in the United Kingdom, encouraging people to be more in touch with their emotions, to avoid bottling things up, and to share their problems. We see celebrities talking more openly about their challenges and the value of mental health support; and rather than being slated by the press, they are increasingly praised for openly talking about the issues they have faced and for emphasising the value of seeking support. We are starting to talk a better game.

But whilst we are making the right noises, how many people actually spend the time to reflect on the way they are thinking and the way they feel? How many people understand why they are behaving in a certain way or making certain decisions? How many people truly understand the people that they are? How many people then use this knowledge to try and make changes, and to challenge and improve the aspects that they do not like? I don't have the statistics, but I expect we would all acknowledge that the number is extremely low. Whether due to time or inclination, very few of us make the effort. This means that despite the rhetoric, progress is painfully slow. And ultimately, one of the reasons for this, is that our mental health is a truly complicated issue that should require complicated discussion, and yet nothing has moved beyond the very basic concept that "it's good to talk!"

So why is this? Why do so many of us never take the time for self-reflection? Why do so many of us dismiss the need for psychological or professional help? We all have behavioural issues that negatively impact what we do on a day-to-day basis, whether it's emotional "baggage", a lack of self-esteem, fears, phobias or problems with confidence, stress or anxiety. Whether we classify them as such, they are all mental health problems. With something physical like pain, we know there's a sliding scale from the small pain (of a snapped fingernail) to the severe pain (of say a dislocated shoulder), but wherever we are on the scale and whatever our ability to deal with that pain, we still call it one thing. Pain! At the low end, we may decide we don't need to do anything and will just put up with it, in the middle we'll probably take a painkiller, and further up or if it persists, we'll go to the doctors. But we identify them all as pain, we acknowledge what we are feeling, and we find a coping strategy or cure. So why don't we do the same with mental health? Why do we treat severe conditions like they are something completely different to the milder symptoms, such that it's only a mental health problem when it becomes serious? This partition means that we have a stigma around people with "problems" and therefore show a reluctance to admit our issues and seek treatment. And because we think we haven't quite slipped into the "problem" category, we pretend we are fine and therefore gloss over and ignore our weaknesses. We all have issues that we would be better resolving, if we were just honest enough to admit it, but few of us seem able to do that!

As described above, the first issue with our mental health is the sense of denial around our problems. But even if we achieve acceptance, there remain several big obstacles to overcome:

1. We admit there is something wrong, but wrongly identify the cause. In many cases, we will see only the secondary symptoms, whether mental (anxiety, frustration, anger), physical (poor health, alcoholism, stress) or tangible (money, family or relationship problems), but not realise or spot the true underlying psychological cause.

2. We admit there is something that we want to change, but we don't think it is changeable. Often, we have that sense that behaviours which developed because of life experiences or the way we were brought up are now a part of our personality that is now fully formed, fixed and unbreakable. We might say to ourselves "That's just the way I am", or like one of my work colleagues told me, "That's because I'm Italian!"

3. We admit that there is something that we want to change, but we don't believe that any of the techniques or professional support will help. If we don't have the confidence that there is a treatment programme that will work, then surely we are better on just finding a way to cope with it, rather than fighting and being unhappy.

4. Even if we get past all of this and believe things are changeable, then sometimes we still don't go through with things, because it feels just too much like hard work and we would just have to make too many sacrifices to get there. Once behaviours and feelings are entrenched, there is no doubt that it can be hard and challenging (both in time and

in emotional energy) to shift things, and time is something that we often lack in our complicated and busy lives.

Considering all these obstacles, it's not exactly surprising that so many of us don't embark on the process. We may look at psychologists or therapists as people who just ask annoying and difficult questions but don't really solve anything, with no knowledge of the different types of psychological support that may be available. We may look at mental techniques such as meditation and mindfulness and dismiss them as hippy claptrap, without having any understanding of what they involve. But most importantly, we probably see coping strategies such as socialising, drinking or shifting our focus onto something "more constructive", as much more effective than some self-reflection. Our failure to address our problems is so commonplace that we even have an expression, "It's better the devil you know", suggesting that we should continue accepting the bad things we are familiar with, because somehow the unknown is even more scary!

And to a certain extent, it's hard to disagree with this opinion. So much success has been achieved by people just knuckling down and getting on with things. You could argue that meeting the challenges in our path doesn't need meditation and self-reflection but just a bit of willpower and determination to battle through and get the job done! Focusing on something, driving ourselves towards our goal of success or happiness, is no doubt a great feeling, irrespective of whatever problems may be lurking in our background. In addition, fighting to change "the way we are" can feel a bit futile, and lead to us failing to accept and love the way that we are. This all feels very plausible, but there are a couple of big problems:

1. If we only had to do something once, then battling through makes sense, but if we're doing something repeatedly, then surely it would be more efficient to fix it! Imagine we have a slow puncture which means we can cycle for two hours

without needing to reinflate the tyre. Well... if we need to get to work now, we should just pump up the tyre and get to work – no point in spending ages repairing the puncture! However, if we cycle every day, and need to re-pump every single day, then surely the investment to repair the puncture makes sense? Psychologically, we are no different. Sometimes, we may be getting through with willpower, but we're making every day harder by refusing to "fix the puncture".

2. We suggest our personality and behaviour is "fixed", and whether shaped by nature or nurture, we may currently act or behave in a certain way, but we can all tell we gradually evolve and change. We may consider this as just natural ageing (e.g. wanting different things now I am older) or learning (e.g. benefiting from a new perspective), but if these changes can gradually happen, why do we not believe we can make them happen? Nobody is perfect, we are all different, and it is important to be happy with the way we are, but if there is something we do want to change, is it really beyond our powers? I personally feel that we are more powerful than we sometimes believe we are!

I have first-hand experience of using denial and private coping strategies to deal with my problems, no more so than in respect of my struggles to come to terms with being gay. In my early 20s, I was wrestling with an inner conflict between the knowledge I was gay and the "straight" life of a traditional family and a passion for rugby, which I felt that I wanted. This conflict had always been there but did not seem that important through my teenage years. As I grew older, however, it gradually became all-consuming. I built a conviction that wanting such conflicting things from my life meant I was doomed to be unhappy, and this cloud over my future brought gloom and despair over my present. But nobody else knew. Despite being very close to my family and having some great friends, not one person in the entire world knew what was going on. My solution was to make myself busy. I was busy enough anyway with work and rugby, but I filled up every gap by going out and socialising. I may not have been drinking, but I was laughing and smiling and looking so happy to the outside world. But it was all a cover so nobody could see my weakness or my inner turmoil! And it wasn't me either. The truth is, the real me is not that sociable. I love to spend time at home by myself, and house parties are my idea of a living hell! I was spending hours and hours doing things that I hated, just to avoid being forced to focus on my conflict.

Fortunately for me, a knight in shining armour appeared and made me realise that being gay was not incompatible with a happy family, and that a family of two with the most amazing person was far better than the dream I had carried in my head. I gradually started to accept the way I was, admitted the truth to myself and then had the strength to admit it to everyone around me. And the rest is history! But had my future husband not appeared at the moment of my deepest despair; how long would I have languished in this state of denial? This is an extreme example, but if we are all truly honest with ourselves, there are probably many smaller things where we are doing the same.

The truth is that we are the only people who see our true self, who truly knows what is going on inside of our head. While with more physical health, a doctor can run a sequence of tests, add together the various evidence and determine what is wrong with us, the same is not true for our mental health. A good psychotherapist can do this, but they are gathering evidence from questioning us and making us talk, and this therefore relies on our openness and honesty. If we're not prepared to open ourselves in this way, then any psychological distress remains private, and those around us (however close they are), may well not see it. This has two big problems. Firstly, it means we can choose what persona we present to the outside world. This is becoming more extreme in social media world, where people can choose to present a "perfect" view of themselves without needing to become that person. But this problem is not new to the internet age. Social media has just created a more public, exhibitionist equivalent of something that was always there i.e. our ability to create stories to present ourselves in the best possible light. And this leads to the second problem, where we devote our energies and focus on protecting the image. While we should be focused on the authentic version of ourselves, so we can either accept it or change it, we are distracted by a character that we have created that is a better version of our real selves.

Whilst overcoming this sense of denial is critical, this is no easy task when we are distracted by our external persona and a bit blinkered to what is really going on. And that is where an outside perspective can be so invaluable. The British are normally too scared to have a therapist, let alone admit to having one, and we prefer to laugh at the fact that every American has one! We are probably wrong to laugh, as talking and self-reflecting is invaluable, but what is the purpose of a therapist? Someone that we see for the rest of our life, or someone who will stimulate a change to either resolve an issue or make us a better person? Whilst the good ones may quickly guide us to resolve our problems, the money-grabbing therapists will be quite happy for us to come back forever – we're providing them with a nice income stream! But just like paying our gym membership isn't what makes us fit, paying regular fees to a therapist is not going to improve our psychological wellbeing. We need to fully invest ourselves emotionally, go past the point of understanding to a place where we can actually identify the problems and fix them. Otherwise, we are just going through the motions, and not taking ourselves forward – it's no different to just having a hobby or a very expensive friend!

There is a joke about a religious man in a flood. With the waters rising, he climbs up on to the roof of his house. A fireman wades through the waters and offers to carry the man to safety, but the man just replies that "God will save me". The waters get higher and higher, and a boat comes across and offers to take the man to safety, and again he says that "God will save me". As the waters are about to consume him, a helicopter hovers above with a ladder lowered down, but the man just looks up and says that "God will save me". The man is then finally consumed by the waters and drowns. On arrival at Heaven, he asks why God didn't save him, and is told quite firmly that:

> He sent a fireman, a boat and a helicopter. What more did you want?

This is clearly a facetious example, but it serves as a good reminder that belief is not enough to take us to safety or success. If we become too blinded by our faith in something and believe that this alone will carry us where we need to go, then we lose sight of our personal responsibility and the decisive actions that are also needed. Clearly this example is painted in a religious context, but this applies just as much to any of the ways we may look at our mental health or our opinions. Self-reflection can be exceptionally powerful but is rather wasted if we do nothing with what we find. Meditation, mindfulness and tai-chi can be powerful tools to focus our mind, but if we do not take advantage of that greater clarity to find a new path, then what have we achieved? Therapists (well the good ones at least!) can be invaluable in triggering this self-realisation by helping to unblock the barriers that we have put in the way to prevent us from seeing it ourselves, but again, the self-realisation and the consequential actions and mindset shifts are dependent on us to take action.

I have a good friend who was my flatmate many years ago, and while we were living together, he was a passionate believer in Buddhism and meditation. He was quite an inspiration to me, as he was very different to anyone I knew, and from what I could see, he seemed very accepting of the fact he was different – something I had not managed at that stage of my life. Although he would spend plenty of time in meditative reflection, I could still sense there was something missing.

I'm no therapist and had significantly less awareness at that time compared to what I have now. However, I do listen, and he talked a lot about a dream to move to Paris. Without understanding the motivations behind this desire, this seemed a simple problem to fix. Despite his open mind, he was classically displaying the "Better the Devil you know" mindset, while my perspective was that he should just go and try and it – he could always move back if it didn't work! More than 20 years later, he is still in Paris, happily married with a wife and children and much more content. However powerful the tools we use, it is the action that really counts!

Once again, if you reflect on the challenges that we face in dealing with our mental health, there are great parallels with our approach to discussions. The barriers to self-reflect on our behaviour, which cause such problems for our mental health, are replicated through our inability to self-reflect on our opinions. We have the same sense of denial that there may be any flaws in our thinking, and by reinforcing this over the years, our views become ever more entrenched. Whilst someone with a mental health problem may have blind-spots to those problems, we can become similarly blinkered. And just as we psychologically create a fantasy version of ourselves, we do the same with our opinions, falsely believing that they are much better informed than they actually are. And if ever we are exposed to that external challenge, we don't properly engage in the process – going through the motions of pretending to listen, or just defending our opinions as if they were a fortress. Through our tendency to listen to the research or evidence that supports our views and criticise or dismiss or undermine any contrary opinions that we hear, we make our opinion almost impregnable.

The controversial Monty Python film, *Life of Brian*, highlighted people's ability to do this in a comic scene where they show Brian being pursued by a large crowd of people who have convinced themselves he is the Messiah. Obviously he is not the Messiah and he is therefore denying it:

"I'm not the Messiah! Will you please listen? I am not the Messiah, do you understand?"

…. but then one of the ardent supporters says:

"Only the true Messiah denies His divinity."

Brian then retorts:

"What? Well, what sort of chance does that give me? All right! I am the Messiah!"

…. And the Followers excitedly proclaim:

"He is! He is the Messiah!"

Now, clearly this is comic exaggeration, but it classically shows how when we have convinced ourselves of a certain point of view, we can take conflicting evidence as means of supporting our argument. In this instance, a denial or an admission were both taken with equal enthusiasm as support for their view. And this happens in the real world too, as was the reaction to *Fire and Fury*, the book on Donald Trump written by Michael Wolff. Fans of Donald Trump perceived it as a reinforcement of the conspiracies against a great leader, while critics considered it an insightful demonstration of the weaknesses of the man. The same evidence, but completely different conclusions based on the predetermined belief that was already there. Similarly, a 2018 survey of Conservative and Labour voters in the UK asked whether they believed that the party leaders (Theresa May and Jeremy Corbyn) were honest. The majority of voters believed that the party they supported was honest, but less than 10% thought the same of the opposition leader. We are clearly never going to listen to the opposite perspective if we are convinced that they are lying!

The fact that these biases lead us to taking such a distorted perspective is exactly why the challenge and contrasting insight from others is so valuable. Of course, we would like people who challenge or criticise us to be constructive in their approach. But as the recipients of that criticism, we need to focus less on how they say things and focus more on the message and the opportunity to get a fresh perspective. This is not about our approach, but about our openness to receive. Progress is stifled when we refuse to accept an informed challenge from an adversary.

This is probably best exemplified by numerous examples from history when great minds and great inventors tried to challenge the pervading thoughts of the time. Think of Galileo, for example, who suggested the concept of heliocentrism, the astronomical model that places the sun at the centre of the solar system. This was met with such fierce resistance that in 1610, he wrote to the fellow astronomer and "believer", Johannes Kepler:

> My dear Kepler, I wish that we might laugh at
> the remarkable stupidity of the common herd.
> What do you have to say about the principal
> philosophers of this academy who are filled
> with the stubbornness of an asp and do not
> want to look at either the planets, the moon
> or the telescope, even though I have freely and
> deliberately offered them the opportunity a
> thousand times? Truly, just as the asp stops its ears,
> so do these philosophers shut their eyes to the light
> of truth.

Whilst he was accumulating huge evidence of a theory that we now know to be completely accurate, this was widely rejected and formally declared as heretical in 1616. Ultimately, Galileo was prosecuted for his views and kept under house arrest for the last nine years of his life.

We may think this is extreme, and mock the Catholic Church for their intransigence, but in fact, we do the same all the time. We hold onto our pre-existing beliefs and viewpoints with such tenacity that we behave just like the "common herd" to whom Galileo is referring in his letter, and we therefore fail to learn from evidence-based challenges that are actually more informed than us! We need to open up to this challenge. There is a big difference between a conscious belief that is built upon information and intelligent thought, and a brainwashed belief that is based purely on distorted perspectives, but we may not see that difference until we accept some challenge with an open mind. We should embrace this opportunity and ask ourselves some questions. Why do we think the way we do? Why are we behaving in this way? Why is my way of thinking the right way of thinking? Do they know something that I don't?

But as is so often the case, this is not as easy as it sounds, because there are a few distorting influences that try to prevent this impartial self-reflection:

Peer pressure: There is immense pressure to follow the crowd and think, act and behave in a certain way. Everyone has probably (at some point in the life) suppressed their opinion from fear of standing out from the mainstream, and this is only a small step from having our opinion swayed. Is our opinion really our own opinion?

Emotion: Positive feelings (e.g. love or excitement) or negative emotions (e.g. anger or jealousy) can lead us to do things in a way that we would never do when we are feeling more calm or rational. This can be a positive thing, as it may release us to overcome hesitation or fear to take a certain action. But it can also be hugely damaging and colour our judgement and lead to us drawing a wrong conclusion. Is our opinion more driven by emotion than reality?

Biased information: Everything we hear or read, however impartial it tries to be, is founded on opinion. We often interpret history or news as fact, when it is just the opinion of the person who recorded the event. If we get a diversity of opinion then we may get a balanced view, but our surroundings, our families, the newspapers and social media feeds that we choose will not always show that breadth of opinion. At an extreme level, this is used to brainwash people as a means of recruitment into cults, gangs or terrorist groups, or as a means of propaganda to conceal corrupt practices. At a lower level, it is probably just giving us a skewed perspective of reality. Is our opinion biased or is it truly based on a balanced view of the circumstances?

Lack of information or knowledge: We often make decisions without properly understanding the facts. Sometimes, this is because of a lack of evidence – despite the saying "we need to see it to believe it", many of us believe in things that are not truly proven, such as our religious beliefs. Sometimes, it's because it depends on future uncertainties – we all made judgements on a post-Brexit future, whether positive or negative, where there were no facts on either side. But sometimes, we just don't bother to find the facts, whether it's voting without knowing what a party stands for or making judgements about people without bothering to ask questions. Have we truly secured all the balanced information to ensure our decision is well informed?

Preconceptions: On a training course, I was shown the classical optical illusion:

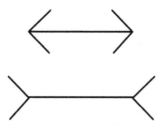

… and we were asked which line was longer. We had all seen this before, and quickly said that they were equal. The problem is we'd all fallen for the double bluff!!! They had changed it so that one line was actually longer than the other.

Our preconceptions just led us to jump to the conclusion, so despite having the clear facts in front of us, we did not interpret them correctly. Interpretation of facts is the critical part of our decision-making process, but this example just showed that we do not always do this right. Preconceptions, assumptions, habits, generalisations, delusions, and the mere fact of our brain running on a sort of "autopilot" can all lead us to misinterpret things. If we could clear our mind of these generalities, would we really hold the same opinion?

These flaws in our thinking mean that we sometimes believe in ideas and viewpoints, that are inherited or influenced or built on a lack of knowledge. We may be passionate about them, but we have been guided into them by the people, circumstances and surroundings in which we have grown up, and these are rarely, if ever, impartial. As such, we may not have reached the same conclusions if we were fed a different diet of information, and because of this, our dearly held opinions may not be right! To truly know and understand and to make the right choices about what we believe, we need to subject ourselves to a real blast of honesty, via some deep and thoughtful self-reflection. Just as a clear understanding of ourselves is amazingly powerful for our mental health, a clarity of thought and understanding is a great strength in a discussion or argument. If we truly understand why we think or believe the way we do, and if we eliminate the flaws, doubts or inconsistencies in our own view by either changing them or reinforcing them, then we will be able to communicate our views much more strongly. Not only will we be able to explain them better, we will be able to stand up to scrutiny and defend ourselves from challenge. If not, we are shooting from a position of weakness. Having the confidence to be open to self-reflection and to fully understand ourselves and our own point of view can give us great insight and will probably give us a better chance of convincing the opposition.

And whilst self-reflection is a private thing, we should never underestimate the value of external opinion in helping us to get the most out of it. Insight from others can cut through our defences and help us to realise why we think a certain way. But we must all remember that it is the consequential actions that we subsequently take that really count. We must be prepared to challenge ourselves and potentially shift our perceptions. We may be right, but we may have opinions that are built on weak foundations, and we need to validate and reassure that our opinions reflect what we truly and honestly believe. We shouldn't even get into an argument before we understand ourselves and why we think what we do! We should turn the lens on ourselves and play devil's advocate against our own view. If we do this and are prepared to keep doing it throughout a discussion, then we have a chance to have a really positive and stimulating exchange of ideas.

THIRD PRINCIPLE

Cherish new insight and use it to self-reflect and challenge your entrenched beliefs

CHAPTER 5

Variety is the Spice of Learning

Smart people learn from everything and everyone;
Average people from their experience;
Stupid people already have all the answers.

SOCRATES

Take pretty much any group of people with a certain gender, nationality, sexuality, occupation or appearance, and we could probably all come up with some stereotypes about that group. We may not necessarily believe all of them or believe that everyone fitting into that box is going to fit the stereotype, but they are there in our mind. They may be oversimplified generalisations, and often exaggerated for comic effect, but if we are very honest with ourselves, there is normally at least a hint of truth behind them. As a gay man, I could take offence at some of the crude ways gay people are represented in popular culture. However, these exaggerations of personality quirks are the bread-and-butter of much of our comedy, and I personally find it hilarious because it creates larger-than-life characters who display exaggerated versions of traits that I recognise from people I know. It's no different to the way that political cartoons may use caricatures to exaggerate the features and personalities of our leaders, to make an insightful and satirical point.

We probably believe that we can see past these stereotypes, but if we are truthful with ourselves, this is not always the case. Very few people who saw Susan Boyle walk on to *Britain's Got Talent* for the first time could honestly say they saw past the frumpy and ungroomed, middle-aged, housewife, and had any expectations of the remarkable voice and amazing performance that she was about to produce. And it's difficult to blame or criticise anyone for thinking this way, because this is a natural part of the way our brain operates. I may be horrendously oversimplifying the neuroscientific explanations, but as we learn from our experiences, our brain is creating neural pathways that allow us to quickly deal with a repetition of the same set of circumstances. As we develop a sense of familiarity from having seen or done something many times before, we start to make the assumptions about what we are expecting to see. Our experience is creating an expectation.

From a psychological perspective, this is invaluable. Imagine a world where everything needed an active and conscious decision – our brain would overload! For those of you who can drive, think back to when you were learning. When we first sat behind the wheel, it seemed horrendously complicated!!!!! The difficulty in learning clutch control and the act of changing gears (particularly when doing a hill start) meant that almost all our focus was on trying not to stall the car and to make it move smoothly. As a result, trying to concentrate on road positioning and our surroundings was a real challenge. However, we reached a point, where we had mastered the basic elements of driving and could do them without thinking. Once these elementary tasks could be completed as if on autopilot, we could focus purely on the more variable aspects such as the layout of the road and the actions of other road users, which is where our attention is needed. As we mastered individual components, established neural pathways have greatly simplified the task, and this is what enables us to complete increasingly complex activities.

So, if these assumptions based on prior experience are all part of our brain operating efficiently, then why is this a problem?

Well, the reality is that, just like when watching Susan Boyle, our unconscious brain doesn't always get it right. A good way of seeing the errors that our unconscious brains can make when trying to interpret familiar information, is to look at an optical illusion. Consider one example below and ask yourself whether Square A or Square B is darker in the following picture.

Most people would see Square A as darker, as our autopilot brain is considering two key pieces of information:

1. The board is a chessboard layout, and so our brain sees the familiar layout with alternating black and white squares, and determines quickly that Square A is one of the blacks, while Square B is one of the whites;

2. There is also a hint of a shadow extending to the left from the blue block, and our brains know that shadows make things appear slightly darker than they are. Square B is therefore clearly a white square, which is taking a slightly grey tint because of the shadow.

Now, superimposing a grey rectangle over the picture, suddenly creates a very different impression, and clearly shows that they are actually the same colour. Even though this evidence was pretty compelling, I still found it hard to believe until I drew the image myself!

The brain misinterprets the information in this example, because it makes erroneous assumptions based on familiar information. But this is not the only mistake our brain can make. The next optical illusion uses context and surroundings to confuse us. Consider the example below, which asks us which of the green circles is larger:

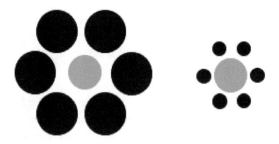

Our brain naturally compares what we are looking at to its surroundings, so when we place a green circle inside a cluster of large circles, it appears smaller than when surrounded by a cluster of much smaller circles. The reality, of course (as you've probably seen this before) is that the green circles are actually the same size. However, this is not what our eyes and brain see!

It is easy to dismiss these optical illusions as tricks of the mind, which are of no great importance. However, the problem is that our brain works in the same way with both people and information. If we see a certain type of person consistently displaying a certain type of behaviour or having a particular attribute, then we create an association between the two, and therefore an expectation that a similar person will behave in the same way. This is not any different to the first illusion – in many cases, we will make the right assumption, but occasionally, the connection or association will be misplaced. Similarly, suppose we receive information from a trusted advisor or from someone we consider an expert, then we treat it differently than if we receive the same information from someone we don't know, don't trust or don't respect. We are treating things differently based purely on the context, just like in the second illusion. Once again, most of the time this is probably correct and helps us to process information correctly, but occasionally this leads us to the wrong conclusion, either relying on false information or dismissing something that was completely valid.

This ability to learn from experience by building connections and associations between things is also the heart of how a stereotype works. The brain helps us to create a very generalised association between people and a certain attribute or behaviour that we may "expect" them to possess. And it is this expectation that is key. Once we have created an expectation, we are in grave danger of failing to treat people as an individual, as we may make the assumption that a whole group of people have that attribute. This is where these stereotypes can become particularly damaging. In its worst form, maybe where we don't like that attribute, this can lead to discrimination, bullying or exclusion. But even in milder forms, wrong assumptions can make us change our behaviour, or make decisions that have a negative impact on someone. Discrimination does not have to be malicious and intentional; unconscious bias can also be very damaging.

Many of us would like to believe we are not doing this, and will convince ourselves that this is the territory of racists, sexists or homophobes; and it may well be true that we are not doing it to such an extreme level. However, the reality is that we are all doing it, just not consciously. Most of us can probably think of times where someone has surprised us with their behaviour. We are only surprised because we walked into the interaction with an expectation, and that expectation has not been met. I remember going into a restaurant where the waiter that approached us had a punk haircut, tattoos across his face and numerous piercings. I was honestly surprised when he was softly spoken, very calm, incredibly polite and provided exceptional service. I took a view based on his appearance that was completely misplaced. In this instance, he had the chance to overcome my prejudices, but this simple example raises a couple of questions:

- How many times do I avoid talking to people with similar appearances and therefore never give them the chance to overcome my prejudice?
- Was his service really exceptional? Am I thinking that just because I had low expectations after I saw how he looked? Or was he truly as amazing as I believe?

This is a relatively small example, but was quite striking for me, as I caught myself in the act of prejudice. Not only was it a misjudged assumption, but it was also an assumption based on ignorance. This wasn't an example of me having had numerous encounters with people with similar appearances that had contributed to this viewpoint; I can't even think of one such encounter that would suggest why I thought the way I did. I can only assume that it comes from the ridiculous connection that as I did not like the appearance, I would not like the person. Clearly the two things are completely unrelated, but I think most of us make this association on a regular basis. This was quite a wake-up call for me, and I would like to think I deal better with similar situations. I know that I am still filled with unjustified misconceptions; but I am hopefully more conscious that I am thinking that way, and I force myself to give people a chance.

But this asks another question. What other prejudices do I have that I'm not even aware of? After all, when I am conscious of my prejudice, I can challenge myself and try to change my behaviour, but this is impossible if I don't realise what I'm doing!

But even when we are conscious of a bias or prejudice that we may hold, we are not out of the woods! How many of us start talking a bit carefully to avoid causing offence? I remember the first time I met a blind friend of my husband. I was talking like I was treading on eggshells. You wouldn't believe how many everyday expressions have words that are vision-related, such as "Let me have a look", until you're fighting the conscious overreaction of feeling like you're saying something inappropriate! Just like noises in the dark feel magnified when you're trying to tiptoe quietly, I became oversensitive to what I was saying. I needed to meet him quite a few times, before I could truly say I relaxed and avoided overthinking. My inexperience of blindness created a heightened awkwardness, and without doubt, it impacted my behaviour.

If we are consciously changing our behaviour to avoid a subject, or being careful with our words, then isn't this discrimination? Sarcastic banter and jokes are commonplace among friends, but should these be avoided if the recipient is "different"? My best friends hold no fear of making jokes about me being gay, and I am glad it is that way. My sexuality should not be treated any differently to my big ears! I should not be discriminated for it, but you shouldn't be afraid to mention it. I find it very refreshing when you see a comedian who is gay or disabled making jokes at their own expense, but we often say that they can "get away with it" as they are in the club! However, I think true success is when we can all make jokes about these things, because we genuinely care about the people on the receiving end, but do not consider their "differences" a big issue.

I've spoken quite a bit about the negative aspects of stereotypes, but it is a misconception that they are always negative. This is not the case. Just like a deluded parent sending their tone-deaf kids onto *The X Factor*, we can sometimes believe in somebody just because of who they are or what they are, and don't really take the effort to find out whether this is justified. A good example of this is the infamous experiment by Stanley Millgram at Yale University in 1961–1962, where people in a psychological experiment were encouraged by a scientist to inflict electric shocks of increasing ferocity on an unseen victim. All participants continued to 300 Volts and 65% continued until the final level of 450 Volts. Despite the screams of pain that told otherwise, these participants were convinced everything must be alright because a scientist was advising them to do it. Participants knew nothing about the "scientist" but were convinced he was an expert simply because of the setting, his professional appearance and his white coat. This shows that appearance can drive positive assumptions or stereotypes, just as much as negative ones.

We can be equally fooled by someone who exudes confidence or charisma, or who shows warmth towards us or an interest in our opinions. We can pick idols or role models because of one attribute, but then follow their views or guidance on things that are completely unrelated. We think better of someone who shares something with us – a faith, an upbringing, an education, a nationality – even though there is no reason for these people to be better than someone else. The Old Boy network was entirely fuelled by this belief that someone who went to the same college or school must be "a good egg"; and I have seen first-hand evidence of people who keep recruiting former colleagues without a thought of the vastly superior people they could find if they looked a bit more widely. Ultimately, we have just as many positive stereotypes around shared experience and admired attributes, that can lead us to making an excessively favourable assumption about a person or situation.

Another misconception is that our application of stereotypes is always directed towards other people. Unfortunately, we can inwardly make the same mistakes, as the desire to fit in with the crowd often results in us imposing the stereotypes on ourselves. We establish the people we are and the things we like to do, and we create the associations as to what that means, the things that we should do and how we should behave. I certainly did that in relation to my passion for rugby and the realisation I was gay. In both cases, I didn't fit the stereotype in my head, and this was extremely damaging for my mental health. At the time, I didn't have the self-confidence to ignore the stereotype, but over a period of time, I managed to detach myself from the image I had in my head of a heavy-drinking rugby player and a party boy on the gay scene; and the stereotype ceased to be a weight that dragged me down. However, I see people in their 30s and 40s, who are still trying to be the person that they think they should be, rather than being themselves, and this has hugely negative consequences.

But just as external stereotypes can be both positive and negative, the same is true of these inward stereotypes, and a sense of belief can be hugely empowering. The four-minute mile had seemed an impenetrable target for many years when Roger Bannister finally cracked it at Iffley Road in 1954. Within one year of him breaking it, 37 other runners had also broken it, and in the year after another 300 had achieved this great feat. He made people believe. We often call out the firsts as they are achieved – Barack Obama being the first black US president, Margaret Thatcher being the first female prime minister, Sam Smith being the first openly gay man to win a Grammy – because things seem more achievable when somebody else has done it, and it feels even more achievable for us if that person fits in the same "box" as we do. We often use a positive association to give us a sense of belief.

As a small example, knowing that someone from my school had successfully got into Oxford gave me a sense that it was achievable, even though I shared nothing in common with these predecessors other than this school. Similarly, a university friend who was the first to get into Oxford from her school had to fight the preconceptions from friends and teachers that it was impossible for someone from her London Comprehensive to get into an "elitist" university. She made it, because she refused to believe their negativity; but again, it takes a certain amount of self-belief to even try. Even though it is totally irrelevant, we use the knowledge that someone "like us" has trodden the same path as a short cut to getting that sense of belief and to help us successfully reach our goals.

However, there is something more than this. Lord Browne (who was chairman of BP and was within a very small minority of openly gay senior business leaders) once wrote about the challenge of believing he could rise to the top without any gay role models he could look up to. Despite his clear talent and the fact that his business acumen had nothing to do with his sexuality, that sense of belief and achievability was important. As outlined above, this is partly because it drives our own self-confidence, but this is not all. Secondly, and perhaps more importantly, it helps to overcome the sense that we may be discriminated against. After all, talent and self-belief can only get us so far – we also need the support from others to make our mark on the world and get the recognition. Whether this is getting promotion or opportunities in a business context, getting people to invest in our thoughts and ideas, being selected into a team or position of leadership, or the marketing, endorsement and promotion of our abilities in popular culture, our own belief is not enough. We also need others to believe in us and avoid seeing our race, gender, sexuality etc. as a barrier. Before we can have that belief that we can reach our goals, we need not only the belief in ourselves, but also the belief that others will see and believe in our abilities as much as we do.

This creation of belief is a big part of why like-minded individuals form groups. In business, there are women's networks, LGBTQ+ groups, associations for young professionals, and societies linking ethnic groups, cultures, professions or many other minorities. These create opportunities for networking, gaining support from people with similar backgrounds and a chance therefore to grow that self-belief, as well as the opportunity to benefit from strength in numbers and potentially challenge a discrimination, bias, prejudice or opinion that may exist. This is perfectly understandable and there is clear value in this, but it also highlights an interesting balancing act that is at play. We do not like to be put in a box as a stereotype, but we often put ourselves in the same boxes. We like to be treated as an individual but tend to form groups. We say that a characteristic does not define us, but we join with people based on that characteristic. By creating these groups, do we help create the strength to break down barriers, or do we reinforce the sense that we are different?

As with most things, both could be true, depending on the aims of the group and the way it operates, and depending on the individual and the motives behind their association with the group. Just like most things in life, there are good empowering examples and negative destructive ones. The same is true of stereotypes and generalisations, whether these relate to our observations of people or our ideas, opinions and concepts. There are times when they help to simplify things in a positive way that enhances our knowledge and understanding, and there are times when they lead to us making serious misjudgements. What really matters is our ability to appreciate the value of the positive examples and to consciously avoid the pitfalls of the negative ones.

So can we do this? Can we leverage all the good things from generalisations and our brain's autopilot mode, without suffering the misjudgements and erroneous assumptions that can also ensue? The key to this is an awareness of some of the pitfalls associated with generalisations, so that we can hopefully stop ourselves when we are falling into some of the following bad habits:

1. Abuse of generalisations to try and win or undermine an argument

You probably don't get many better examples of the abuse of generalisations than in the arguments between a parent and a teenager, and my brother and I had grandstand seats to watch our elder sister try and push the boundaries with my father. Her usual argument was a pretty hopeless generalisation that "Everyone's going" or "Everyone's got one", which my father always calmly dismissed with a "Have you really asked everyone in the whole world?"

This just cued a bit of pantomime arguing, which was great to watch. While our sister was in the middle of it and couldn't see what she was doing wrong, I think it's safe to say my brother and I learned a lot about the wrong methods of trying to win an argument with our dad! The reality here is that my sister over-pushed a generalisation, and my father successfully got his way by just undermining the generalisation. If generalisations are used badly, then all that happens is a slapstick argument; and we miss the point of the discussion. After all the shouting, we never actually got to know why my sister wanted something or how important it was. Now in this instance, this may have been intentional from my father – why go through all the discussion if he was still going to say no! However, when this is something more important, it's a real travesty if we never get into the proper discussion.

When scientific research is conducted, it clearly must be done on a sample – we couldn't test a new medicine on everyone! Deciding whether it is possible to generalise the findings is therefore a key part of research. Science gets round this problem by using statistics, with the goal of proving that a particular outcome is so unlikely to have happened purely by chance that it must have been because of the factor being tested. Without the statistical proof, we have nothing more than a theory or suspicion that requires further investigation. Now clearly, a normal discussion will not involve statistical analysis, but just as in science, a discussion requires us to realise when we are facing a valid generalisation based on sound evidence and when we are just being given someone's opinion. Opinions are fine, and we should not be afraid to use them in a discussion, but we need to be able to differentiate between subjective views and objective facts, both in the way we use them and the way we interpret what other people may say when talking to us.

Reflecting on the discussion of parenting from the earlier chapter, then one of the scientific conclusions in this field is that children benefit from having two parents in a stable relationship. This is a reasonable and scientific generalisation. It does not mean that all children from single parent families are doomed to fail. It does not attempt to deny that many single parents do an amazing job despite the challenges of taking on the impossible job of parenting on their own. It simply looks at statistics and draws a factual conclusion that there are a bigger proportion of problems in children from single parent families. There is plenty of useful discussion that could be had in this respect. Is it purely the fact that there is a single parent or is it more the circumstances that are connected to single parent families (e.g. divorce, bereavement, teenage pregnancies)? What can a single parent do to minimise the chances of their children having issues? Are there similar traps that cohabiting couples could fall into and can therefore learn from in this research? However, we rarely progress to these useful discussions, because of a tendency to dismiss the statistics by undermining the "generalisation".

How many times have you heard someone reply by saying something like, "I was brought up by a single parent and I have no mental health problems"; or "Most single parents do an amazing job"; or "Don't criticise my parenting". Without meaning to be rude, this is irrelevant nonsense! Finding an exception to something doesn't make it wrong. There will always be exceptions and trying to pretend that this disproves a valid generalisation, is basically reducing a good discussion based on fact into a slapstick argument with a teenager! In other words, it does nothing but undermine the quality of the discussion.

This is just one example, of a widespread practice of finding an easy way to dismiss uncomfortable information. Probably the greatest exponent of this is Donald Trump who could dismiss Nobel Prize winning research as "fake news". However, although he takes it to pantomime levels, we are all guilty at times. We need to recognise when somebody is using a valid generalisation against us, and where that is the case, we need to avoid the cheap route of undermining the accurate generalisation and find a better way of winning the argument!

2. Assuming we know the facts and failing to investigate properly

A few years ago, my partner and I were thinking of adopting. This is obviously a hugely significant decision, and as a result, there are a lot of steps in the process that apply checks and controls to make sure we have thought it through properly, and to make sure that we would be suitable parents. One of these steps is an interview with some social workers, and having injured myself playing tennis, my husband and I made our way to the council offices with me on crutches. The interview generally went well, and we could have guessed many of the questions that were coming our way, but there were some things that caught us by surprise. The first one was when we were talking about our family and our support network, particularly when they said they would go to meet my partner's parents. So, we asked the obvious question:

"Oh… you're going to travel over to Brazil, then?"

Surprised looks on their faces as they realised their error; before they clarified that they would need to do it by phone. Second obvious question:

"So, you speak Portuguese then?"

To be honest, we both found this one pretty amusing, although it was a little concerning that people who were making such critical judgements about our suitability were making assumptions. However, they then managed to take it a step further, with a question that caught me completely by surprise!

"Are you going to be able to cope running around after the kids in that condition?"

"What condition?"

"That one! The crutches!"

It actually took a while for me to realise they thought I was disabled, which firstly I didn't think was that relevant, but secondly, was completely inaccurate. In their job, how could they possibly be making such erroneous assumptions? What if they hadn't asked the question, and then had rejected me based on their assumption? What other assumptions are they making that they haven't made the effort to clarify?

It's easy to criticise, but we all do the same. I've asked when somebody's baby was due, to find out they are not pregnant. I've congratulated somebody on their wedding after they changed their name, only to discover they'd gone through a painful divorce. I've asked someone if they hurt themselves at the weekend, only to find out they've got an artificial foot. We all do this, unfortunately, and although it can be hugely embarrassing when we publicly get something wrong, this is the good side of the situation, as we get the chance to clarify our error. More often than not, when we're making such assumptions, we think we know "the facts" and we don't even seek to clarify the situation. If we know the answer, why would we bother asking? And this is one of the biggest problems with generalisations, our illusion of knowledge prevents us from applying the right level of investigative scrutiny. And if we don't ask the questions, we won't really know what's going on. There are some great expressions in this respect, such as "You can't judge a book by its cover" and "You don't know what goes on behind closed doors", which emphasise the importance of avoiding assumptions and clarifying the details. We do not know what other people are thinking, unless we take the time to ask and find out. However, our presumption of knowledge often discourages us from making the effort.

3. We believe generalisations that are not fact and they distort our judgement

A recent survey found that four to eight year olds had already determined that builders, footballers, lorry drivers, engineers, doctors, farmers, mechanics, electricians and plumbers were "male" jobs, while beauticians, nurses, shop and bank workers and vets were "girls" jobs. So very young, and yet the children had already formed opinions, largely aligning with gender stereotypes, based on the information that they have received. Now the problem with surveys is that they often make us think of a follow-up question, and we don't have the answer. In this case, I want to know exactly what question they were asked and what this actually means – i.e. what are the children meaning by a "male" or "female" job? I may not fit into this age range, but when I go into a hospital, I will see more female nurses than male nurses. As a result, depending on how the question was asked, I could easily say that nursing is a female job. The key point is whether there is a consequence of the opinion i.e. would the boys avoid being a nurse? Ultimately, the fact that children may give this answer does not matter, but if it distorts their judgement, and potentially makes them avoid a suitable career path, then we have a problem.

Now I said earlier that a problem with surveys is that we don't have the answers to the follow-up questions we would like to ask. However, an even bigger problem is that we often seem to believe that we do; and we believe that we know more than we have actually been told. A better and more serious example of this is the Brexit negotiations. I discussed in Chapter 1 about the calamitously inadequate arguments we saw in advance of the vote. However, the situation did not change after the vote, with hideously oversimplified generalisations of what the voters were thinking. As we voted for Brexit, the focus is obviously on the Brexiteers, and what mandate they have given. Advocates of a hard Brexit seem to "know" that the voters wanted complete detachment from the EU in every respect from immigration to law to trade, while Remainers seem to "know" that Brexiteers did not understand what they were voting for, and that we should vote again now that they "know the truth".

Well, the only reality here is that we don't know any of this information! We know the people of the UK voted to leave the EU, but we don't know what type of Brexit they wanted;

and we should not seek to presume this information. We also don't have any evidence that they didn't understand what they were voting for. These presumptions of assumed knowledge can paralyse progress, as they can sound plausible and powerful and convincing, but in fact, they are completely missing the point. Our leaders could spend ages trying to understand what Brexiteers were thinking, but this is a pretty impossible task, seeing as they don't know who voted for it. In addition, the vocal Brexiteers (as on any controversial topic) are always at the more extreme end of the spectrum and will not necessarily represent the mainstream that voted that way. What the leaders therefore need to do is focus on the one bit of fact that they have (i.e. we voted to leave the EU), and use their knowledge, understanding and expertise to apply this in the way that they believe is best for the country. No presumption of what type of Brexit we voted for, no presumption of why we voted that way, just stick to that one single fact and then act in our best interests.

Sadly, this form of erroneous assumption is endemic in politics. In many countries, there are just a handful of major political parties, and it would be a miracle if one of those parties was in complete alignment with every single one of my beliefs. I am therefore looking for the best fit. This may be a single policy that is of real critical importance, a way of thinking, an inspiring leader, a balanced review of policies or a tactical decision to eliminate an even less desirable option. There are many different motivations for voting a particular way, and the only thing we can say with certainty is that the voters for a particular political party are not all thinking the same. However, politicians tend to believe they know so much more than this and will use it to justify every bit of small print from their manifesto. In reality, all we have decided is that the winning party is best able to act in our best interests. We took a view on the people, the way they are thinking and things they are saying and decided who we think will be best for our country. Nothing more than that should be assumed, no specific details or assumptions behind the motivations behind our decisions, just a belief that they are broadly on the right track, and that they need to keep making good decisions if they want to stay in power!

But this failing extends well beyond politics and into every aspect of our life. These generalisations are the things that create our blinkers when we believe in something, "helping" us to ignore and dismiss any counterevidence that could diminish our strength of opinion. They are also the generalisations that can allow us to misinterpret things when we have suspicions or self-doubt. In the absence of facts, it is incredibly easy to combine some circumstantial information and create that generalisation, or as it was beautifully put in an award-winning short film called *Balcony*:

> When nobody knows, folks tend to fill in the
> blanks with their imagination.

We need to try and make sure our judgement is based on the truth, and not an opinion that has been cobbled together from an unwarranted extension of the truth.

4. We oversimplify and judge the book by its cover

In the land of fairy tales, it's always so simple – we have a hero we should love, who is dashing and beautiful and intelligent and kind and so full of charm they are universally loved. Then we have the villain who is evil and manipulative, often with some physical affliction, and with an offensive manner that is universally loathed. The gap between them is exaggerated to an extreme, and so there is no room for debate, something that is explored further in Chapter 8.

In real life, it's much more complex than that. Nobody is completely perfect, and nobody is 100% evil. People may appear so, because of what they keep hidden from view. They may be concealing the flaws or weaknesses that they do not want us to see as they try to project the best possible image of themselves. Alternatively, at the opposite end of the spectrum, they may be hiding their softer, more human side as they try to project an image of ruthless toughness. We see what they show us, and we fail to see the elaborate and multidimensional spectrum of qualities that lies underneath. In addition, our view of them is subjective. We all like different things, and in just the same way, we connect and relate to different people and will therefore react differently to what we see.

Despite this complexity, we still tend to oversimplify things. The world may be complex and multidimensional, but we treat it as black and white. A close friend of mine was horrendously bullied by a research supervisor; and not only was he being bullied, but one of his female colleagues was suffering mental health issues because of the treatment from the same supervisor. Unfortunately, nobody at the university believed them because their supervisor was charming, successful and vivacious. She had successfully created a friendly persona, which further enhanced her reputation as a successful psychologist and fooled everyone, except those who had the misfortune to work for her.

Sadly, this sort of thing is not that unusual. We have seen the recent exposure of so many celebrities who were guilty of sexual abuse but were left unchallenged because of who they were. This is the tip of the iceberg in terms of "private" crimes (i.e. those happening behind closed doors with just one victim), where a positive public image is used to dismiss the thought that they could have committed heinous acts in private. How could such a lovely person be guilty of child abuse, rape or domestic abuse? But we have the same issues at the other end, where we will create suspicions of guilt because of someone's characteristics or beliefs, finding it so much easier to believe that someone we do not like could be capable of committing evil acts.

Celebrity trials such as the highly publicised ones of OJ Simpson or Michael Jackson are often a good demonstration of this where before the trial has even started, we have crowds of people either proclaiming their innocence or condemning their guilt. How do these people possibly know? The reality is they just have their perception of a celebrity, based on everything they have seen in public, and use that to make a judgement of their guilt. Or putting it more simply, they are judging based on whether they like the person or not!

In fact, our legal system reinforces this with the concept of a character witness. The defence will get character witnesses to describe the many wonderful qualities of the accused and will also undermine any prosecution witnesses by dishing the dirt on their private life and their integrity. The prosecution will do the same in reverse. Both know the power of perception and how our feelings about the people we are seeing, good or bad, will have an enormous sway on the judgements we ultimately take. If the evidence is not absolutely compelling, then our personal judgement of the individuals is effectively the deciding vote. The importance of this was shown in the infamous trial of the Liberal politician Jeremy Thorpe, who was charged in 1979 with conspiracy to murder a former lover. In his closing speech before sending the jury to consider the verdict, the judge heavily emphasised the distinguished public record of Jeremy Thorpe, while dismissing his lover as a fraud, a sponger, a whiner and a parasite before accepting "but of course he could still be telling the truth". Even the judge was steering the jury to make their judgement on the "credibility" of the key characters involved in the trial.

I have referenced some extreme examples to emphasise the point, but our presumption that we know people based on the external evidence we see is pervasive in every interaction that we have. Ruby Wax once cut down a lazy interviewer who was confusing her with her onscreen character, but we are all guilty of that. Every time we are talking to somebody, whether a new person we are meeting for the first time, or an old friend we have known for years, we draw conclusions about them as a person, which go far beyond the information we are actually getting from the conversation. Our brain is working overtime to see the connections and associations between the new information we are receiving and the things we already "knew".

Hopefully these examples help to demonstrate how pervasive these pitfalls are in our everyday interactions. Considering that the problems are entrenched, combined with the fact that it is a natural process of our brain to simplify and connect things, then how can we possibly stop ourselves when it is leading us into poor judgements? How do we avoid making the mistakes of unconscious bias? One way of looking at this was described beautifully in a theory I was once taught on a work course, which resonated with me, and is something I have consistently remembered, used and shared ever since. It basically described the cycle of learning as follows:

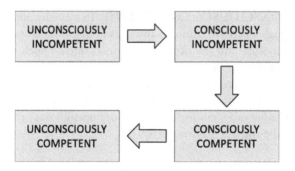

Talking through the stages in the cycle:

UNCONSCIOUSLY INCOMPETENT: At the start, we are not necessarily conscious of our failings, and we can continue blindly. This means that we are making assumptions and poor judgements, but without realising. This is not any different to the addict, who is yet to admit there is a problem. This is the most dangerous phase, because we will blindly continue, getting things wrong, without any awareness we are doing this.

CONSCIOUSLY INCOMPETENT: Next comes a bit of self-realisation. This is like my incident with the waiter, when I made my snap judgement, and caught myself feeling surprised when he was calm, friendly, thoughtful and attentive. I haven't fixed anything but having caught myself in the act, I suddenly became conscious of my failing!

CONSCIOUSLY COMPETENT: Once we are aware of our failing, we can start to do something about it. This is not at all easy, but once we have an awareness of being judgemental, we can stop ourselves, and force ourselves to ask questions to clarify our understanding. This can feel a bit awkward and clumsy, especially if our questions just reveal we were right in the first place! However, it is rewarding when we find out something new or surprising.

UNCONSCIOUSLY COMPETENT: This is the ultimate end-goal, where we are just naturally curious and questioning and can walk into any situation with a completely open mind. Being realistic, we will always struggle to do this in every situation – there may be certain blind spots that we struggle to overcome; or situations that get us angry or frustrated and prevent the calm, rational thought. But hopefully, we can do it naturally when it really matters.

So, the first thing we need to do is admit that we do it. Seeing as we will never completely eliminate our tendency to make judgements, this just requires a bit of honesty. Secondly, we need to accept that this is probably not going to be an easy change. I regularly do crosswords. When I get a clue like "wind", I might start thinking breeze, gale, hurricane etc., so when none of these are the correct answers, it just feels like a dead-end. Then I look up the answer and discover the answer was "coil", a synonym for a completely different meaning of the word "wind". I had set my mind on a certain track, and got myself a bit blinkered, failing to see the alternative meanings. After my brain had been thinking a certain way for a couple of minutes, it was already difficult to redirect it. Imagine trying to change the thought patterns we have had for many years. Once prejudices, judgements and biases are entrenched, they can be incredibly hard to shake, and we will therefore need to be prepared to fight through this.

Reality shows often demonstrate this battle to overcome our prejudices as they like to put together opposites to provoke a dramatic reaction. To get something out of the experience requires that ability to fight through the judgements and keep going. The best demonstration of this that I have seen was in an episode of *Faking It*, a show where people were dropped into a very different world, given the challenge of learning something, with the goal of convincing some judges at the end that they were not the one that was "faking it". One particular episode involved an army officer being tasked with becoming a drag queen. Seeing someone with strong homophobic prejudices, who initially refused to participate, moving through the stages from prejudice to tolerance to acceptance, and then to actually start to see the people behind the drag queens and start to appreciate them as people, was truly amazing. He showed what we all need to do, which is to fight through our prejudices and get ourselves to the point where we can truly treat the people in front of us as individuals. This is hard but is both achievable and hugely rewarding.

Fascinating insight can be gleaned when we ignore superficial appearances, and get past the stereotypes and generalisations, but it is important that we want to do that. Battling to overcome our prejudices requires a hunger and desire to face up to this challenge and to get to the truth. Too often in life, we do not make the effort, as a character suffering from prejudice said in *Balcony*:

> You'd think they'd want the truth, but they just
> want what makes them feel better.

Sometimes the truth hurts. Sometimes the truth makes us step out of our comfort zone. Sometimes the truth makes us change our mind. Sometimes the truth takes us to an uncomfortable place. But as Churchill told us during the Second World War:

> The great thing is to get the true picture, whatever it is.

During wartime, he needed to know exactly what was happening, however good, bad or ugly it was. Only with the true picture, could he make the right decision. At times of peace, and in our normal day-to-day worlds, the reality is no different.

When we want to get to the truth, then we will start to ask questions. Too often, our prejudices are based on a lack of knowledge, with us learning things from the media or from those around us, who suffer from the same biases as us, and know little more than we do! Asking questions can help us to dismantle this. I remember once getting on a train, and seeing a young Korean girl sitting close to a couple of drunk guys and looking a bit uncomfortable. I went to sit nearby, just to make sure she would be fine. In fact, the guys left after a couple of stops, and we ended up chatting, and somehow the conversation strayed on to the fact that I was gay. She literally said that they "don't have gays in Korea", but it was said with a real innocence; followed by a desire to try and understand. For a start, she could not comprehend that I would sit there if a supermodel walked onto the train, and not be attracted in the slightest. That question had to be asked three or four times, before she accepted the answer! But she then just asked question after question after question. From her zero base, she probably left the train 30 minutes later with a better knowledge of homosexuality than most straight people, because she just took the opportunity to ask. It was extremely refreshing to be on the receiving end of questions from someone who really wanted to know and understand, but also quite inspiring as to how I should approach people or concepts I do not understand.

But we need to go a step further than just asking questions, we need to listen, understand, interpret and analyse what we are hearing to build some new insight. Grayson Perry did a fascinating documentary called *All Man* about cage fighters.

You could probably not find a presenter further adrift from the world he was seeking to understand. But he refused to just dismiss the fighters as violent, and the guys engaged with him and did not dismiss him as different, and between them they uncovered fascinating backstories. They all admitted that "there's a story behind every fighter", and this included specific and personal stories, such as one fighter who was motivated by a troubled childhood in which his brother (his only family) had committed suicide.

Asking questions and getting some interesting personal stories is lovely, but does not really progress our thinking, and Grayson Perry showed us this by digging deeper to turn the stories into insight. He realised that there may be individual stories, but there were also strong influences from society and history. Just as anywhere, the guys wanted to prove themselves, and unable to do this financially, this represented a great way of standing above their peers. But on this occasion, it was more than that. The mining heritage produced a hard man, very tough on the outside, who was at the heart of the community, and the male figures therefore took the role of "strong, stoical providers". Even though the mining industry was no longer there and the previous "ideal" was no longer necessarily what was needed to meet the demands of the current workplace, the heritage and culture of the mining days was embedded in the mindset. With this backdrop, they considered their tough attitude and behaviour to be "100% normal" in a way that may not be the case in other environments. He managed to turn his curiosity into insightful interpretation.

Getting to this level of insight and understanding feels like a pretty good achievement, but we are not quite yet done. Truth and knowledge are fantastic, but we also need to use the newfound insight to think about things differently. We need to look at things from an alternative perspective and incorporate this new knowledge and insight to change the way we think. My favourite example of thinking differently (you may be surprised to hear), relates to the lift! After its invention, one of the great challenges to engineers was trying to make the lift move more quickly. Many great minds were focused on the mechanics, trying again and again to make technical alterations that would help solve the problem, without success. More and more people tried and failed to come up with a solution. Eventually one bright spark suggested we should distract the passengers and then nobody would mind that it was moving slowly. He came up with the idea of putting a mirror inside. Simple, cheap, immediately implementable, and although a completely different solution, it had the same impact of ensuring passengers did not get bored or irritated by the slow-moving lift. So, when you're getting to the truth, challenge yourselves to think a bit differently and avoid just following the crowd. By doing this, we will truly get to learn from the other perspective, and get the opportunity to learn about ourselves, and to challenge the people that we are.

Now I've walked through some steps, but basically, I've just suggested we should talk to others, learn from them, and use that fresh knowledge to change our perspectives. This is not exactly mind-blowing guidance! However, it is extremely important and to be successful, there are *three barriers we need to overcome*. The first of these is getting access to different perspectives. In building friendships and networks, whether in the real world or on social media, we often look for commonality and therefore tend to surround ourselves with people who may think in a similar way. Newsfeeds on social media and the internet tend to reinforce this as they preselect stories and views that align with our interests. We need to overcome this. In the workplace, everyone talks about diversity and pushes for a mix of gender, race, sexuality etc, which is invaluable as it provides *access to a diversity of thinking*. But we shouldn't get completely distracted by the societal labels and focus more on the way people think and how much they will challenge us and our opinions. I am introverted, structured, analytical and I value stability, so I learn most from people who are extroverts, who act spontaneously with their gut feeling, and who embrace change and the opportunities it brings. People often say that opposites attract, and that is true if we embrace the differences.

The second obstacle is our desire to be right, which makes the act of questioning and learning much more difficult than it sounds. Assuming we have found someone with a different perspective, and we are making the effort to ask questions, then we need to make sure that we genuinely **seek to listen and understand**. The main pitfall is that as soon as we hear something we disagree with, we tend to challenge, which stops that learning process. Wait! Hold yourself! Seek to understand what they really mean, and why they are thinking that way. We should do what Grayson Perry did and try to get to the real story underneath, before we start to make our judgement as to whether it is right or wrong.

The third obstacle is taking the time and effort to **utilise that new-found knowledge**. Busy lifestyles can be the first thing that gets in the way, as we need to be wary of just moving onto the next thing, and not taking the time to reflect on what we have learned. But even if we do reflect, then just blindly believing what we always have done, is a much simpler path than trying to change beliefs, to alter our direction, or to set off on a path that feels much more uncomfortable. Long-held beliefs can feel like a comfort blanket, particularly where they are shared with those around us. However, my husband and my best friend are people with great hunger to learn and change and to take the difficult path. So, let's be inspired by them, take the time to reflect, and decide what is right and not what is easiest. Even if doing this does not change our mind, we will at least understand what the opposition is thinking and even more importantly, why they are thinking that. This can only help our chances of engaging with them and will also greatly enhance our changes of influencing them!

We must avoid the easy trap of assuming that we are right and know better. In doing so, we will start to appreciate people with different perspectives, content in the knowledge that an intelligent, knowledgeable and insightful person may come to a completely different conclusion to us on any given subject. We should actively seek out those people, be prepared to listen to them, so that we understand and learn from their perspective. Having gained this insight, we should initially resist the temptation to try and persuade, staying focused on thinking and asking questions to truly understand the other person. We can then repeat the lessons of the previous chapter to turn the spotlight on ourselves and to question and challenge our own beliefs. Only then should we start to engage, as debates and discussions are so much more powerful when we have properly taken the time to understand both sides before we steamroll in with our own argument.

FOURTH PRINCIPLE

Explore the perspective of others with curiosity and a desire to understand

CHAPTER 6

Right for me is not Necessarily Right for you

Every one of us is different in some way, but for those of us who are more different, we have to put more effort into convincing the less different that we can do the same thing they can, just differently.

MARLEE MATLIN

Many people would say I'm pretty weird. In fact, one particular friend would probably take great pleasure in coming up with a long and brutally honest list of reasons why he thinks I'm weird! For most people, however, it comes down simply to the fact that I don't drink alcohol.

A lot of people ask me why I took the decision, and there is not a simple answer. Ultimately, it just felt the right thing to do. Like many people, I started drinking when I was a teenager. I was particularly influenced by the fact that I was playing a lot of rugby – a world that was surrounded by a heavy drinking culture. The peer pressure was intense and so I went with the flow. I never drank that much. I was drinking considerably less than those around me, but I was trying to be inconspicuous about that, which meant drinking just enough to pretend I wasn't completely pathetic! But basically, for whatever reason, I just felt inside that I did not want to drink. I was just drinking because everyone else wanted me to, and at the age of 18, I decided that was ridiculous. So I gave up. The choice was not easy, because of the peer pressure I was facing, but I decided to go for it. From a self-confidence perspective, this was significant for me, as I was standing up to the opinions of others and saying, "This is me!" for the first time. But from an "alcohol" perspective, it was a simple choice. There was no judgement as to whether drinking was right or wrong, or whether other people should drink, just a simple personal choice that shouldn't affect anyone else.

And I would like to think it doesn't affect anyone else, because I don't impose my choice on anybody. I may not be drinking alcohol myself, but I do not for a moment consider that those around me should do the same. In fact, I look back over my many years as a non-drinker and have so many fond memories of fantastic nights out when everyone around me was drinking. As a rugby player and as a student, I would go as far as saying that alcohol was a pretty key part of my life, even if I wasn't drinking it! Before I made the choice to give up, I found the presence of alcohol immensely uncomfortable. But once I had quit, I grew to love the drunken shenanigans. At the rugby club, I evolved from lurking on the side-lines to an active part in the drinking games where I was made to down pints of Coca-Cola or fizzy Ribena, whilst those around me were downing beers. We bonded through the rowdy singing, the rude jokes, the funny stories and the crazy dancing, which I joined as energetically as the drunkest of the drunk! In fact, most people who watch me dancing express great disbelief when they realise that I'm not drinking. Whether this is a compliment about my undoubted enthusiasm or a slight on my lack of style, I am never quite sure!

The reality is that despite the fact I was not drinking, I truly valued the role alcohol played in those evenings. I may not have consumed any myself, but I appreciate that the evenings would have undoubtedly been considerably less fun if nobody was! It's hard to describe quite why it was so important, but alcohol somehow assumed a significance far greater than just the fact that it helped people relax. I was actively feeding off the atmosphere from the drinkers around me – it created an atmosphere, a mood, a buzz that is hard to describe until you feel it. I would get so caught up in things that I soon realised I needed to park my car a good walk away from the nightclub. Jumping behind the wheel too quickly, while I was still buzzing from a great night, was probably just as dangerous as drink driving! Ultimately, quitting drinking was the right choice for me, but I am perfectly happy that not everyone makes the same choice.

And this is what life is about. It's about personal choice. Some choose to drink, and some choose not to; some choose to smoke, and some choose not to; some choose to take drugs, and some choose not to. Whether because of the taste or the effect, there are some hugely positive aspects to alcohol, cigarettes and drugs, which is what makes them so tempting. But we equally know that there are some hugely negative consequences, whether that is the dreaded hangover in the short-term or the potential health implications in the long-term. We all get different levels of "reward" from these stimulants and have different perspectives on how much negative consequence we are prepared to accept. As a non-drinker who associates no pleasure with alcohol and is happy to be the first person on the dancefloor in my completely sober state, then the idea of binge drinking and writing off the following day is an alien concept. But for others, the rewards of the amazingly entertaining and fun evenings they have, the stories and memories that they will hold for long after and the bonds of friendship they develop, are sufficient to make the suffering the following day completely worth it. These are vastly different perspectives, but neither is right or wrong.

Even when the negative consequences are much more significant, such as the link between smoking and diseases of the lung and heart, then in most cases we are purely increasing a risk and not creating a guarantee of problems. As a result, in a similar way to how we have different perspectives on our positive emotions, we also make very different decisions in evaluating the level of risk we are prepared to accept. I may choose not to smoke, and consider it a major health risk, immediately conjuring up memories of my school education on smoking. This included a visit to a man with emphysema who had to talk through a hole in his throat due to damage to his trachea. In my mind, this made smoking too much of a risk. However, I was happy playing rugby and knew smokers who thought that rugby was far too dangerous and a level of risk that they were just not prepared to take. Smoking and rugby may be an odd comparison, but in reality, this just shows how different perspectives on the associated pleasures drive different views on the acceptable level of risk. Neither of us was right or wrong, and neither of our choices were "superior", they were just different.

However, whilst in theory it is correct that our decisions as to whether we drink, smoke or take drugs are purely personal choices and we are free to make any decision we like; the reality is not so simple. We are heavily influenced by those around us. This was beautifully demonstrated by a good friend of mine who was a social smoker. The two of us were part of a group of four people from the office who lived fairly near each other and used to meet up socially away from the workplace. For most of the time, I was the only non-smoker in the group, which was fine, and I would often pop outside the pub to keep talking with them while they were smoking. However, suddenly two of the group decided to try and quit smoking together. Suddenly my friend was the only smoker in the group. The first time we met up afterwards, he headed outside on his own to have a cigarette; which we all laughed about and dubbed "antisocial" smoking. But ultimately, because he had been spending a lot of time with people who were smokers, he gradually started to smoke more and more.

There is not necessarily anything wrong with this if he is choosing to be a smoker, but this is a classic example of where influence is superseding choice. Spending a lot of time with two smokers had caused him to smoke more and more, but the fact that these other people suddenly stopped had the completely opposite impact. Something that should have been a personal choice became a consequence of circumstance. And this is not unusual. We are impacted by the places we go, the things we are doing and the associations we hold with those places. We are influenced by the companions we go with and whether they want to drink, smoke or take drugs, and how much effort they may make to try and tempt us! We are impacted by our state of mind, the levels of stress we are facing, and the desire for a bit of escapism. But we are also tempted purely by the products themselves, whether because of any addictive tendencies or just because of the pure pleasure we associate with them. However much it is our choice as to whether we partake or not, the combination of temptation and our surroundings may well coerce us to do more or less than we would ideally choose.

On reflection, it was this societal influence and the associated peer pressure that made it such a hard choice to be teetotal. The opinions and comments of mainstream society created a sense of expectation of what I should choose. All my struggles to give up drinking centred around the impression it gave to make that choice and the way I thought that others would treat me or perceive me, largely because the social importance of the pub and its association with alcohol is indelibly ingrained into our society. Alcohol is used to help us celebrate and to commiserate, to meet new people and to bond with old friends, to lift us up and to help us relax. Apparently, the younger generation are turning less to alcohol, with the 16–24 age group being those least likely to be drinkers, and this may help people of that age make different choices. But that was not my experience as a young adult in the 1990s when the choice not to drink was making me different from those around me.

At that time, I was particularly susceptible to efforts to persuade me. Drinking was considered cool and grown-up, and the pressure of expectation was intense. The insults, disapproving looks and even the occasional refusal to buy me a soft drink were a real challenge, which is why I went with the flow for so long. After making the decision to stop, I only kept on my chosen path because of an innate stubborn resilience and refusal to budge, although it was certainly helped by the clarity of my choice. It may seem slightly weird but saying that I didn't drink was far easier than saying that I did drink, but I didn't want to drink tonight. Even to people who found it rather difficult to comprehend, the black and white nature of my decision rather disarmed their attempts to influence me.

As I have grown up, the attempts to persuade me have never really gone away, with my wedding day being a particularly good and amusing example. Even people who were close to me and my husband were assuming that we would have a glass of champagne for the toasts. At that point in time, I hadn't drunk alcohol for about 13 years, and personally, I didn't understand why I should drink something I didn't want on such a special day. Despite this, some close friends struggled to comprehend why we weren't following the "tradition". As far as I am concerned, we did follow and embrace the tradition, but whilst we focused on the speeches and the toasts, they were much more focused on what was inside the glass!

Fortunately, whilst I still get comments and there remains a presumption that I should drink, things just don't impact me in the way that they used to. This is partly because my increased self-confidence means that I am no longer embarrassed to tell anyone I am a non-drinker, but in addition, most attempts to persuade me are much less confrontational. Normal tactics are to tell me that "alcohol is good for you if you don't drink too much" or to try and convince me how wonderful it tastes. I am sorry, however old I get, nothing tastes better than fizzy Ribena!

These comments may seem innocuous, but they are good examples of how our personal choices are muddied by the opinions of those around us. This can make our decision-making exceptionally difficult. As a small, but typical example, suppose we are asked to go for a drink after work. Simplifying this scenario, we have three choices. We can give the full "YES" and enjoy the evening out with colleagues. We can give the full "NO" and decline the offer. Or we can opt for the middle ground, and agree to go for one quick drink, before heading home or to our other plans. On paper, picking one of these three choices sounds incredibly simple, but it is never quite as easy as it sounds, because we are not just thinking of what we personally want, but of any other priorities we may have and how people may perceive our decisions:

- If we say yes, are we embracing the opportunity to enjoy time with colleagues we like, knowing that we will have a great evening and that we have no other commitments? Or are we being swayed by the persuasiveness of the person who is asking or what people will think if we say no and we are just getting our priorities wrong?

- If we say no, is that because we know we are not going to enjoy it, or we genuinely have more important things to do? Or are we just being a bit antisocial and missing a chance for some fun or to network with colleagues that would be good for us?

- If we say we will go for one drink, are we genuinely trying to get the best of both worlds and spend a bit of time with friends or colleagues whilst also leaving time to do something else? Or are we just saying that to be polite when we don't really want to go, or deluding ourselves that we will actually manage to leave after one drink?

We are all different, and our circumstances are different, so there is not one choice that is right for everyone. The right decision for one person is often the wrong decision for someone else. However, there is probably a decision that we should be making, and the question is whether we are successful at making that decision. Now clearly for one night at the pub after work, then in most cases, this is not that important. If we get the decision wrong, then normally that just impacts that one night, and the next day we are back to normal! Yes – it is possible that there may be something amazing we missed because we turned the offer down, or there may be negative consequences of something else we fail to do when we are out having fun. But this is rare, and it may therefore seem strange to put so much emphasis on little decisions like this. However, these decisions are not normally a one-off, as we tend to make the same decisions over and over again. The little choices therefore tend to blend into bigger decisions and effectively become the lifestyle choices that shape our lives. In these cases, it therefore starts to become critically important that we make the right decisions, rather than just drift with the tide. After all, as the author, Dan Brown, once said:

> Life is filled with difficult decisions, and winners
> are those who make them.

These decisions apply to all facets of our life. While we choose whether we drink, smoke or take drugs regularly, occasionally or never, we do the same with everything. We do it with our religion, where we can be a devoted worshipper, a non-practising believer or an atheist. We do it with our lifestyle choices, such as exercise, where we can be extremely committed and competitive, do a bit of light exercise to keep fit or try to avoid it at all costs. We do it with our social life, when we can be a wild party animal, someone who pops out for one or two drinks before heading home, or a bit of a social recluse. Our lives are defined by these balances, and where we place ourselves on the scale between the extremes. It is worth reiterating that there is no right or wrong place. What matters is that we personally make the choice of where we position ourselves, with our knowledge of what is best for us. We shouldn't drift with the crowd and do what those around us are doing or get influenced by the temptations, but we should remain true to what we really want and what is right for us. We need to show the wisdom of choice as per the Chinese proverb:

> A wise man makes his own decisions. An ignorant man follows public opinion.

This is important because public opinion can be incredibly unhelpful. Nobody knows us as well as we do, and people who influence us are often directing us towards what suits them, and not what is best for us. This can be seen by the way we look at people who end up getting into trouble, whether with drugs or crime, and we remark how they "fell in with the wrong crowd". But this happens to all of us on a smaller scale. As we are influenced by those around us and go with the flow, we may see the many positives associated with being part of a group. However, the hidden negatives of ignoring our own wishes whilst we strive to fit in with others can ultimately end up being much more significant to our mental health, personal wellbeing and happiness. I can really relate to this, because reflecting personally, the times when I have drifted with the tide, have generally coincided with the unhappiest periods of my life. This is because I was living the way that other people wanted and not the life that was right for me.

The first example would be my shambolic approach to drinking in my late teens. At the start of the chapter, I focused on the successful end to this period, when I finally made the decision to quit. However, that ignored the years and months running up to that point, when I just went with the flow and drank or tried to pretend that I was drinking. This time was dreadful. With my family, everything was fine, as they never pushed me to drink. But away from home, I hated every social interaction, as I battled to negotiate the evening without being exposed as a lightweight. This led to me becoming increasingly antisocial as avoiding social occasions seemed the much easier path. When I did force myself to go to a party, I used every coping strategy to survive it, including hiding in the toilet, or sneaking out and coming back an hour later and pretending I had been there the whole time! I even remember an away rugby match, when I was sitting on the coach on the way up, thinking whether it would be better to lose as there would be less pressure to drink! No wonder it was such a relief when I made the decision not to drink. I had drifted with the flow and got myself in an immensely unhappy place. It just needed one decision to get me back to where I wanted to be, which now seems so ridiculously simple and obvious, but it was anything but that at the time.

The other main example in my life was when I was struggling to come to terms with my homosexuality. I have talked a bit about this earlier in the book, but it's worth re-emphasising how I drifted into behaviours that helped me avoid thinking about my situation. Although I am much more relaxed in social situations since I quit drinking, I am still not a particularly social person. I enjoy doing things I really want to do, and I enjoy seeing people I really want to see, but the act of being out or going to a party gives me no real pleasure. In fact, a house party, unless I know most of the people, is my idea of a living hell! However, at the time of my life when I was struggling with my sexuality, I chose to start socialising more and more. Basically, I was either at rugby training or out with friends; which meant I was always out of the house! The quiet time at home that makes me most happy was completely sacrificed, because time to myself meant time to reflect on this major problem I saw hanging in front of me. By going out, I deadened the discomfort of thinking about the fact I was gay, something I had still not accepted. Whilst constant socialising made me immensely unhappy, it felt like the lesser of two evils. I may have looked happy, and may have been doing what happy people do, but for me, it was the very opposite. I was doing everything I did not want to do as an "easy" fix that was not fixing anything!

Eventually, I got honest with myself and realised the crazy situation I had created for myself. I accepted that after 12 years, my sexuality wasn't a phase that would miraculously come to an end. I accepted that this was the person I was, and that I had nothing to be ashamed of. But I also accepted that I wanted all my friends and family to embrace the real me, and that if anyone didn't like that, then they weren't the right people to be sharing my life with. This process of acceptance sounds so easy when I write it down in a few words, and it also seems so obvious that I should think this way. But trust me, this was a seismic shift in my thinking. The weight of pressure had been building and building over my years of denial, and everything just burst in an extremely difficult way. But it triggered the start of a new journey in my life, which gradually transferred me to a much happier place. Being truly honest about who I was and what I wanted was liberating and transformational.

Once we have escaped from those difficult times, it's easy to look back and see the stupidity of the situation we were in. With my rational mind, it is hard to comprehend how I allowed myself to drift into patterns of behaviour that made me so obviously unhappy. But the truth is that when we are in the middle of it, we don't look at our circumstances with the same lucidity. In both instances, I had decided the person I ought to be and the public image that I wanted to portray, and everything then felt like a justifiable self-sacrifice in the protection of that image. Although it may have been the opinions of others or my perception of cultural expectations that had pushed me into the situation, it was actually me who maintained that status quo. By investing all my energies into convincing the world that I was a heterosexual drinker, I almost convinced myself that this was what I wanted to be! And this is the real danger of drifting. Our perception becomes skewed and the blinkered thinking that is the consequence of this can make it hard for us to step out of that fast-flowing current and get ourselves back onto the right path.

Whilst I suffered greatly from those blinkers when I was trying to convince myself that non-drinking was right for me, I am now fascinated by the weird experience of some drinkers applying that same self-justification in reverse. In fact, this is probably the most common reaction I get when I am meeting someone new and they discover that I don't drink. I don't judge them for one moment, and never ask them about their drinking, but they start telling me things like "I don't actually drink that much anyway, you know, just the odd glass every now and again" or "I'm quite capable of going out without having a drink". It is not important to me, so why do they feel the need to tell me?

Before we answer that question, we need to consider a different one. Is it accurate? Throughout my difficult times, I was projecting an image to the outside world that was simply not true, so are they doing the same? In a fascinating documentary called *Drinkers Like Me* hosted by Adrian Chiles, he said:

> Like most enthusiastic drinkers, I've diligently
> avoided working out just how much I am
> putting away.

He also said that:

> The amount of alcohol we buy in the UK is
> roughly double what we admit to drinking.

This suggests that whether through ignorance, denial or dishonesty, the average person is underplaying how much they are drinking. This also probably suggests that many of the people who are self-justifying their drinking to me are significantly under-calling their consumption. So why would they do this?

The most likely explanation is they are trying to manage my perception of them. If we are asked about the number of sexual partners we have had, we will give a completely different answer to our mates in the pub than we would to our grandmother! So maybe they are just implying a lower amount in front of a non-drinker then they would in front of likeminded drinkers, as they think that would be more palatable to me. The desire to underplay their drinking is magnified, because there is no doubt that a lot of people who abstain from something can be a bit smug and righteous about it. Going back 2500 years, Confucius said that:

> The superior man thinks always of virtue; the
> common man thinks of comfort.

This is good guidance in making choices but was not intended to give people an air of superiority because they have followed the path of "virtue". Even if I don't think that way, they don't know that yet! Without knowing what I am thinking, then it is no surprise that some people choose to get their defence in first! That was my approach when I felt people were looking down on me for not drinking, so it is only reasonable that drinkers would do that as well.

But is that all? In my difficult times, I wasn't just spinning a story to the outside world, I was lying to myself, and it was this internal self-deception that was so much more damaging. So, are they trying to convince me that they don't drink too much, or are they trying to convince themselves? Are they genuinely happy with how much they drink, or are they drinking more than they would like and desperately trying to convince themselves everything is fine? Within reason and if alcohol is being enjoyed rather than being abused, it doesn't matter how much somebody drinks. It is a personal choice and what matters is whether they are drinking an amount they are happy with. And when I say happy, I don't mean thinking they are happy because their judgement is distorted but being truly happy with an unimpaired and objective perspective. I ask this because in the extreme case of an alcoholic, we all know that the first challenge is for the drinker to admit they have a problem. But is addiction the only time we should be concerned? Looking at my two issues, I had no addiction or dependency, but I was becoming increasingly downcast because I had drifted away from my happy place. The reality is that anywhere on the scale can be a problem once we lose that sense of objectivity, and to overcome this, we need to subject ourselves to a real blast of honesty! Are we being sincere about what we are doing? Are we happy with what we find? Do we need to change?

This chapter may have initially concentrated on our relationship with alcohol, but the same applies to all facets of our lives. Things happen that distort our perspective, pushing us to see false positives, and we lose that ability to be honest with ourselves. This causes us to maintain friendships or relationships that are toxic or one-sided or exploitative because we get a bit blinded by a certain positive and allow that to overwhelm the downsides. It can lead us to spending money on material items that we cannot afford in our desperate attempt to "keep up with the Joneses" and paint the impression that we are successful. It may mean we stay in jobs that we hate because we have a couple of good friends there or a misplaced sense of loyalty, or simply because the effort of finding a new one is just too hard. We get caught up in routines and habits that we find oppressive but fail to see that there are no shackles preventing us from introducing a bit of spontaneity. In all aspects of our lives, when we fail to look at ourselves with that sense of impartiality, we tend to get drawn into some damaging cycles that are incredibly difficult to escape, because the gradual slide was never a conscious choice and we are almost not sure how we got there! Whilst it should be a personal choice, we have lost the power to choose. And these consequences are often negative, because outsiders don't know us as well as we do, and so their influences are often not right for us.

But it's not just our habits or behaviours that fall prey to the influence of others, the same applies just as strongly to our opinions. Are our choices in politics or religion or morality purely what we believe? Or have we just drifted into that viewpoint based on the influences around us? When we are surrounded by people with a common belief, our preference for blending with the crowd means that everything conspires against our capacity to maintain that balanced perspective and make a true choice for ourselves. Many of us will share the beliefs of our surroundings, whilst some may rebel and jump to the contrary position. Either way, opinions are often a reflection of our surroundings, rather than an honest, open-minded assessment of the differing arguments that allow us to dig deep into our conscience and get to know what we truly believe and feel. Do we really understand where are opinions came from? Have we gathered a diverse range of facts and opinions and come to an honest and truthful viewpoint? Or are we just repeating what others say? And when we share those opinions, do we understand the circumstances of other people and if, how or why this will change the "truth" or give them a different perspective?

Unfortunately, the answer to this question is often a "no" and we suffer the basic confusion that things that work for us or make us happy are going to apply to those around us. We seem to mistakenly think that our personal tastes and preferences are going to be just as relevant for everyone else. Without understanding the personal circumstances of other people, we somehow make this incredibly unintelligent assumption! This is crazy! I may choose not to drink, or only want five hours of sleep a night, or think that meditation is ineffective, or avoid social media, or hate going to parties; but that doesn't mean that is right for everyone. Before I start proclaiming that this is the way to go, I need to understand the perspectives of the people I am talking to. Maybe they do not feel the same way. Maybe they have a hugely positive relationship with alcohol, or suffer with reduced sleep, or gain great empowerment from meditation, or value the friendship, opportunities and ideas that they earn from social media and from parties. The fact that they are not for me, does not have implications for anyone else. We can both be right even though we have reached completely opposite conclusions! The world is richer when we appreciate those individual differences and allow people to make their own choices.

When you stand back and observe just how different we all are, then it does seem strange that most of us fall into the same trap of oversimplistic generalisations. So why does this happen? Probably, it is simply because we enjoy sharing our opinions and making it look like we are knowledgeable. We seem to have precious little reluctance to share a view that is based purely on personal experience or gut feeling, and because it is well-intentioned, we fail to notice that it is poorly informed. Social media has exacerbated this problem as it makes it so easy to air our views without much thought and consideration. But this is not a new issue, the internet has just broadened our reach.

Now before anyone jumps to the wrong conclusion, this doesn't mean we should never try and persuade people round to our own point of view. What it means is that we need to have applied some intellectual scrutiny before we do it. Not only do we need to properly challenge and understand our own viewpoint to make sure it is factually sound and not just the outcome of outside influence, but we also need to understand how it is going to impact others and determine whether it is right for them. This is important enough if we are just influencing one person as we should never underestimate our ability to influence people, and the possible impact if we put them on the wrong path! But clearly this becomes even more important when we are reaching a wider audience or are campaigning for more widespread change, however justified we believe that may be. First and foremost, we must remain conscious that there will be others who will disagree or be negatively impacted. Before we push too far, we need to acknowledge and understand the consequences for those with a different perspective and we need to be comfortable that the greater good justifies the hardship that others will face.

Gaining a proper understanding of opposing perspectives introduces huge amounts of additional information and makes things significantly more complicated. With our one-sided viewpoint, decision-making is so much easier, and so avoiding the complexity of knowledge is incredibly tempting. With too much information, we are probably all inclined to follow the approach described by Ben Macintyre in his great book called *Double Cross* about secret agents in the Second World War, when he wrote:

> Like most official bodies, when faced with
> competing factions and equally unpalatable
> alternatives, MI5 opted to do nothing, but wait,
> watch and worry.

Too much information tends to have an almost paralysing impact, something which is beautifully explained in the wonderful book, *A Road Less Travelled*. In one section, M. Scott Peck compares two military leaders, one of whom cares little about his troops, other than their capability as soldiers, while the other shows great empathy, knowing them as people and knowing all about their families. In effect, the first leader has simplified his decision-making. It is likely he will be able to benefit from the detachment and focus purely on the military goals without the fear of consequence from sending his troops into battle. However, he therefore bears the risk of being a bit gung-ho as he does not consider the human risk associated with the decisions he is taking. On the other hand, the second leader may know too much, placing excessive focus on the human side and therefore worrying too much about the consequences of any decision. This creates a grave risk that he is prevented from taking the correct military decision because he cares too much about the people involved.

Whilst we can probably all understand the desire to keep things simple, it is clear that a truly powerful general would be able to gain a clear understanding of the people in their charge and yet still be bold enough to send their troops into battle when justified by the military goals and when the balance of risk was correct. And even if most of us will never be in a such a life-or-death situation, the same principle applies to many of the decisions we take. True power in decision-making and therefore true power in discussion comes from knowing the detail so that we fully understand the impact of our decision, whilst still being able to impartially balance the conflicting views and make the right choice. This means understanding the complexity yet simplifying it into a manageable framework of information from which we can make a coherent decision. This is easy to say but is incredibly challenging to accomplish, which is why the desire to avoid complicating the arguments with other people's views is so very appealing!

But our failure to consider the complex patchwork of facts is not purely driven by our desire to keep things simple. Our inability to truly engage with and understand other people's perspectives is another significant factor. This is partly driven by our blinkers to people's individual differences that we discussed earlier in the chapter, and our unconscious bias that others will or should think or feel the same. But even when we successfully manage to peel back those blinkers, our lack of empathy also gets in the way! As discussed in Chapter 2, it is incredibly rare for us take our listening skills to the level where we are truly feeling what the other person is saying; and when we feel our argument, but don't feel theirs, it is no surprise that our argument seems so much more powerful. This can lead our biased brains to the mistaken belief that our argument is somehow "better" and as soon as we are feeling superior or starting to be dismissive of what someone else thinks, then any chances of discussion are doomed. If we stand back and reflect on many of the poor arguments we have, so often this is the consequence of us being dismissive of the opposition. In fact, this sense of superiority is inevitable when our views are so heavily biased or distorted by our personal opinions and preferences.

Once we reach this stage, when our views are so blinkered, then anyone who does not share our view is likely to completely ignore what we think. We saw this happening in the emotional rages between Remainers and Brexiteers, but there is an even better example of this from the world of American politics, and in particular, the case of a Republican candidate in Alabama in 2017 who had been accused of sexual misconduct with a minor. You may expect party loyalists to defend the candidate and to potentially argue that he is innocent until proven guilty or to defend his policies. You may expect that fellow Republicans are more likely to presume the best whilst rival Democrats would be likely to jump to the opposite extreme. But would you expect someone to say:

> I'd be fine with a child predator in the Senate so
> long as it would keep the Democrats from stealing
> this seat. Child molesters are evil, Democrats are
> even worse.

These were the words of the right-wing activist, Eric Dondero, whilst an author Carroll Bryant also expressed some similarly shocking and extreme views.

> I'd rather have a pedophile in office rather than
> a democrat any day of the week and twice
> on Sunday. Pedophiles only screw kids while
> democrats screw everyone.

Whilst we can focus on the extreme and hateful nature of these comments, this is not what we should be noticing. The real concern is that these individuals have completely lost their perspective and any ability to be impartial, and it is incredibly challenging to recover from this. Anyone with a different viewpoint is going to ignore everything they say, because they appear completely deranged.

And whilst this can be shocking when the views become so extreme, we see the same problems on an everyday basis. If I reflect briefly on alcohol and smoking, which formed the start of this chapter, and then throw some illegal drugs in the mix; we can see exactly how our personal preferences have an impact on our views. The UK laws surrounding these three stimulants are crazily inconsistent with the relaxed licensing of alcohol, the heavily restricted licensing of tobacco and the illegality of drugs. But how many of us could genuinely say that we manage to look at these policies impartially? A heavy drinker or party goer may be delighted by the freedom to drink alcohol and the relaxing of licensing laws allowing late-night drinking, whilst abstainers may bemoan that town centres can become a bit of a war zone on a Friday or Saturday night. A smoker may be frustrated by the ever-increasing restrictions that are imposed on their habit, whilst a non-smoker may be celebrating the cleaner air in pubs and clubs or even wish that the restrictions went further. A recreational drug user may struggle to comprehend why they are criminalised when alcohol and smoking carry an equivalent (at least!) level of health risk, while the non-users may think that this is sending the right message and is a habit that should be discouraged. All these opinions are valid, but ultimately, they are so skewed by personal preference and lacking understanding of other's perspectives that they are a major impediment to debate and discussion.

However passionately we may believe in something and however biased we may therefore be, we should never ignore the views of others. If we can avoid making assumptions about what they may think or why they may think that way, and make the effort to find out, then we are getting more information and new perspectives, which leaves us better informed. It may allow us to find a "compromise" solution, where we can achieve our goals without trampling over the feelings of others. But even if this is not possible, it will allow us to think through everything, arm ourselves with the best possible information, and just like the general deciding whether to send his troops into battle, it will ensure that we are aware of the consequences of our opinion. Once we have gathered this new insight, we may choose to discount some pieces of information to simplify our decision-making, but at least this is done consciously, rather than being a consequence of ignorance or laziness. Moreover, we are doing this with the benefit of the intellectual scrutiny that I was requesting earlier on. This scrutiny ensures we enter the discussion with the required level of knowledge that is essential for the subsequent exchanges to be insightful and thought-provoking.

However much we already know, we should always aspire to enhance our understanding, ensuring we have actively established our own beliefs and have not just drifted with the crowd. Once we are comfortable with our own view, we must realise that it is just our choice. There is no right or wrong because of the individual differences between us. People are different and circumstances are different, and as a result, alternative views may be just as valid. What is right for us is truly not necessarily right for everyone else! As a result, we should make the effort to find out why others think differently and to understand their circumstances, only sharing our opinion if we know it is informed, relevant and genuinely for the greater good of the recipient. Having considered all of this, we will be able to communicate in a respectful and insightful way, combining facts with emotion to both inform and persuade, in a way that combines our personal beliefs with an appreciation of individual differences. I know this is not easy, and in fact, it may sound slightly overwhelming, but do not fear. Actually just having the right intentions will take us most of the way.

FIFTH PRINCIPLE

Appreciate our individual differences before you share your views

CHAPTER 7

Curiosity Killed the Cat, but Dodgy Assumptions Killed the Discussion

Your assumptions are your windows on the world. Scrub them off every once in a while, or the light won't come in.

ISAAC ASIMOV

Immigration has had an enormous impact on the United Kingdom, with an influx of people and their descendants making a massive contribution to the country's success over its long history. At times, this has been actively encouraged, such as in the aftermath of the Second World War when immigration from Commonwealth countries was desired to help rebuild the nation following the extensive loss of life during that conflict. At other times, it has happened more naturally, whether as a result of an attraction to opportunities that Britain presented or a desire to escape problems and issues people may have experienced in their homeland. Or in many cases, a combination of the two.

The combined effect of multicultural immigration and indigenous emigration has steadily shifted the racial and ethnic diversity of the population. According to the last UK census of 2011, 86.0% of the population of England and Wales identified as White, a reduction from 94.1% in 1991 and 91.3% in 2001. Moreover, while 87.5% of the White ethnic group identified as White British in 2001, this fell to 80.5% in 2011. These numbers may be steadily changing on a national basis, but depending where we live, we get very different experiences of this. Whilst in London, white people represent just 59.8% of the population, white people represent more than 95% of the population in North-East England, South-West England and Wales.

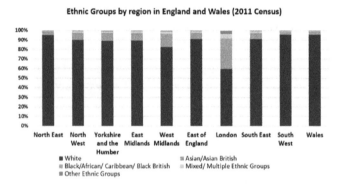

Ethnic Groups by region in England and Wales (2011 Census)

Whether it is because of the varied level of exposure to diversity, or because of elements of our personality or upbringing, we also perceive the impact of the new arrivals in very different ways. Some relish the evolution of the country with new perspectives, ideas, languages and cultures, creating a varied and vibrant atmosphere that greatly enhances the country. Others fear the changes and the risk of losing some of the heritage that they value and cherish and feel this diminishes what makes the country special. Similarly, when we look at the new arrivals, they react and behave in different ways. Some want to actively bring their cultures into their new surroundings, maintaining many of the elements that they loved about their homeland and sometimes choosing to openly celebrate this with a new audience. Others tend to be more inclined to assimilate with the indigenous culture of the land they are entering, honing down some of their differences (at least in public) as part of blending in with their new surroundings and the existing culture.

None of these perspectives is individually right or wrong, and it is perfectly valid for us to see the world differently. Some people actively embrace change and variety, and it is therefore no surprise if they see the diversity of people and changes in their surroundings as positive and life-enhancing. On the other hand, some people are very resistant to change, whether because of their personality or because of traditions or religious beliefs in which they do not see space for flexibility. As a result, it is no surprise that they have a fear of change. These are just different perspectives that make the world more interesting.

Whilst many of us would like to feel we fit into the first category that embraces the evolution of the world, the reality is that most of us probably fit into the second category. Away from the specific confines of immigration, our fear of the unknown means that helping people to deal with change is big business. There are hordes of psychology books guiding us on how to deal with change and how to adapt to new surroundings. There are also many consultants making big money from guiding businesses to manage change more effectively within their organisations, as it is known to de-motivate and de-energise their employees. And this is highly relevant as perfectly summarised by Imam Shpendim Nadzaku of the Islamic Association of North Texas who said:

> Immigration strikes at the very heart of a
> central metathesiophobia, or fear of change.

Although this fear can have hugely concerning consequences in a racial context, when considered in this light, such a reaction from many of us is not really that surprising.

One of the key elements that helps people to deal with

change is having some sense of control, and it is no surprise that a lot of the immigration discussions around Brexit have focused around control of our borders. The other key message, however, is that we need a bit of time to ease through the process. Where it is forced on us too quickly, it meets with firm resistance that can be difficult to overcome; but when we are taken on a journey, it feels so much more manageable. It is no surprise therefore that negativity around immigration tends to use emotive language that suggests it is uncontrolled and coming too fast. We often hear mentions of a "flood" of people coming into the country, as that sense of a rapid and uncontrolled influx exacerbates that fear of change.

If we look at migration statistics over the last 50 years, it would be accurate to say that immigration has accelerated in the last 20 years. From the mid-1960s until the mid-1990s, net migration was extremely low. It was slightly negative until the early-1980s (i.e. more people leaving the country than arriving) and then slightly positive thereafter. However, from the mid-1990s, this started to steadily increase, contributing to the shifting racial diversity of the country.

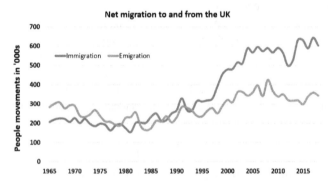

Net migration to and from the UK

From the language in the Brexit debate, you would think that this all came from the European Union, but this is not the case. Net immigration of both EU and non-EU citizens have contributed to the effect. Non-EU citizens drove the initial growth in the mid-1990s, and the EU impact followed in the mid-2000s, primarily after the so-called EU8 (Czech Republic, Estonia, Hungary, Latvia, Lithuania, Poland, Slovakia and Slovenia) joined the European Union in 2004. For sure, the EU8 have had a material impact on EU migration to the UK as approximately 40% of EU citizens in the UK are from those eight countries, even though they represent just 16% of the total population of Europe. This acceleration is a fact, but whether we consider this problematic or a "flood" is probably very much down to our perspective and the impact in our own community and our own life.

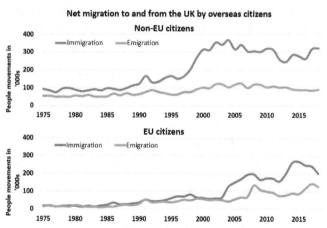

These contrasting perspectives are something that I can absolutely relate to. Having grown up in the South-East of England in an area that was greatly lacking in terms of racial or ethnic diversity, my upbringing was exceptionally sheltered in this respect. I would encounter people of different ethnicities from time to time, but my circle of friends and acquaintances were almost exclusively white middle-class and not exactly challenging my "traditional" perspective. But this all changed rather rapidly when I met my husband-to-be, who had been in the UK for just three years and was studying to learn English while working part-time in catering.

To my mindset at the time, he was effectively from another world. This includes, obviously, his upbringing in Brazil, but even in London, his experience was about as far removed from mine as possible! He had British friends, but also a whole range of friends and acquaintances from Europe and beyond, who had moved to the UK to learn English, experience the culture or to make a new start. With him, things just clicked and despite our usual introversions, we could talk endlessly for hours. But with his friends, it was quite a learning experience for me. This was not because there was anything strange or wrong or even different about them. It was just because the anecdotes of shared experiences that had previously connected me to people no longer held any weight. Putting it bluntly, I needed to learn how to have conversations with people from a very different background!

Not only did he introduce me to a varied and multinational group of people, but he also introduced me to the world of immigration. I will never forget one of our early holidays, when we chose to drive to my brother's wedding in Switzerland. Coming back by ferry, he received a bit of a grilling from an immigration officer about what he was doing in the country, where he was studying, whether he was working, how many hours was he working etc. This was totally normal stuff for him as a standard part of any travel; but an eye-opening window for me on the immigration system. This was just the start, as over the years I got first-hand exposure to the formal processes managed by the Home Office; whilst also seeing some examples of the dodgy underworld of fake marriages and bogus language schools, which was enabling some people to stay. A whole hidden world that was right under my nose as I went about my daily business, but I didn't even realise was there.

All of this was extremely revealing. The chance to see the real lives that are stuck in the system gives you a fresh perspective on the whole issue of immigration. I became aware of the honest and good people, who were escaping miserable conditions or were here for such positive purposes and were abiding by all the rules – and yet seemed to be given a tough time. But I also saw the other extreme, the scammers who were lying and breaking every rule and yet just seemed to get away with it! It just made me realise what an impossible job that the Customs and Border Control officers have in trying to establish between the two. How on earth are they supposed to tell in a short interview at the airport or a ferry terminal?

But as well as learning about the immigration system, I learned hugely from the ethnic diversity of the people that I met. Rather than see them as someone from a particular country or race, I increasingly started to see them as individuals. I made the rather obvious realisation that they are not this amorphous collection of likeminded people, but they are all completely different to each other. Just as we would experience if we went to a school reunion, we will like some of them and will develop a great connection, while with others it just won't click. Some of them will seem exciting and engaging, whilst others will just seem a bit dull. We will get the full spectrum and we will realise they are not that different from us – the culture and upbringing may give them a different wrapper, but underneath we are all just people!

As discussed in Chapter 5, as well as the chance for new friends, this diversity gives us the opportunity to learn. Whilst most of this will be positive and informative, providing a new and different perspective on our lives, we can also be surprised by the negative perspectives or generalisations that may be applied against us. I remember a Spanish friend who told me that his best friends will always be Spanish, because he relates better to Spanish people and they share a culture and upbringing. I remember a French employee who expressed great surprise that I didn't behave in exactly the same way as her previous boss – because we were both English, she just assumed we would be the same. I was quite shocked that people would think that way – applying such a broad generalisation to me as an individual or blindly grouping me together with all my countrymen. When we are on the receiving end, it feels completely wrong, but do we perceive it the same when we do this to someone else?

Sweeping generalisations and alignment with our "own kind" are a key theme in a wonderfully thought-provoking book called *Why I'm No Longer Talking To White People About Race* by Reni Eddo-Lodge. At one point in the book, she describes a conversation with a French girl she had recently met, in which she was sharing an experience of discrimination when applying for a job. The conversation was going well and the two of them were connecting nicely until the author said how she had later discovered that the position was given to a white woman of a similar age and similar experience. At this point, the French girl challenged:

> You don't know if that was racism. How do you
> know it wasn't something else?

Take out any feelings or sense or emotion about being on the receiving end of discrimination, and you might be thinking this is a perfectly valid question. Being honest, that was my initial reaction, and I battled quite a bit in trying to challenge my viewpoint. However, a few of my friends reinforced that you sometimes just get this sense or feeling that you are being discriminated against. You don't need the evidence, because you can just tell it is happening. They therefore completely understood the situation the author was describing. This was further reiterated by my experience at the time I was reading the book. I was on holiday in Barbados and as my husband and I were both wearing the same wedding rings, we were obviously identified as a couple in a homophobic country. I did not need direct abuse to my face to know what they were thinking, I could just sense it from the way they looked at me and talked to me. It was obvious, just as it was obvious to the author what was happening when she was overlooked for the job.

Whether intentionally or subconsciously, the white girl was defending her "own kind". By dismissing the possibility that there were racist connotations, she took the contrary position to the author. As a result, she became a white person defending a white stranger, whilst dismissing the opinion and perspective of the black person that she was talking to. She was a good example of a "white moderate" referred to by Martin Luther King in a letter he wrote from a Birmingham jail. Within this beautiful narrative, he writes:

> I have almost reached the regrettable conclusion that the Negro's great stumbling block in his stride toward freedom is not the White Citizen's Councillor or the Ku Klux Klanner, but the white moderate, who is more devoted to "order" than to justice; who prefers a negative peace which is the absence of tension to a positive peace which is the presence of justice.

He went on to say that:

> Shallow understanding from people of good will is more frustrating than absolute misunderstanding from people of ill will.

If we dig into our conscience, then Martin Luther King is accurately describing most of us. We may not be racist, but we feel uncomfortable with any sense of confrontation and therefore seek to dismiss that there are negative reasons for the way our "compatriots" have behaved. We may not be racist, but when someone seeks to provoke that difficult conversation and give us an uncomfortable feeling of guilt, perhaps we are defensive or dismiss them as a troublemaker. We may not be racist, but when someone behaves badly or acts in a racist way, we are too afraid to put our heads above the parapet and to challenge it. If so, then we may not be racist, but we are allowing racism to happen. Whether by blocking the conversation or by making insufficient effort and therefore failing to understand the issue from the other person's perspective, we are protecting the status quo that serves us well rather than exposing ourselves to the discomforting truth.

A good example of this arose following the murder of Stephen Lawrence back in 1993. This was a racially motivated stabbing in South-East London of an 18-year-old black man. The severely flawed police investigation ultimately led to a public enquiry that was launched by the Home Secretary in 1997 and published in 1999. The conclusions of this report not only highlighted the severe flaws in the investigation, but also concluded that the Metropolitan Police was "institutionally racist". Ultimately, we started to get to the truth, but this was many years after the murder. In the immediate aftermath, the mainstream media jumped to the defence of the police, acting to smear and discredit the family. Whilst the truth was the horrendous racially motivated murder of a black youth and the brave family standing up against police failures, the storyline was hostility and suspicion towards a black family who were being openly critical of one of our institutions. The mainstream was pulling together against a more disruptive truth.

This story has resurfaced many times, with the family deserving great credit for their persistence despite the flak that they received for long periods. One of the many notable resurrections of the story was after two of the attackers were finally convicted of the attack in 2012. Just two days after the trial, in a Twitter discussion with a journalist who was questioning the use of the term "black community", the MP Diane Abbott wrote a tweet saying: "White people love playing 'divide & rule'. We should not play their game #tacticasoldascolonialism." Irrespective of whether this is right or wrong, or whether it was tactfully voiced at that point in time, this was not the news story. The news story was that there had been a terrible racist murder and that it had taken 19 years to bring two men to justice because of institutional racism. However, we managed to turn this into a story about inverse racism because of one tweet.

And this is exactly where this becomes highly relevant to the art of conversation. This is a classic tactic that is used to avoid a difficult conversation or to save ourselves in an argument that we are clearly losing. When all else fails, we often look for an inappropriate comment or phrase or word in the middle of a wonderfully well-constructed argument, as a means of diverting the discussion from the real issue. I am sure I'm not the only person who has done this when receiving some valid criticism from my partner. Rather than face the ugly truth, I managed to turn it into an argument about an annoying comment he made to one of my friends at dinner last week! We do it when rowing with our partners, but we tend to do the same on all sorts of controversial topics. Rather than allow the conversation to drift on to a topic where we feel exposed, we shift it towards something where we can be on the attack. This is clear obfuscation to avoid the real issue at hand, as beautifully summarised by Jean-Jacques Rousseau:

> Insults are the arguments employed by those who
> are in the wrong.

Sometimes, this is a wholly intentional tactic, but sometimes I wonder if it can be equally driven by ignorance or unconscious bias. Being married to someone who was born and raised overseas, I get the chance to see first-hand how a migrant can be perceived and the comments that are directed towards them. In this respect, the comments I find most strange are those showing a refusal to accept his Britishness. Considering that one of the common complaints about immigrants is their failure to fully integrate into British society, or that they would put their birth country first, why are people so resistant to accept someone who has genuinely made that shift?

My husband never felt a great affinity or connection with the country where he was born and grew up with the feeling that he wanted to leave. As a young adult, thanks to the unimaginable kindness of his best friend, this is what he managed to do. He has now lived in the UK for more than 20 years, has taken up British citizenship, given up the passport of his birth country, learned English and having lived and breathed and studied and worked in English for that time, it is genuinely his first language. He has not visited his home country for many years, and absolutely cherishes the British culture, particularly the comedy. He is completely oblivious to the news and politics from his birth country, as it is the politics of his home that matters to him. Although he is not the most avid sports fan, he would successfully pass the controversial "Tebbit Test" about who would he cheer for in a sporting match between the two countries. In fact, because he has experienced the support and opportunity and feeling of belonging in the UK that he felt he greatly missed when growing up, I would suggest that he is more proud, patriotic and appreciative of this country than many people who were born here.

You would think that would be enough for most people, wouldn't you? Well strangely, it seems it is not. Because of his slightly Hispanic appearance, people are obsessed with asking where he is from. The conversation normally then follows along the line of:

"Where are you from?"

"I'm British"

"No. Where are you really from?"

"I'm British"

"No, where are you originally from? Where were you born?"

Having managed to draw that out of him, they triumphantly declare that is his real nationality! He can't change it. It's immovable. That is just the way it is. Really? Someone who wants to be British, feels British, is British, and yet many people cannot handle that. People who will say that they want people to integrate, to fit in and embrace our culture cannot accept it when someone has done exactly that? They fear that their cultures and traditions may be over-run, but when someone arrives and completely accepts and cherishes those cultures and traditions, then they still say he is not one of us! I am never quite sure whether they simply cannot imagine dropping their own nationality in that way, and therefore fail to comprehend how someone else can do it, or whether there is a more malicious intent. However, either way, they just impose their view that he cannot change, and never seek to truly understand why he may think that way. They cannot appreciate that he has made a shift that they feel unable to do. The greatest sadness about this is not necessarily the way they currently think, but that they are so insistent on their belief that there is never a chance for a discussion. Just as with the French girl who denied the uncomfortable possibility that there could have been racist intent, they reinforce a focus on differences without any chance for discussion.

Now this particular example with my husband is mildly annoying but it has deeper undertones, as highlighted in the case of two German footballers of Turkish origin, Mesut Özil and İlkay Gündoğan. Following the poor performance of Germany in the 2018 Football World Cup, Özil became the scapegoat for the team's exit. Despite a poor team performance, it was the player of third generation German-Turkish extraction who bore the brunt of the criticism. The meeting of the two players with the Turkish president a couple of months before the tournament was apparently further evidence that they were not truly German and not truly committed to the cause. The comments led Özil to state that:

> I am German when we win, but I am an
> immigrant when we lose.

This sentiment neatly represents the sort of fake integration that we have to a large extent in wider society. We show great tolerance and support in the good times, but we tend to get a bit obsessed by the difference when something goes wrong. In an interview in early 2019, Liam Neeson demonstrated this by describing an incident where a friend of his was raped, and on discovering that it was done by a black man, he descended into a primal rage eager to pursue revenge by killing another black man. Now this is extreme, and I do not suggest for a second that many of us would take our innate discrimination to such a level; but the reality is that we all react similarly at a lower level. We continue quite happily in diverse groups, ignoring the differences between us, until something is done that hurts or upsets or annoys us. As soon as that happens, the differences that were previously irrelevant become highly relevant. And they are not only considered just relevant, they are blamed and identified as the cause of the issue.

If you do not believe this, then just read the reporting of negative stories about terrorism, crime or benefit fraud. If it is committed by an immigrant, then this suddenly becomes hugely significant. We describe their race, nationality or heritage like it is an element of huge detail, in a way that we simply do not match when the person is White British and was born in the country. Even if it is not specifically said, we allow the impression that race, ethnicity or nationality is the cause of the problem. And it is by no means just race that we do this for. We roll out our stereotypes on gender, sexuality or any other chosen prejudice as soon as someone with that label does something wrong.

The result is that we blame the label irrespective of its relevance. I remember a discussion with a friend, who was telling us about a relationship between a wealthy Brit and a much poorer Moroccan. He was talking about how this was a common imbalance between Westerners and Africans, and how this was causing relationship issues between the two of them. He made the clear implication that the races of the two individuals was somehow relevant. However, the issues that were described sounded identical to some of the challenges that I faced on meeting my husband, when I was working in the City and he was doing part-time work in catering, or an investment banker friend who was engaged to a nurse. Great imbalances in wealth or income levels can absolutely cause problems if there is either a superiority complex or inferiority complex, one way or another. However, it does not necessarily have anything to do with race. We need to be careful not to blame the obvious difference as it is not always the real issue.

But we need to be careful that we do not go the other way and fail to notice that important difference because we are trying too hard to ignore it. Another very interesting topic from the book of Reni Eddo-Lodge is her discussion of "colour-blindness" and how white people are generally taught to ignore the difference, while black or mixed-race people are often taught to focus on their racial identity. There is some truth in this, as I remember a friend of mine who married a South African man and moved over to Cape Town. Soon after she arrived, she was told that she needed to talk differently to people, depending on whether they were black, coloured or white. To both me and her, this seemed an alien concept to treat them differently. That concept of treating people equally and fairly, as if we were "colour-blind" had been drilled into us from a young age.

Reni Eddo-Lodge goes on to make an incredibly thought-provoking point:

> In order to dismantle unjust racist structures, we
> must see race. We must see who benefits from
> their race, who is disproportionately impacted by
> negative stereotypes about their race, and to who
> power and privilege is bestowed upon – earned
> or not – because of their race, their class and
> their gender. Seeing race is essential to changing
> the system.

However well-intentioned is the concept of colour-blindness, it does create the risk that we are so focused on ignoring the difference that we do not notice it when it is highly relevant. Going back to both the French girl denying the discrimination and the media and police not accepting the valid criticism of institutional racism, both are clear examples of this. Whether malicious intent or brainwashed naivety, these are instances where our failure to observe the differences in treatment and the impact of colour, have meant that we have failed to get to the truth.

So, if colour-blindness is not the answer, then do we need to go the other way and apply positive discrimination, a concept that is much loathed in many circles? A lot of this comes down to whether you believe we live in a meritocracy. Reni Eddo-Lodge puts it succinctly when she says that:

> You'd have to be fooling yourself if you really think
> that the homogenous glut of middle-aged white
> men got there purely by talent alone. We don't live
> in a meritocracy, and to pretend that simple hard
> work will elevate all to success is an exercise in
> wilful ignorance.

Firm language, but it is virtually impossible to argue with the sentiment. Things may have improved over the years, but there is absolutely a legacy of history that has benefited white men and put them into a position of influence and privilege. Once we have put this group into such an advantageous position, then there is no longer a level playing field. When recruiting somebody for a new job, an interviewer may be completely "fair" on the interview day and give everyone the same opportunity, but privilege has meant that some candidates arrived with distinct advantages.

Firstly, privileged people know people! Even if the old boys' network is not quite as powerful as it used to be, so much opportunity comes from "working your network" whether this is a new job, a business deal or just some inside knowledge. A few years ago, my department gave some work experience to a young university student. He was good and hard-working and a pleasure to have in the team for a few weeks; but he got the opportunity because he was the son of a family friend of one of the senior managers. The underprivileged just do not get these sorts of opportunities, and that distinctly puts them at a disadvantage when they are looking for chances in the future. Reflecting away from business into a different circle, think of how many current actors, actresses or pop stars are children of former actors, actresses or pop stars. Do we all believe that they are necessarily better than other people we have never heard of? They have talent, yes, but the legacy of their parents, and the resulting network and experience is certainly giving them a leg-up.

Secondly, the success of parents has often created wealth, and this gives a further multitude of opportunities. It is true that money does not buy happiness, but it certainly can buy private tuition, public school, homes in affluent areas where you can improve your network, and the ability to afford unpaid internships, university education and gap-year experiences. All of these add polish, making people look better, such that they stand above less-privileged people with the same ability. There is no doubt that the middle-classes are particularly adept at working this to their advantage. Their experience means that they know and understand the system, so they school their children to overcome their shortcomings and shine to the maximum of their potential. Nobody would deny them doing this, as they are simply trying to get the very best for their own child, but history and circumstance is giving them more opportunity to do this.

The combination of these two things means that when we are interviewing a candidate, history has potentially given one of them access to opportunities, experience, education, tuition, guidance and "polish", that the other one has not received. Placed in this context, does it make sense to completely ignore that legacy of history that has given one of them such a big advantage? If the one in a position of privilege is marginally better, are we doing the right thing by choosing them because they were slightly better on the day? Or should we be looking beyond this, understanding the extent of opportunity that they have been given and acknowledging that the rival has more innate talent and ability and we should be going for them?

The latter may possibly be correct, but this is incredibly difficult to do. How on earth do we assess the level of benefit that the privileged candidate has received, and therefore what margin of difference is acceptable? A few years ago, I helped at an assessment centre, where we were evaluating candidates through a range of tasks, group activities, roleplays and interviews; with the goal of determining who we would bring onto our graduate scheme. The vast majority of the applicants were final-year university students, but there was one candidate who had left university, been to work for eighteen months in an investment bank, before deciding this was not the right route for her and making the brave decision to start again on a different path. She was fantastic in the interview. However, I was wholly conscious that she had highly relevant experience that many of the other candidates just simply did not have. Was she better than them? Or was she just benefiting from the extra experience and it was making her look better?

Now, this example has nothing to do with race, and the issue of a failed meritocracy does not have anything specifically to do with race. But race does become relevant when the privilege and therefore the opportunity and the subsequent advantages are predominated into a specific racial group. Despite some exceptions in specific countries, if we look on a global scale, history has put white people in a position of power, and this is the case in the United Kingdom. This is highly relevant, because whilst Reni Eddo-Lodge acknowledges that discrimination can go in both directions, she draws a very interesting distinction between discrimination and racism:

> There are unique forms of discrimination that are backed up by entitlement, assertion and, most

importantly, supported by a structural power
strong enough to scare you into complying
with the demands of the status quo. We have to
recognise this.

Again, it is difficult to argue with this view. Discrimination
from the powerless can be offensive and upsetting, but ultimately
this is something we experience in the moment it happens.
Discrimination from those in a position of power will have a
much more lasting impact, and she is absolutely correct to
highlight this distinction. And this provokes a realisation that
whilst we may not be prejudiced and may be using our "colour-
blind" upbringing to treat everyone equally, this is not necessarily
good enough to overcome what has happened in the past.

This point had never resonated with me until I was sitting
in a work presentation on the gender pay gap. The presentation
was giving the normal view of men in power protecting their
own kind by promoting them more and paying them more.
Listening to this as an individual who is convinced that I do
not do this, left me somewhat detached from the conversation;
understanding the issue but not feeling personally responsible.
So, I drifted off and started thinking about what did make
me decide how much I would pay somebody. My primary
consideration was what they were previously paid, and then
suddenly it clicked! I may not be discriminating against them,
but if they were underpaid previously, then I was reinforcing
the problem. I was not thinking about gender or discriminating
in any way, but by ignoring it, I was potentially reinforcing a
historic issue.

I am not sure why presentations never focus on this angle.
By focusing entirely on discrimination at the point of the
decision, it sounds like they are only talking to the extremes of
society. Shifting the tone of the discussion would make more of
us think. It would draw attention to the "white moderates" that
Martin Luther King referred to, or the well-meaning but silent
majority who are not actively discriminating, but somehow

allow the perpetuation of the prejudice. Positive discrimination may be a bit of a blunt solution, but there is some logic when we perceive the issue in the context of history. I do not know if it is the right answer; but when we have a mainstream process with loads of applicants then we need a simple tool to facilitate doing this in an efficient way.

However, this book is not about recruitment when we need to filter a selection from hundreds of CVs or make a quick decision in a 45-minute interview! This book is about conversation and in a conversation, we don't need to be so simplistic. We can get into the detail, the complexity, the hard truths that get us to the nuts and bolts of the issue and allow us to understand it properly. We can ask the difficult questions and take the time to properly understand what is going on. We can spend the time to identify when something like race is relevant and pertinent to the issue, either directly now, or because there is a history or legacy that makes it relevant; or whether it is just a distraction from the true issue. Just like a psychotherapist or a doctor can get distracted by the superficial symptoms and needs to delve under the surface to identify the real source of a problem, we need to explore with an open mind to get to the heart of the matter.

This is where conversations on race and immigration become so disappointing. As soon as a white person is dismissed as racist, or a black person is admonished for "playing the race card", then the conversation is over. Valid concerns over the impact of immigration policies just get lost by dismissing the opinions as bigoted. Dismissing proponents of open borders as anti-British or dismissing their criticisms as reverse racism are similarly effective debate crushers. By doing this, we just dismantle any chance of a good open discussion and therefore any chance of getting a full and thorough understanding of the motivations behind people's beliefs or behaviours. This is a major opportunity wasted.

Reflecting on the comments of Liam Neeson, should we not value his honesty even if we find his actions distasteful?

Should we not relish the chance to consider the points he makes, and acknowledge that although his response was extreme, the underlying prejudice may be uncomfortably prescient? Should we not face the uncomfortable truth of how we might behave if we were faced in a similar situation? As per some of the examples from earlier, should we not discuss the fact that most of us instantly see "difference" when something bad happens, in a way that we fail to do when the world is good? These thoughts are difficult and challenging and require self-reflection and the confession of guilty secrets. But they also present an opportunity to progress the conversation and to learn. It is a real shame when we take the easy route, distancing ourselves from the subject by just dismissing him as a racist.

With these overly simplistic and disparaging retorts, we not only close the conversation, but we close the opportunity to understand the perspective of the individual we are talking to. We immediately put them in a box with other racists, or unpatriotic renegades, depending on which way we lean. We make the wrong but easy mistake of dehumanising the individual and treating their thoughts as identical to a giant swathe of people that we have categorised similarly. Opinions are not that simple. People are not that simple. In a film called *The Beguiled* where a group of young ladies are treating an injured enemy soldier during the American Civil War, one of the lead characters realises during the process that:

> The enemy, as an individual, is not what we
> believe. His visit has taught us an important lesson.

By squashing the conversation, we deny ourselves the opportunity to learn that lesson.

Not only do we curtail that individual conversation, but we create an atmosphere where people feel wary of asking for details to better understand. Once something becomes a controversial topic, as no doubt is the case for race and immigration, then any conversation can feel like we are treading on eggshells. It can feel like one bad comment and we're a bad person. Having to over-think and be careful with our words is not the foundation of a good open conversation. In Chapter 5, I celebrated a Korean girl on a train striking up a random conversation and asking plenty of open questions about homosexuality, actively seeking to understand the concept and how it felt. How many of us would be truly prepared to do the same? How many white, able-bodied, straight people would be prepared to ask someone how does it feel to be black or disabled or gay? I think we would all agree that the number would be incredibly low. Just like the age-old guidance about avoiding conversations on religion, politics or money, we tend to avoid any potential for awkward conversations by sticking to safer ground. But we are all worse off for doing this.

I have talked a lot about race in this chapter, but the reality is that we have these same issues on any topic where we are engaged in a passionate debate. Where we hold a strong opinion, then we can be very fast to see this as the explanation for a whole range of consequential issues, even though the reality may be different. Once we have decided that drugs, big business, our parents or right-wing politicians are our pantomime villain, then we tend to blame them for everything! Just like people who are accused of "playing the race card", our blinkered one-dimensional perspective stops us from seeing the full story. At other times, we are the equivalent of colour-blind. Whilst the real explanation is blatantly obvious to an independent observer, our conviction that there is nothing wrong with our drug-taking, our capitalist society, our parents or our right-wing policies means that we cannot see the most plausible or realistic explanation. Our views and biases stop us from seeing the reality in its glorious complexity.

As we go through life, it is only naturally that we will gradually accumulate assumptions, biases, blinkers or prejudices, but it is important that this does not lead to shortcuts in our path to knowledge and understanding. This requires an open mind so that we walk into a discussion with a readiness to listen and ask questions. But we must also strive to keep this going throughout the discussion. Even where we get irritated, annoyed or offended by anything we hear, we should avoid the temptation to close the conversation with throwaway insults or slip into frustrated assumptions that can lead us to completely misread the situation. By staying calm, we can guide ourselves through the details and the complexity of the issue at hand until we have full knowledge and understanding. Only when we are comfortable with its inherent complexity will we be empowered to make the right judgements.

SIXTH PRINCIPLE

Don't oversimplify with assumptions. Dare to face the complexity!

CHAPTER 8

Good Monsters and Bad Angels

Everything has beauty, but not everyone sees it.

CONFUCIUS

The NHS is a great institution, which has been a key element of the fabric of the United Kingdom since its introduction back in 1948. From day one it operated on three key principles meeting the needs of everyone, being free at the point of delivery and being based on clinical need, and not the ability to pay. Through the years since then, the NHS has changed and evolved, but these core principles remain and now form part of a broader constitution that was more recently implemented with seven guiding principles:

Principle 1: The NHS provides a comprehensive service available to all

Principle 2: Access to NHS services is based on clinical need, not an individual's ability to pay

Principle 3: The NHS aspires to the highest standards of excellence and professionalism

Principle 4: The patient will be at the heart of everything the NHS does

Principle 5: The NHS works across organisational boundaries and in partnership with other organisations in the interest of patients, local communities and the wider population

Principle 6: The NHS is committed to providing best value for taxpayers' money and the most effective, fair and sustainable use of finite resources

Principle 7: The NHS is accountable to the public, communities and patients that it serves

These principles, supported by values such as respect, dignity and compassion have been key to the high-quality service that has been provided to so many people since its formation. The detachment from an "ability to pay" is especially important, ensuring that nobody is deprived of care because they are unable to afford it or do not have the appropriate insurance. It is hard for anyone to deny that it is a good thing to have a service that will step in for people when they most need it, regardless of their personal circumstances. It is therefore a real credit to the UK that this has remained in place with the organisation responding to the challenges of the ever-changing world.

These principles are immensely honourable but incredibly difficult to deliver. This is the most enormous operation, spending in excess of £100bn per annum, with over half a million doctors and nurses, hundreds of thousands of other qualified and non-qualified staff and interactions with a million patients every 36 hours. This is no mean feat! Now consider that some of these interactions are quite literally a matter of life and death, and that most of the service users are seeking relief from pain, suffering or some sort of condition that is negatively impacting their lives. That should help to crank up the pressure a bit further! Now consider that the workload is growing at an alarming rate due to an ageing population, with medical research helping to generate new procedures, extend the range of options available and prolong life expectancy. With all this in mind, the success of the NHS is an absolute miracle!

However, as with anything of this size, it won't be perfect. Talk to anybody and they can probably reel off both positive and negative experiences of interactions with the NHS. As a rugby player who found out midway through his career that he had a blood clotting disorder (not the ideal combination!!!!), I have had my fair experience with hospitals; and I would echo this sentiment. I have experienced plenty of excellent treatment, but at different times, I have faced the extremes of good and bad that you may expect when interacting with a behemoth of an organisation.

My longest and probably weirdest stay in hospital was for two weeks and involved a combination of planned and unplanned procedures. Having gone into the hospital for a knee reconstruction on the Monday morning, I was largely recovered by the end of the week. However, because of my bleeding disorder, we all agreed that it was best to err on the side of caution and to keep me in through the weekend. This ended up being a decision of pure genius, when a rapid decline in my health on the Sunday afternoon was eventually diagnosed as appendicitis! To the great amusement of the anaesthetist who asked me "What on earth are you doing back here?", I had an operation on my appendix a week after the one on my knee! This therefore gave me the pleasure of a second week in hospital. Just to add to the drama, they felt I had used enough morphine in the previous week, so they gave me a substitute that triggered the most horrendous hallucinations – so bad that no pain relief was preferable. Safe to say that was not the most enjoyable week of my life!

This stay was a great case study as I experienced both extremes of nursing care. One of the nurses at the Royal Free at the time was a guy called Barry (and I use his real name as he was an absolute credit to the profession). After my full recovery,

I went back to see him to say thank you, because he was simply amazing. He was extremely efficient in the way that he carried out his duties, so when he was with me, I would never know how incredibly busy he was. He had that magic touch of taking the time to talk, making me feel like I was his priority and that he had all the time in the world for me, even though we both knew that was not the case. He would listen and remember, so that I never needed to tell him the same thing twice. He identified the personal things that I would really appreciate, and then went out of his way to do them for me, as soon as he had a little bit of time. I had some very low times when I was struggling with pain and hallucinations, and he was there for me whenever I needed and helped me through the process.

Unfortunately, he was not there when the appendicitis symptoms started to kick in! Sadly, my duty nurse at that time was the opposite extreme. She would come in and do her observations with no patient interaction when I was awake, and with a desire to talk when she disturbed my sleep! When I tried to ask for something, she would just snap "What?" and ignore the request, and most worryingly, she just ignored my declining condition. When I was feeling terrible on the Sunday evening, and after no response to my patient alarm after 30 minutes, I had to drag myself on crutches to the reception to see my nurse plus two others just chatting in reception. Face-to-face, I wasn't so easy to ignore, and suddenly I had attention and doctors appeared, but I should never have been pushed to this limit. One hospital visit in one department and two completely contrasting experiences.

But the highs and lows are not isolated. I have made numerous trips to the haemophilia clinic at the Royal Free hospital, and without fail, the treatment is exceptional. The staff are friendly, attentive, precise and caring in everything they do; and the process of having blood tests or blood transfusions became a remarkably pleasant experience! Go to my local GP, and I get the mixed response. It is potluck as to which GP I see, and therefore chance as to the quality of service I get. Some of the doctors are caring, inquisitive and knowledgeable, with the time to explore my issues and concerns; while others behave like they are just simply ticking through a list. Then there are other healthcare facilities where the service is consistently bad, such as one nameless hospital department where I visited someone over several days. Other than on the procedural basics, no nurse or staff member spoke to my friend for the entirety of his stay. But it was not just their complete lack of warmth or friendliness, it was also their standard of care, probably best demonstrated by the initial request to keep his urine as it was "needed for samples". None of the samples were ever collected, so after a few days, the open receptacles piled up in the bathroom until the whole room started to smell. Nobody was prepared to remove them because it "wasn't their job", and eventually I just took matters into my own hands and emptied all the bottles. Every facet of the care was a disgrace and before you leap to their defence, they certainly had time. Every time I went to get them when they were ignoring an alarm call, there were plenty of nurses to be found chatting, just ignoring the alarm because he "wasn't their patient". Service is driven by the individuals and unsurprisingly, the variety is huge.

Even from a procedural basis, you get enormous variety. The 111 service is much maligned, but I have had nothing but good experiences, and it has been a godsend at some key moments. On multiple occasions, I have benefited from sensible advice over the phone and quickly arranged "out of hours" GP appointments to better assess the condition, with subsequent fast-track transfers into hospitals where needed. My experience has been a good process, efficiently operated and getting me to the right service quickly and efficiently. Compare this to my partner's experience in A&E with something stuck in his trachea and impairing his breathing – quite urgent you would think? After twelve hours in A&E with no sign of a doctor and his condition severely worsening because they had not let him drink any water since he arrived, we decided it was time to leave and try and find somewhere that actually cared! But no – apparently, he couldn't leave because he needed a doctor to discharge him. Seriously! If he could see a doctor, we would not need to go!

So even from my personal experience, it is very clear that the levels of individual service and procedure can operate at very different levels. And this is not that surprising. Consistency of high-quality service is one of the hardest things to achieve in a big organisation, and organisations do not get much bigger than the NHS. However, when we try to point out these issues, then an interesting thing happens, as we tend to get one of two reactions:

1. Point the finger of blame at the pantomime villains:

There is a ready list of baddies who are the most likely recipients of the blame for anything going wrong. First on the list is those nasty managers and bureaucrats, who "really don't understand what it is like on the front line" and who are obsessed with targets that lead to dysfunctional behaviour. Then there is the interference from central government (who are often the people coming up with the targets!), with the criticism seeming to escalate when the Tories are in power. Then we have the evil bankers, who caused the austerity measures and the acceleration of cost-cutting and efficiency. Finally, and probably as a combination of this evil trinity, we have all the paperwork, admin and cumbersome processes that are imposed on the staff and get in the way of their care.

2. Defend the good guys irrespective of the facts:

Where the criticism is pointed a bit more directly at frontline staff, then some real defensiveness tends to kick in. Criticism of an individual is often taken as a criticism of the whole profession; and a real sense of denial is displayed. Poor service is blamed on the system, the pressure, the long hours, the admin. We are told how the front-line staff are the victims, just as much as the patients on the ultimate receiving end.

There is clearly plenty of truth in these arguments about increasing pressures. With an ever-growing demand for services, and new treatments constantly being identified, then we must either throw more and more money into a bottomless pit, or we need to make some tough economic and commercial decisions. This will have to mean unpalatable policies, efficiencies and difficult choices, putting the staff into uncomfortable and challenging positions in front of their patients and stretching resources to breaking point. We also live in a world of legal action, with patients suing for mistakes, and sadly, this therefore inevitably leads to bureaucracy and paperwork as we try and evidence that we have done the right thing. These things undoubtedly clog up time and resources and drain the amount of time available for patient care. However, this is not the only problem. As with any organisation, there are good and bad people at all levels and in all types of roles.

Let's start with the front-line staff, also known as "the goodies". Of course, most of them are wonderfully caring staff, and I am sure there are a significantly higher proportion of caring people than you would find in the wonderful worlds of banking, sales or accountancy! However, there are people in these front-line roles, whether by nature or by circumstance, who are no longer providing that sense of care for the customer. There are people, whether by nature or as a result of the pressures that they are under, who are cutting corners and making mistakes. There are people, whether by nature or by training and policy, are behaving rigidly and failing to react to the unexpected circumstances that are unravelling before them. Ultimately, these people have an incredibly challenging job, and while the majority do it brilliantly, others will fall short and simply do not provide the standard of care we would want or maybe even expect. As much we wish it to be true, the front-line staff are not universally the heroes.

Now let's look at the hospital managers, also known as "the baddies". Of course, there are some managers who meet the caricature, who are totally focused on targets and the cold, hard numbers; and will prioritise this at the expense of patient care. However, this is not a manager, this is a bad manager! However much we may resist it, the truth is that there are also great managers who abide by the seven underlying principles and manage to balance that impossible tightrope between providing "the highest standards of excellence and professionalism" with the patient "at the heart of everything", but whilst "providing best value for taxpayers' money and the most effective, fair and sustainable use of finite resources". Whilst we are lampooning them, these non-clinical staff are guiding us through the minefield of political targets, funding constraints, legal challenges and patient complaints. Do the critics understand just how complicated that is? Ultimately, this is an incredibly challenging job, and while some will fall short and impose the bureaucracy and cost-cutting we detest, others will rise to the challenge and provide the balanced leadership and decision-making that are fundamental in creating the amazing health facilities that we are able to visit. As much as it is convenient to claim, the back-office bureaucrats are not universally the enemy.

One of the key jobs of "management" is looking after the huge budgets of the hospitals. Back in 2015, Lord Carter who was chair of the NHS Co-operation and Competition Panel, highlighted some of the considerable wastage and inefficiencies in the NHS. In particular, he pointed out the costs associated with poor procurement choices.

> I've been surprised by the variation in performance
> in getting the very best care for patients and
> delivering value for money within the NHS. It's
> clearly the case that some of our hospitals are the
> envy of the world in terms of both quality and
> performance – so what we must do now is resolve
> to bring all providers up to the standard of the best.

One very specific example he highlighted related to hospitals that were regularly spending £1.50 a time on soluble tablets for liver failure when non-soluble versions could be bought for 2p each. Soluble tablets are only needed for young children or people who have difficulty in swallowing, but the cost of inappropriate purchasing on this one tablet alone in one hospital was £40,000 per year! Money that could have been directed into front-line treatment was being lost because of poor decision-making. It is clear that inefficiencies like these need to be stopped, but who should be responsible for this?

If the baddies are the waste of space they are often portrayed, then we need to ask the front-line medical staff to make the purchasing decision during their busy day. Knowing how time-pressured they are, this would probably mean a quick decision based on the suppliers that they already know about or currently use – in other words, a decision without the full information as to different options and therefore the potential savings. Alternatively, if they think about things properly, then they need to step away from where they are most needed. Even if they eventually get to the right answer, we are losing valuable patient time. Neither of these are optimal solutions, so let's give it to one of the baddies, locked away in a back room of the hospital. According to the caricature, their eyes will light up when they do the research and see the opportunity to spend 2p per tablet, rather than £1.50 per tablet. They will therefore take the money-saving option, and put the cost saving before the considerations in patient care, which is great until a young child gets a tablet stuck in their throat! This is also suboptimal and is the behaviour that we describe and what we imagine is happening.

Now suppose that the back-office baddie does the research, and prepares a summary of the different suppliers, the different drug-types and the associated costs, with estimates of the annual spend for the different providers. They can do this quickly and clearly, because this activity is in their sweet spot, resonating with their skills and expertise. At a suitable time, they show this to one of the clinical leads, highlighting the level of saving that can be achieved by switching to non-soluble tablets, and asking if there is any reason why we cannot make the change. The clinical lead is then able to make a quick decision without any disruption to patient time, because they now have all the information in front of them. They point out the patient groups who need the soluble tablets but approve the change for the rest. Employ some collaborative working with everybody performing a role that aligns with their areas of knowledge and expertise, and we efficiently get to the right answer with minimal impact on patient care.

Now, I'm sure this sort of collaboration does happen in most of our well-run hospitals, but we undermine this completely when (from the outside at least) we create an "us" and "them" tension between the hospital staff and management. Isn't this crazy, when this close working arrangement is what we want? The Queen seems to think so! In a meeting of the Sandringham Women's Institute in early 2019, the Queen said a few words about the need to be more collaborative in discussions:

> As we look for new answers in the modern age,
> I for one prefer the tried and tested recipes,
> like speaking well of each other and respecting
> different points of view; coming together to seek
> out the common ground; and never losing sight
> of the bigger picture. To me, these approaches are
> timeless and I commend them to everyone.

This was considered as a thinly veiled reference to Brexit negotiations, but it could probably be applied just as readily to the NHS. While we are watching a Hollywood movie, the separation of the goodies and baddies is fun and entertaining, but in the real world, dismissing well-meaning people as baddies is not constructive, particularly when they are fighting for the same goal. When we think of them as the enemy, it is easy to lose sight of the fact that the hospital management also want an efficient service of a high quality that is delivered with care. They want the same as the front-line staff. The only difference between the two sides is the amount of emphasis placed on the different pillars that are needed to achieve this challenging goal.

Management are probably more focused on efficiency to ensure we can keep the service running with finite funds, and the design of a high-quality service with procedures and controls that prevent errors and mistakes. The front-line staff are probably more focused on implementing the high-quality and critical services to the patients and providing the care and attention that is needed at difficult times. The implications of these different perspectives influence heavily the decisions that they would make when faced with a life-and-death situation. While front-line staff who are at the coal face, may want to try a drug or procedure that has a low chance of success because they have a specific patient who would benefit from it; management takes the perspective that we should save the money from a likely lost cause in order to save resources for other "more worthwhile" causes. In fact, this is a debate between which NHS principle takes precedence when there is a conflict. Principle 6 says that with limited resources we need to provide "best value for taxpayers' money", but Principle 4 says "the patient will be at the heart of everything the NHS does". Unfortunately, we can't always do both, so which is right? There is obviously a "nicer" answer, so it is not surprising in this context that we portray the goodies and baddies in the scenario. However, the reality is that we just have two sets of people with a different viewpoint on a very difficult decision.

When we are faced with such challenging decisions, then rather than focus on a simplistic question of good (clinical staff) against bad (management), we should emphasise the importance of having the highest quality people on both sides. If we have recruited the best people, then rather than being the enemy, managers could be the inspiring leaders. They could be the ones creating the caring culture, setting the example as to how everyone should be operating, taking the lead on training and developing the staff, and knowing how to stamp out inefficiency without negatively impacting patient care. A good manager would encourage the open collaboration between staff, ensuring that decisions combine the commercial and clinical expertise that will lead to the right choices. A good manager will also have high standards to ensure that the service provides the "highest standards of excellence and professionalism" as per the NHS principles. This means nurturing and developing staff to improve their performance, but also being prepared to make tough decisions around disciplining and removing those who are not operating at the standards we expect, whether this relates to back-office or clinical staff. After all, good standards require good people!

This is where the defensiveness, the second issue highlighted earlier, becomes a major problem. At the start of the chapter, I gave a few examples of poor service from my personal experience, but I also have two examples from close friends who work in healthcare – one in the NHS and one in the charity sector. In both cases, formal complaints were made about staff members because of poor quality care. In the first instance, a nurse witnessed a colleague verbally and physically abusing a patient in a mental health facility, and therefore formally reported the abuse to the clinical manager. In the second instance, a nurse reported that they were being bullied and harassed by the nursing manager on the ward. In both cases, the bully remained in their jobs, and the complainant ended up leaving. These may be isolated cases, and I am sure that there are plenty of examples where the complaints procedure works better, but these cases happened. Alleged "goodies" performed the mistreatment and then other "goodies" covered it up to prevent the reputational damage and to protect their friends. Distorted predeterminations of the good guys can have real consequences.

The implications of this is that those who dismiss this criticism in the pretence of protecting their profession are causing a huge amount of damage. Their actions stifle progress and allow instances of real abuse to go unchecked. Failing to confront poor performance and bad behaviour from staff is the very worst thing from the patients' perspective. Moreover, hiding issues does not instil confidence in the public. Confidence comes from swift and decisive resolution of the issues that arise, and swift and decisive resolution comes from having an open mind in response to criticism that is received. No "goodie v. baddie" bias whereby we fail to notice the bad points in a "good" person and fail to notice the good qualities of a "bad" person, but an open-minded and impartial assessment of the facts that has the best interests of the institution at heart.

But this pantomime view of good and bad is not restricted to the world of healthcare. It is something that we apply in so many areas of life, and it leads to the same blinkers. Occasionally it is driven by societal views or principles of right and wrong, as for example, there is probably a consensus of how we would attribute Hitler and Mother Teresa between the two categories! But in many cases, our categorisation is more a consequence of our personal choice. Our tastes in music, sport or politics will define what and who we perceive as heroes or villains. Our relationships and upbringing will define our perspectives on family members and create deep feelings of love or occasionally of resentment. Our relationships and life experiences will define what we think of people, places and companies that we meet, visit or interact with, and we each reach different conclusions as to what we love, what we hate and what opinions we form.

Even in some extreme cases, we can come to very different conclusions on good versus bad. Consider an infamous murder trial in the United States. In 1989, two brothers – the Menendez brothers – aged 18 and 21 in an affluent family in Beverley Hills shot and killed their parents while they were watching TV. The father was shot point-blank in the back of the head, while the mother was shot in the leg as she tried to flee and was then subsequently shot several times in the arm, chest and face leaving her unrecognisable. The brothers then went to the cinema to give themselves an alibi, before returning and calling the police when they got back home, claiming that they had just found their parents. They were not initially suspected, and so were not immediately charged. They started to arouse suspicion as they went on a major spending spree over the coming months but were only charged after one of the brothers made a confession to his psychologist. The delayed arrest as well as disputes over the admissibility of evidence that was recorded by the psychologist without permission meant the case did not go to trial until 1993 in a high-profile televised case.

The prosecution and all of us would ask how did the boys become such monsters? Who would commit such a brutal and unprovoked attack on their middle-aged parents while they were sitting watching TV? Who would shoot their mother so many times that she was unrecognisable? How could they do this to parents who had given them so much wealth and opportunity? How could they possibly justify doing this just to get their hands on their parents' money more quickly, or to avoid being written out of the will? How evil must they be to have done this?

However, the defence had an answer for this. In some harrowing evidence that shook the case, they revealed the years of sexual, emotional and physical abuse which the boys had suffered. Witnesses to the case have suggested that the boys were either incredible actors, or their testimonies must have been true, as there were huge amounts of emotion and feeling in the room. A cousin went to the stand confirming that many years previously, one of the brothers had told them about the sexual abuse. The sheen of loving parents was peeled away, and a much more sinister family was portrayed. The descriptions were of a cruel, vindictive paedophile of a father and a selfish, unstable, substance abuser of a mother who allowed everything to happen unchallenged. Having confronted their parents and fearing for their safety, are their actions suddenly more justified? Is what they did excusable or at least understandable? There may be no dispute that they killed their parents, but does this shift things to manslaughter or self-defence, rather than the evil and premeditated murder that the prosecution described?

We have been taught from as early as we can remember that murder is wrong, so the thought of applying some sympathy and saying that it is understandable in certain circumstances is incredibly difficult to stomach. But conversely, if the evidence of the abuse is to be believed, then the boys have been through an unbearable ordeal over many years. To have no shred of empathy for the unbearable pent-up emotions and misery and distress that the boys have been carrying for so many years would therefore seem completely unfeeling and callous. The poor juries on this trial (there were two following the trial – one for each brother) could not cope with this ambiguity of sentiment and emotion and simply could not reach an agreement on whether this was murder or manslaughter.

The juries' inability to decide reflects the polarised opinions on this case. There are those who do not believe a word of the abuse story, believing this fabrication is another layer to the evil murderers who so callously slaughtered their parents just to get their grubby hands on their parents' fortune. There are others who are convinced by the accusations and are overwhelmed with sympathy for the victims of many years of abuse who lashed out inappropriately but understandably, considering what they had been through. Steering a course between one of these two opinions is uncomfortable, and so the brothers tended to be labelled as either manipulative murders or misguided victims.

The retrial in 1994 rather removed this ambiguity as most of the evidence around the sexual and emotional abuse was deemed inadmissible (as it was considered unproven). Without this, the case for a murder prosecution was compelling. The brothers were therefore sentenced to life imprisonment without the option of parole. They remain in prison some 30 years after the murder with no current option of release. This gave a clear verdict, but probably did little to change the opinions of anyone who had sat through the first trial. Witnesses to the first trial had created an emotional connection that extended well beyond a summary of the facts, creating either a deep hatred and abhorrence of their heinous acts or an overwhelming feeling of sadness and sympathy for the rough hand that the poor boys were dealt. These emotional connections are much harder to shake than a fact-based opinion into which we throw some new evidence.

Strong emotional connections in themselves are not necessarily a problem, but the fact that they become so entrenched does create real issues. The problem is we put so much weight on the emotional connection that contrary factual evidence loses its power to persuade us; and this can have disastrous consequences as outlined in the preface to a booked called *Sway: The Irresistible Pull of Irrational Behaviour* by Ori and Ron Brafman. They describe the true story of a two-year old girl who was brought into hospital with severe abdominal pains. Although this could be a symptom of a whole range of conditions, it can be also be something very benign like indigestion. The mother was flustered and anxious, and in the eyes of the doctors, she appeared to be greatly overreacting, and they therefore sent the girl home without running any checks. The mother and daughter returned the next day, with the mother's behaviour reinforcing the doctors' views of her as a hypochondriac and so for a second consecutive day, they sent the child home without running any tests. On the third consecutive day, the doctors were even more convinced by their initial view of the situation until the child lost consciousness. By this time, it was too late to recover the situation and the girl passed away. There were so many missed opportunities to run some tests and realise their error, but they missed these, because of their deep-rooted conviction that the mother was wasting their time. The doctors (despite their medical training) allowed a negative emotional judgement of the mother to interfere with more fact-based evidence. It is horrific when the consequences are so severe, but the reality is that by labelling people, concepts or ideas, we all fall into this trap.

Our flawed use of labels is fantastically demonstrated in the musical *Wicked*, with the concepts of good and bad being a central theme of the storyline. The plot includes a particular emphasis on erroneous presumptions of good and bad, and the role that labels play in creating these misconceptions. One of the songs, 'Wonderful' appears to be motivated by the much-quoted phrase:

> One man's terrorist is another man's
> freedom fighter.

.... as the lyrics highlight situations where positive or negative opinions result in us creating positive or negative labels to describe what we are talking about. We do this all the time, as I could for the examples I was discussing above by asking if the brothers are ruthless murderers or misguided victims, or whether the mother was an irrational hypochondriac or a concerned and loving parent. These labels accurately reflect our positive or negative perspectives on the individuals concerned, and this is what makes them so valuable. They can help us to simplify and rationalise our views on a subject, and provide a good way of communicating our opinions, in just a simple word or phrase.

The song 'Wonderful' takes things a little further by subsequently highlighting our discomfort with ambiguity. Once a label is created, we tend to pick one side or the other and act as if there is nothing in between the two extremes. With people, this means we tend to assign the chosen label to the whole personality of the individual. If we consider the Menendez brothers to be victims, then this will excuse them of all their negative traits, and not just this single action. Conversely, if we do not share this sympathy and believe them to be guilty of murder, then we consider them evil in all aspects of their life. This reminds me of a cartoon I once read, showing two inmates and one saying to the other that:

> You are not a murderer; you are just a person who
> murdered someone!

This tries to assign the ambiguity to the situation and suggest that the person should not be defined by a single act, however abhorrent it was. But we struggle with this concept. This is like a question asked by F. Scott Peck in *A Road Less Travelled* when he asks whether we can think of any positive qualities of Hitler? Having dismissed him as evil, this is almost impossible, even though it is perfectly possible for an evil person to have some positive traits.

We do this when we create a negative perspective of someone, but we do the same with positive associations. If we find a celebrity that we greatly admire, we tend to create an awe of them, which extends far beyond their talent as a singer, actor or sportsperson. Marketing has long taken advantage of this, using celebrities to endorse a whole range of products, knowing that we will be tempted to buy them just purely by their association. This would be completely logical in their chosen field, such as a footballer endorsing football boots! However, we go so much further and are influenced completely irrespectively of whether our idol knows, likes or uses the product they are recommending. In social media, this has evolved into the concept of "influencers" who cultivate a mass following via regular postings on a topic of great interest or expertise. In a similar way, once they have a loyal following, their influence can extend so much more broadly, and we buy into their personal brand. As a result, we are now influenced well beyond the original niche.

In summary, we tend to create oversimplified generalisations at either extreme. When, we have labelled people as good, we over-glorify their qualities and become blind to any failings, but once we have labelled them as bad, we write them off in all respects and become equally blind to their good qualities. This behaviour saves us from the sort of moral ambiguity that the song describes and which we find immensely uncomfortable.

As well as being a flawed safety measure, labels also drive us to these polarised views as they give us a distorted sense of comparability. Using a very simple example to consider this, let's think about my age. Last year, I turned 45. Moving from 44 to 45 did not feel like anything had really changed. However, suppose I filled out two surveys, one the day before and one the day after my birthday, and as is common in surveys, they categorised my age. Just one day had passed, but I have now passed from 35-44 to 45-54. This feels like I have aged ten years in a single day – it must have been a good party!!!!! The impact of the label tends to exaggerate the difference between the categories (as I see the gap of ten years between the ranges) but underplay the variety within the range (as I tend to ignore the ten-year range within the group).

Now, filling out a survey is hardly that important, unless it happens to dent my self-esteem. However, this happens everywhere and can sometimes be far more serious. Consider when we are sitting exams, where someone scoring 70% in an exam is recorded as an A-student. This is a great performance, and these high-performing students are unsurprisingly perceived very differently to a B-student. However, some of those B-students may have scored 69.9%! Not only do we consider these students considerably worse than a rival who scored just 0.1% more than them; we exacerbate this injustice by considering them the same as someone who scored 60% (i.e. 9.9% less than them!). Presented this way, it feels crazy, but that is exactly what we do. Moreover, doing it feels completely normal! Ultimately, to simplify the way that we communicate exam performance, we feel the need to draw some lines, but on occasions, these lines can create a totally distorted impression. Some small differences of 0.1% are exaggerated and some large differences of 9.9% are eliminated!

And this serious impact does not just happen when there is a clear scale as with age or exam grades. Suppose we are comparing people with and without a criminal record. When thinking of a "criminal", we are usually thinking of someone who has committed a reasonably serious crime. This is the mental image for that label, but whilst the criminal could be a predatory serial paedophile, the label also covers a parent who confiscated some ecstasy pills from their child and got caught in possession. Similarly, a clean record normally suggests a good person and that is the mental image that we have, but it would also include a troublemaker who is regularly in fights but has had the good fortune of not being arrested. Our mental images for the labels tend to underestimate the sense of variety within that label (i.e. criminal = criminal, good = good), but rather overestimate the difference between contrasting labels. Our mental images do not consider the people at the boundary who we have pushed either side of the threshold as thinking of them makes things a bit more difficult!

Even on fundamental labels such as gender, we have created the same problems. As discussed in Chapter 5, we have created definitions of the male and female labels, even if that is something that we are now trying to unpick. The female stereotype describes them as emotional, caring, nurturing homemakers who need protection. The male stereotype is a strong, rational, insensitive breadwinner who can protect and provide for those around him. Clearly everyone is different, but these labels have created the sense that "Men are from Mars, Women are from Venus" as per the famous book. Maybe we are different by the time we get to adulthood, but the reality is that this is probably more driven by the societal view of the characteristics, behaviours and roles of the different genders, than being caused by any underlying difference between men and women.

Our brain's enthusiasm for simplification means it naturally reinforces these blinkers. Firstly, when on the receiving end of a stereotypical label, we tend to talk and behave in a way sometimes described as the chameleon effect. This reflects the animal's infamous protection strategy of blending in with its surroundings. What this means in relation to the above example is that boys grow-up trying to behave as close to the male stereotype, whilst a girl will do the same with the female stereotype. As explained by a guide called Improving Gender Balance Scotland:

There is more variance within groups of boys
and within groups of girls, than there is between
boys and girls. Gender differences are learned,
not innate.

More generally, this describes our tendency to act up to our labels and reinforce them from within. Tell someone they are bright and intelligent, then they will tend to study hard and feel confident about tests and exams, resulting in an over-performance. Tell someone they are a stupid troublemaker, and they will probably think their efforts to prepare are a waste of time and approach the test lacking belief and probably underdeliver against their true ability. Working against the tide of external opinion is hard and constantly challenging people's misconceptions is exhausting, so we often don't bother. As a young Muslim girl said in the wonderful short film, *Balcony*:

I tell them what they're already thinking.

In summary, most of us spend time living up to the labels that we have been given, not just in the way we behave but in the opinions that we share, and this is what makes labels so relevant to discussions.

But that's not the only issue, it gets worse! When we are the observer, we apply something called "confirmation bias", as briefly mentioned in Chapter 2. This is the psychological explanation for our tendency to place more credence on evidence that supports our current beliefs, and to be much more dismissive of counterevidence. If we see a strong, ambitious and competitive man, we see it is as evidence that the label is true; but when we see an emotional caring man, we just see him as untypical and do not perceive this as contradictory. But confirmation bias is even stronger than this. It's not just about how we react when evidence comes along, as in addition, we actively behave in a way in which we try to reinforce our current beliefs.

From a psychological perspective, this expression was coined by the English psychologist Peter Wason, who demonstrated this in his Rule Discovery Test that was first performed in the 1960s. In the test, he came up with a rule connecting three numbers, and then gave an example of three numbers that met the criteria. He then asked the participants to try and work out the rule by coming up with alternative sets of three numbers, knowing that on each occasion, he would confirm whether their suggestion also satisfied the rule. What happened, almost without fail, is that participants quickly determined what they thought the rule was, and then come up with suggestions that would prove their own hypothesis. Suppose for example, that they were given the series "2, 4, 6", participants would come up with a hypothesis such as:

- Even numbers (and start suggesting "4, 8 ,10", "6, 8, 12", "20, 22, 24"); or
- Increasing by 2 (and start suggesting "3, 5, 7", "8, 10, 12", "11, 13, 15")

When each example did satisfy the rule, this increased their conviction that they were correct. However, when told that this was not the rule, they would keep trying the same hypothesis, feeling that more examples just added more and more evidence that they were right; even though the tester was telling them they were wrong.

The reality in this test is that the participants would learn more if they tried to come up with series that they did not think met the criteria (e.g. odd numbers, increasing by bigger amounts, fractions, minus numbers, descending numbers) and then problem-solving based on the answer. Getting a mixture of positive and negative responses is helpful as we then start to look for the differences between them and can use this to build a view of what the rule is. However, this simple test showed that we often do not do that. We often set out to prove that we are right; and can remain stubbornly fixed on that path, even when we are told we are wrong! We seek to reinforce our own bias, and then get even more firmly entrenched in our conviction as we get more and more positive affirmations. The fact that we are getting positive affirmations because we have asked questions that would lead to positive affirmation is rather lost on us!!!!

So, we have a real problem here. Mental labels may be an incredibly powerful tool that facilitates our understanding and communication of important concepts and greatly eases our lives, but they also cause us great problems. They make us oversimplify things as black and white, distorting our sense of comparability and preventing us seeing the grey in between. And they make us blinkered, so that we get excessively swayed by irrelevant information that supports us and dismissing factual evidence that contradicts us. We make these fundamental errors in our judgement of people, but also in our assessment of views and opinions. The perceived big gaps between right and wrong already make it difficult to persuade us to change our minds, but it becomes even more challenging when we have such a skewed impression of new information that we receive. Referring back to *Sway: The Irresistible Pull of Irrational Behaviour*, the authors quote a psychologist Franz Epting who puts this fairly neatly when he says that:

> We use diagnostic labels to organise and simplify.
> But any classification that you come up with,
> has got to work by ignoring a lot of other things
> – with the hope that the things you are ignoring
> don't make a difference. And that's where the rub
> is. Once you get a label in mind, you don't notice
> things that don't fit within the categories that do
> make a difference.

This sounds terrible, especially when we exacerbate this with our confirmation bias, meaning we keep reinforcing our distorted perspective. But as I have mentioned before, understanding our failing is the key to finding the solution. Just as in the number game, where we need to suggest series that would break our personal hypothesis, we need to do the same with labels. It's hard to do this with everything, but if we are honest with ourselves, we know the labels that are important to us. We know the labels where we have strong opinions and where however right we are, we are likely to be a bit biased. We therefore know the labels where we must try and force ourselves to overcome the confirmation bias. In other words, we need to go out of our way to give the contrasting view the benefit of a good hearing to overcome our blinkers!

Consider the case of Southampton University Student Union president Emily Dawes who vowed to paint over a mural of graduates at her university, because it depicted only white men. She later said that her "intention was to promote strong, female leadership". Her strong views on this topic unsurprisingly created intense opinions on a picture that did not reflect the diversity that she believes was appropriate for the university. Suppose she was more conscious of the potential for bias and therefore asked a few more open questions about the picture? If so, she might have found out that the mural was a commemoration of all the young students who went off to fight in the First World War and never returned to collect their degrees. There was, in fact, a good justification for the lack of diversity; but a strong opinion or label about the significance of "white men" meant that it felt unnecessary to find the facts. Knowing we have strong opinions on a topic and that our ideological lenses are distorted is the time when it is most important to find the facts; and when it is most important to process and absorb those facts. This is our remedy to the problem.

Reflecting on the healthcare system, this means avoiding the desire to jump to the simplest conclusion and to blame the obvious targets. It means being prepared to sift through the details of what happened and to draw an honest conclusion as to what is causing an issue. Sometimes it means championing the cause of hospital managers who are trying their best, within a difficult system. Sometimes it means acknowledging that the true failing was in a lack of care from front-line staff and that any challenges provided by the system were not actually the cause of the problem. But always, it means actively overcoming our preconceptions, getting to the heart of the matter, finding the truth and finding the right solution by attributing accountability to the appropriate cause.

This is incredibly easy to say, and incredibly difficult to do. When we are looking at something objectively, we all appreciate how informative factual evidence can be. We also know how much we want other people to be objective in the way they treat us. However, objectivity quickly falls away when we are passionate about something. Our intensity of opinion triggers emotion, and these emotions can create a real sense of certainty and conviction that is difficult to resist. As a result, resistance to this emotional bias is critically important. Without it, we are blind to the strengths of our opponents' arguments and we are blind to the weaknesses of our own.

By ensuring we are aware of our preconceptions, we have a fighting chance of avoiding being derailed by them. We give ourselves the chance of being passionate without becoming irrational and blinkered. By accepting that our view is not perfect, and that the counter-opinion is not completely misinformed, we can maintain a good, intellectual discussion rather than an incoherent argument. By managing to see the good in the bad and the bad in the good, we can spot the flaws in our own view and see the nuggets of genius within the views of our enemy. This will guide us to the truth and allow us to truly benefit from the knowledge we get when we combine our strengths.

 SEVENTH PRINCIPLE

See the good and bad in everything and always aim to find the truth

CHAPTER 9

Don't you want to know how Amazing I am?

It is already hard enough to understand what someone is saying. Discussion is just an exercise in narcissism where everyone takes turns showing off. Very quickly, you no longer have any idea what is being discussed.

GILLES DELEUZE

When I was a child, people often used to say to me, "Enjoy your schooldays, they are the best years of your lives". I absolutely loved my schooldays and have nothing but happy memories of my childhood and upbringing; but even then, I found it a rather depressing thought that my life was going to go downhill from there!!!! I'm glad to see this has not been the case. I can genuinely say that I've enjoyed my life more and more as the years have gone by. Yes – there have been some blips on the way. Yes – there have been some periods or times when things have gone wrong and everything has just seemed hard. Yes – there have been times when I wished for the innocence of childhood when I didn't have to carry the burden of responsibility. But these blips were temporary, and the general trend has been upwards.

I previously mentioned the debut appearance of my partner and I at a local gymnastics club. We were two 40-somethings who had never done anything like this, so the instructor started gently. All around, there were young kids doing backflips, aerial vaults and tumbles as they prepared for a competition, whilst next to them, we were starting with forward rolls. But while many youngsters were trying to impress those around, I was getting sheer personal joy from successfully achieving my first ever cartwheel. Finally achieving something that most six-year-olds can do! And why was I enjoying it so much? Because I was enjoying it for myself, focused on my own personal achievement, not worried for a second what other people might be thinking of me. If there was anybody laughing at my appalling efforts, then I would not have noticed and certainly would not have cared. I was enjoying my own personal victory, and totally focused on that.

And that's been the joy of growing older for me. Maybe I am weird for being a gay, teetotal rugby player who loves dancing wildly in nightclubs, but hates parties. Maybe it's old-fashioned that I don't want to use Instagram or Facebook or Twitter, and that I prefer pen and paper to organise my life. Maybe it's childish that I laugh more at pantos than any of the children around me, that I think it's unfair when there is an age limit on bouncy castles or that I have still failed to find a drink that tastes better than Ribena. Maybe it's a little strange that I'm in my mid-40s and I've still got a crush on Robbie Williams after nearly 30 years, or that I enjoy singing country music with a "bad" American accent! Maybe! But that's the way that I am, and I am happy with it. I don't need to pretend I'm straight, or pretend it's cool to be a bit rebellious, or pretend I drink sometimes but just not tonight. I don't need to have the latest phone or go to the swankiest bars or clubs to impress anyone, because I like the person that I am and if others don't agree, well…. not everybody is going to like me, and I'm OK with that.

But it wasn't always that way. As a youngster, probably like most children, I spent huge amounts of time worrying about what people thought of me, and I wanted to be accepted by my peers. Particularly in my teenage years, I worked exceptionally hard to pretend I was like everyone else. I wasn't prepared to admit that I was gay and so I used to pretend I liked lads' mags and would randomly pick actresses or pop stars that I would claim to fancy. I wasn't prepared to admit that I was a bit antisocial, so I had to shield the fact that I wanted to stay at home with my family on a Friday night. I wasn't prepared to admit that I was a bit straitlaced, so I never told anybody that I thought alcohol and cigarettes were the absolute opposite of being cool and grown-up. I wasn't prepared to admit that I was a swot, so I underplayed how much effort I put into my homework to try and look a bit cooler in front of the rugby lads! I hid so much of my true self to hide my differences.

And when we are cultivating our image, it is immensely embarrassing when we get exposed. I'm sure the pressure has ramped up so much with the increasing powers of celebrity and the influence of social media, but even in the late 1980s, there was a lot of pressure. I remember the humiliation when not only did I accidentally say "orgasm" (instead of "organism") in a Biology lesson, but it became quickly apparent that I was the only person in the room who did not have a clue what an orgasm was! I also remember feeling hugely embarrassed standing at school in my diabolically naff Dunlop Green Flash trainers, when all those around me were modelling their fancy labels.

I have intentionally chosen two tiny examples of childhood nightmares, because although they seem so trivial when I look back as an adult, they felt absolutely crushing when they were happening. And they felt so crushing because I had a great fear of revealing weaknesses or differences that could leave me exposed. Being isolated or different or weak made us an easy target, so fitting in with the crowd and having friends not only made our schooldays so much more enjoyable, but it also became a bit of a means of survival. Putting on that act and concealing our weaknesses and differences was critical, even though doing this on a day-to-day basis was draining.

So, what did this mean in the school playground? Ultimately it meant being as close to average as possible! In an ideal world, we didn't want to be too clever or too stupid, too rich or too poor, too fat or too thin, too "pretty boy" or too ugly. And we needed to like the "right" things and follow the trends and fashions that came along. It never mattered whether we actually liked those things or not, just as long as we went along with it and didn't rock the boat.

At a young age, I found this reasonably easy to navigate. My strange hidden mix meant I could relate to most people, so I found I could get on with everyone. I was academically good and loved Maths, so I could get on with all the geeks. I loved sport and was quite competitive, so could join in with all the playground games. I was good at rugby and able to handle myself, so I could get on with all the rough and tough guys. But I also had a more gentle side that involved me getting the lead female role in *Bugsy Malone* at my all boys school, so… I'll just leave it at that! Basically, I could get on with pretty much everybody and I found this hugely helpful; because when we're getting on with people, they are a much easier audience. I could superficially play along with the pretence that I fitted in with everybody, without getting too much scrutiny. Small differences and indiscretions were just overlooked, and I could carry on along my path.

As I got older, however, it started to become more challenging. Rebelliousness, alcohol, cigarettes and sex suddenly became quite central to the behaviour and conversations of the groups at school, and so my conservative, well-behaved, innocent, prudish and introverted nature diverged further from those around me. My outlook on life probably correlated most with my friends from the Maths class, but they did not share my interests away from the textbook or my sense of humour. The rugby boys and some of the more social groups better shared my tastes and interests, but they were all drawn to girls and alcohol, so were starting to push me in a direction that I didn't want to go. I found ways of happily negotiating my way through the school day, but things became so much harder away from school when the external temptations were more accessible for my friends.

To get through everything, I still had three big advantages. Firstly, the fact that I was a big-hitting rugby player meant that nobody suspected my big secret – I had a cover story without having to come up with a lie! Secondly, getting on with everyone allowed me to continue flitting from group to group, which acted as a great defence mechanism. I was effectively in every group, but in none of the groups – in the sense that they all allowed me in, but none of them got to really know me. Thirdly and finally, I had the comfort and love and support of my wonderful family, and I was very happy to retreat into that safety net. These advantages all helped to minimise the pressure, but particularly in relation to alcohol in my rugby surroundings, I still felt great pressure to conform.

Take away some of the securities that I had, and I can only imagine what a nightmare the effects of peer pressure must be for some children who feel different to the mainstream. Choose to be ourselves and the differences can lead to isolation, teasing and bullying, as well as a lack of self-esteem as our young brain often sees popularity as the measure of success. When the fear of these consequences is so strong and so real, doing something we don't like to fit in with the crowd often feels like the best thing. But unfortunately, this just creates different problems. Choose to go with the crowd, and we can fool everyone externally, but the suppression of ourselves can feel like an ever-increasing pressure cooker of emotions that grows stronger as we are led further from the path we should be following. In different ways, this can also make the school experience unimaginably hard, with coping strategies that are equally unhealthy to our mental health. I found a way of coping, but that is not manageable for everyone, particularly if their differences are more visible, if they are lacking the cover story that would enable them to blend, or if they are not blessed with the family support from which I benefited so greatly. I did feel "abnormal" for much of my childhood, but also appreciate that I was actually pretty lucky with my dysfunctionality!

For me, the peer pressures I struggled with most were alcohol and sex; two things where I did not want to follow the crowd but lacked the confidence to stand alone. But peer pressure can relate to so many things, because not only do we have our concept of "normal" (i.e. the looks, characteristics or behaviours that are shared by the mainstream), but we also use it to control people's taste. One way this happens is through trends and fashions. Trends are fairly pervasive across all aspects of our life such as the clothes we wear, the hairstyles that we have, the accessories we buy, the gadgets we need to have, the brands that define us, the games we play, the music we listen to, the apps we should download, the music we listen to and the things that we do. They tend to be quite specific as they can be a very precise way that we should wear our clothes (e.g. sagging) or a very specific thing that we should do (e.g. the ice bucket challenge). Some can operate in a niche demographic (e.g. Fortnite), whilst some can much more widespread (e.g. Gangnam style) and even end up with presidents and political leaders being asked to join in! These can often seem quite fun, but it is fun when it is something that we want to do, and not when it becomes a bit more of a compulsion. And that is often the way, as although failing to follow every single one is not necessarily a problem, people tend to draw wider implications from our choice to abstain and we get a "reputation"!

Another way we can control taste is by the way we tend to rank our preferences. This can apply to our tastes in clothing or sports or music or entertainment, our physical or social media appearances, and the things that we do. In many cases, the preference will vary according to the demographic or the clique to which we belong. For example, whilst some younger groups might consider hip-hop to be superior to pop and certainly to opera, an older more affluent crowd may flip the order into reverse. And while in some cases, the taste is probably driven by popularity (e.g. football being the "best" sport), other preferences may be driven by perceived quality (e.g. classic literature in comparison to "chick lit"). Their generic nature does make them different to trends, but they are very similar in the way that we draw wider ramifications from the choices that people make. We tend to equate unusual choices in music or sport or pastimes with an unusual or different personality; meaning that being "different" requires real confidence. Once again, it can feel better to pretend to have some mainstream choices than be ourselves, if we don't want to get a reputation as a weirdo!

And psychologically, we don't like to be that lone wolf. We don't want to be the person who is different and who stands on their own. Dr Solomon Asch conducted an amazing bit of research back in the 1950s where he asked a group of participants to look at a set of images with one line on the left, and then a group of three lines on the right-hand side. In each of the sets of images, one of the three lines on the right-hand side would be the same length as the one on the left – line B (I hope you would agree!!!!) in the image below.

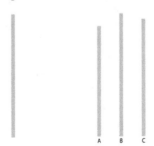

The trick was that only one of the participants was a true participant. The others were part of the experiment, and after choosing the right solution the first few times, they were then asked to start giving the wrong answer. After a few rounds, the true participant (giving their answer fourth in the group) was therefore in a situation where all three predecessors had consistently given an apparently wrong answer. The participant basically had to choose between following the group (and therefore being wrong) or being different (but actually being correct). Whilst in a standard trial with no actors, the error rate on questions would be less than 1%, this jumped to about 37% when the actors were giving misleading answers.

Analysing more deeply, only a small minority followed the actors every time, but 75% of participants made an error and were following the actors on at least one of the questions. The main reason highlighted was a "distortion of action" where they knew the right answer but did not feel they could defy the majority on every occasion. This suggests we are prepared to stand alone, but not on a consistent and recurrent basis. However, there were some who followed the crowd more consistently who showed a "distortion of judgement" whereby they started to believe that they must be misinterpreting the question as the majority must be right. This is effectively a sense of brainwashing whereby a mainstream view is consistently applied, and we eventually start to believe it must be true, even though it contradicts our own judgement. Even within the group who gave the correct answer throughout, the vast majority highlighted a real sense of discomfort about the fact that they were giving different answers to everyone else. For some reason, this is hugely uncomfortable; and strangely, many of us are happier being wrong than different!

This action of publicly conforming to the group is something called "normative social influence". This is believed to be a natural behaviour reflecting the fact that we are social creatures and positive interactions with others has always been key to our survival and prosperity. We try to be likeable as research shows that this helps us to establish satisfying relationships, facilitates our personal and professional fulfilment and makes us healthier and live longer. One of our main tools to likeability is to blend in, and to align on the values and behaviours that encourage social cohesion. As the experiment shows, this is so natural that we even do it with a group of strangers, that we have never met before and will never meet again. It is therefore no surprise that these incentives for alignment are therefore even stronger amongst friends, families and acquaintances where we have ongoing relationships, and therefore an ongoing benefit from our interaction.

But whilst there are positive incentives to conform and align with the group, there are also good reasons to avoid the sense of exclusion. Separation or isolation is known to create a state of psychological stress, like the "fight-or-flight" stress we feel when we are threatened. When we are on our own, our body effectively prepares itself to deal with external environmental threats; something that is greatly reduced by the sense of safety and security we get from being with other people. With isolation and exclusion triggering these feelings of stress and anxiety, we naturally try to avoid them, and following the crowd or blending with our surroundings are a good way of securing that comfort from having people around. This also reflects why those with low self-esteem or lacking confidence are more likely to follow the crowd, as they will be more attuned and more sensitive to the stresses associated with their isolation.

We sense these stresses as soon as we feel isolated and alone. However, the feelings will be exaggerated and become more acute when this is highlighted or exposed in public. Sometimes the act of highlighting this can be with malicious intent, either via teasing or ridicule that we are different or standing alone, or via intense peer pressure or harassment to push us to conform. This bullying behaviour greatly adds to the stress, both through the unpleasantness of the act itself, but also in the way that it can emphasise the sense that we do not belong. However, the same can happen without such malicious intent when we are a bit naïve about the differences between us.

I once went on a work training course, where we were being trained to be authentic leaders. The idea of the course was to accept the type of person we are and to act in a way that aligns with that personality; whilst also understanding how to adapt our style in certain situations. At one point on this course, we were asked to stand in two groups, based on whether we were an introvert or an extrovert. The initial and oversimplified explanations of these personality types were hugely irritating, but when someone had the guts to challenge them, it broadened into an excellent open conversation about some of the differences between us.

As this was a two-day residential course, we talked about drinks in the bar the previous evening. One of the extroverts explained how she wanted everyone to enjoy themselves and that was her main preoccupation. If somebody suggested they might leave, she was intent on persuading them to stay as she didn't want anyone "to miss out on the fun!" I explained how uncomfortable this made us feel because we genuinely did want to go back to our rooms. Having been round people all day, we just craved a bit of time to ourselves before we went to sleep. This was a bit of an alien concept to her!!!! But giving each other the chance to talk helped us to both learn a great deal about our differences.

As an extrovert, it had never crossed her mind that she was trying to make us happy by getting us to do what would make her happy. The reflection helped her realise that she was pushing her tastes on to people who did not share those tastes – it was the opposite of what we wanted. She needed to be more conscious of what other people wanted before she started to try and persuade them. As an introvert, I learned that there were good intentions behind her actions. At the time, when I was feeling that peer pressure persuading me to stay, it felt quite hostile and malicious. This started to make me draw wider conclusions about her as an individual, potentially for example, that she was a bit of a bully. However, listening to her the following day; it was clear that this was not the case. It made me realise how I had misinterpreted the situation through the uncomfortable emotions of stress.

Although I did feel the influence to conform on this occasion, the stresses of peer pressure were minimal compared to the terrifying emotions I experienced as a child. As a younger person, I would have stayed having drinks, pretending that I was having a good time in a desperate attempt to avoid disappointing those around me. The discomfort would therefore have lingered for longer, gradually building in intensity, and the feelings of irritation with the "bully" would have been much stronger. As a grown-up, I did not allow this to happen. The feelings when they were trying to persuade me were intensely uncomfortable and the act of walking away was therefore stressful, but I had the confidence to do it. This meant that at the time I wanted, I managed to retreat to the safety of my room, for some personal space and a nice book!!!! The peer pressure was still there, but the negative feelings of succumbing to the pressure were replaced by positive feelings of self-confidence for overcoming the situation, imposing myself and doing what I wanted.

There were two facets to the self-confidence in this situation, but they are closely interrelated. One was purely just being comfortable with the person that I am, liking the person that I am and therefore not being so embarrassed to show that publicly. I did not have any fear or shame in being honest and open, even where I perhaps looked a bit boring! The other side, however, is that I no longer fear the consequences. If somebody is irritated by the fact that I walked away from the drinks, then I am not going to lose any sleep over that! As it was so beautifully put by Dr Seuss:

> Be who you are and say what you feel, because
> those who mind don't matter, and those who
> matter don't mind.

Thinking back to my reminisces from school, what was so apparent was that I wanted everyone to like me. My likeability was measured simplistically in numbers – the publicly observable statistic. If we cast our mind back to Valentine's Day at school, the focus was on how many cards that we received. Whilst I am now very happy to get one from somebody who really loves me, the focus at the time was all about getting quantity. This very simplistic measure absolutely had the effect of reinforcing my behaviour. My ability to get on with everyone and therefore be "friends" with everyone appeared to be a shining success. In my young mind, by flitting from group-to-group, I had managed to resist the peer pressures and avoid getting drawn into things I didn't want to do, whilst being a well-liked person. My strategy looked like a win–win! However, the harsh reality is that I left school with no friends. My survival techniques and my lack of authenticity had meant that I built no strong relationships outside of my family. After the day I finished, there was only one person from school that I ever met again socially; and that friendship was founded around tennis and didn't last for long. Even after university, when I moved back with my parents and so I was living in my hometown for a couple of years, I still did not meet up with anyone from school. In reality, I had gone 20 years without making one friend!

It still took me many more years from that point to start to realise the importance of quality over quantity; and the fact that we need to be ourselves to get that quality of relationship. However, I still have my moments! There is a very interesting interview with Simon Sinek when he talks about our relationship with virtual friendship and social media, and the positive dopamine effect of being liked. This explains why we get a buzz when somebody likes a social media post we have shared, or when we get a message from a friend. Even though my focus is now much more on the quality of relationship, I absolutely resonate with a behaviour that he described. He explained how when people are feeling low, they tend to fire off a simple text or WhatsApp message to about ten people; just hoping that one of them will reply! Despite having some very deep relationships with my husband, my family and a few close friends; sometimes in the moment, getting a few messages feels incredibly comforting, even if they are from some distant acquaintances! I have evolved, but I haven't completely shed that desire for popularity!

In a book called *Popular: The Power of Likability in a Status-Obsessed World*, the author Mitch Prinstein who is a professor of Psychology and Neuroscience, outlines that there are two types of popularity. One of these types is around being likeable, and this generally has the positive impact that I discussed earlier. When we are just being a kind and amiable person, we gain the benefits of camaraderie and collaboration, which are good for our success, health and mental wellbeing. However, when this veers into a more visible status-oriented bid to become "popular", then the impacts are much more negative. The pursuit of popularity for status and extrinsic measures can lead to short-term boosts, but various research has suggested that it ultimately results in increased levels of discontent, anxiety and depression. It can result in distorted perspectives of what other people may think and "rejection sensitivity" as we get increasingly nervous and uncomfortable where we do not get the level of love, support or recognition that we think we deserve.

As so often in life, this is best explained by the wonderful lyrics of Robbie Williams! In his ironic song 'Handsome Man' where he talks about adulation, he sings about his popularity and how this is effectively proof of how wonderful he is. However, he goes on to emphasise that he is now completely dependent on this love. Without it, he would be nothing. It is the perfect reminder that if we are not careful, this excessive pursuit of popularity can become a bit of an addiction and be just as unhealthy for us and those around us, as the addictions we would better recognise. Or ultimately, as for Robbie and many other celebrities, can just be a precursor for those other addictions. Popularity through being a likeable version of ourselves is hugely positive; but status-driven popularity through being a fake or exaggerated caricature is likely to be hugely detrimental. There is no doubt that the celebrity culture and the rise of social media make everyone a little bit more susceptible to this hazard and maintaining the schooltime focus on quantity. There are undoubtedly huge benefits of the modern world, but also great dangers of which we need to be aware.

Ultimately, successful navigation of these hazards comes from being a likeable version of ourselves; and bizarrely, this makes me think of my early experiences of watching *Sex and the City*! I was young at the time and had not accepted my sexuality – even though you would think that my enjoyment of the show was probably all the evidence I needed!!! However, being uncomfortable from a sexual perspective, I initially hated the character of Samantha. As well as being beautiful, she was brash, overconfident, promiscuous, and would speak her mind (particularly about her sexual exploits) without a care of the consequences. These were far removed from qualities that I admired, but mainly because they were far removed from the person I was. Over time, she evolved to be my favourite character – not because she changed, but because my perception did. Why? Because, she believed in what she was doing, accepted how she was, and behaved in the way that she chose, not worrying about what others thought of her and what others wanted her to be. Even though her personality was completely opposite to mine, I started to realise that she was just being herself, and I found that confidence to be yourself without fear of recriminations hugely admirable.

The other interesting thing about *Sex and the City*, although certainly not unique to that show, is that you have a group of friends who are so different from each other but love each other because of or in spite of those differences. And thinking back to the introvert v. extrovert story, this is the other real lesson. Not only do we need to understand and be happy with ourselves, but we should also understand and appreciate the differences in other people. Relationships where we are very different and complement each other in terms of strengths, skills, knowledge or experience can be really inspiring and beneficial.

There are wonderful examples in nature of mutual symbiosis where different animals gain great benefits from their togetherness. There is the oxpecker bird that eats ticks from the zebra's fur, but also warns them of impending danger. There are crocodiles that let a bird called an Egyptian plover into their mouth to pick out meat that is trapped in their teeth and to pick parasites from their gums. There are also animals that have been known to hunt together, such as hyenas and wolves, with hyenas benefiting from the wolf-pack hunting skills, whilst the wolves benefit from the hyenas' sense of smell and their ability to break bones and rip through garbage. We can get surprising benefits when we acknowledge what others can do, appreciating our rivals (or our prey!) rather than trying to destroy them.

This is also very true in sport. The great rivalries tend to enhance reputations rather than undermine them. I discussed Roger Federer in Chapter 3. Even though he has won 20 Grand Slam championships, he would have probably won even more if it wasn't for the presence of some other great players at the same time – particularly Rafael Nadal and Novak Djokovic. Over the 15 years from 2004 to 2018, 50 out of the 60 Grand Slam titles were won by these three players. If I add in Andy Murray and Stanislas Wawrinka, who have each won three Grand Slam titles, then 56 out of 60 Grand Slam titles have been won by just five players. Now suppose only one of these five players existed, then that one would probably have a significantly better record and have won more titles. However, they would not necessarily be so well known or so revered. The rivalry has made them significantly raise their levels and the epic matches have made them so much more memorable. Dominance can get a little boring, and without the competition, Roger Federer would have probably retired many years ago. It is the competition and rivalry that brings out the best in them all and has created what many consider a golden era in men's tennis.

When we are watching these tennis stars, we see their competitive nature in action. This comes across in their gladiatorial instincts and is crucially important in the heat of a match, as it fills them with an insatiable determination to win. Obviously, they are trying to play as well as they can, but that isn't what matters to them at that moment in time. It's all about the victory. Whilst critically important, I consider this a fairly "negative" type of competition as it removes any focus on quality of performance and is all centred around beating the other person. Moreover, whilst this type of competitiveness may get them through a single match, it is not what makes them a champion. The champion qualities come from a form of competitiveness which goes on behind closed doors, during the hours and hours and hours of training that precede what we see on court. They might show a competitive spirit on the day of competition, but if they have not shown a determination to work hard and meticulously develop their skill, their fitness and their technique, then they will not be successful at the higher levels of competition. As per the old adage, "failing to prepare is preparing to fail", and it is the hard, unglamorous work behind the scenes that is really the key to the success. This is all about making themselves better and better and better until they are not only the best they can be, but they are better than everyone else. Putting themselves through this requires an intense, inward-facing competitiveness, which is hugely positive as it is totally focused on quality of performance, with the knowledge that victory will come as a natural consequence.

These different types of competitiveness are also reflected in our conversations. In some discussions, there is positive competition. We show that preparedness to engage with diverse people with differing opinions, without feeling threatened in any way. We value the different views, are prepared to engage and work hard to understand them, and whilst we think we are right, we focus on absorbing the varied insight to give us the full understanding. In positive competition, we are focused on quality. We know that relentlessly engaging in robust and insightful discussions means we become more aware, more informed and more skilled in the art of conversation. Rather than winning debates because it is our sole purpose, we end up winning as a by-product of our knowledge and awareness. This is in complete contrast to other discussions, where there is negative competition. We worry less out the best solution, the full facts or the opportunity to gain any deep insight and place all importance on getting that personal victory. And whilst we may win in the short term, we stand still in terms of knowledge and personal development.

Thinking about discussions involving negative competitiveness and it is hard not to make a passing mention of Brexit! The post-referendum situation quickly became farcical, with everyone wanting to point fingers at everyone else. For me, however, there was always one underlying problem at the heart of Brexit, which fully aligns with the concept of bad competitiveness. As we listened to most inputs, whether from the EU or from the UK, and whether from Brexiteers or Remainers, then winning became more important than discussion, compromise or a good solution. We got statements about how uninformed or intransigent the other side was. We got unworkable proposals that sounded fanciful but that were clearly not acceptable to their opponents. We got unprovable criticisms that "I would have done a better job if I was in charge". Fortunately, it seems like common sense prevailed at the bitter end with a no-deal looming, but until that last minute, we had pantomime.

But Brexit is one of many such examples where people are too focused on trying to win rather than trying to problem solve and find the best solution. Moreover, in many such cases, the outcome is often not that important! So why do we do this? Why do we so often resort to bad competitiveness in our daily discussions? Why do we make winning so important when there is not even a competition? It is probably because we enjoy the feeling of victory. It gives us that dopamine hit, just like the "boosts" of popularity and it makes us feel good. We therefore look for places where we can get that buzz of victory, picking small battles where we think we can win. It's like the conversational equivalent of beating another car away from the lights or sneaking in front of them in a traffic jam – it still feels good even though the other person did not know they were competing!

In discussion, this shows up in the way we love to get our opinion across and make it sound amazing! A common opportunity for this sort of mini-victory is when we start giving advice on things like dealing with a relationship problem or a bereavement, or guiding people on how to lose weight or to get fit, or where someone should go on holiday. Without spending the time to properly understand the person or the situation, we pluck an anecdote to share, trying to sound like the hero riding in with a silver bullet or a nugget of genius that will solve all their problems. But the sentiment gets even stronger when we slip into an argument. Once the red mist descends and we are deep in the argument, that victory is all that matters! The problem is that we get this same hunger to win the discussion, irrespective of our understanding of that topic. We are happy to wade into arguments with strong opinions based on scant knowledge, armed with nothing but a keen desire to pretend that we are informed!

And it is this enthusiasm to launch into subjects that extend well beyond our knowledge that is most aggravating. Discussions spring up on topics that we may find hard to comprehend because they are far beyond our own personal experience, and yet this does not hold us back from having strong and forceful opinions. We put ourselves in the shoes of someone else and use our limited experience to imagine how they must be feeling, remarkably unconcerned about how inaccurate our assumptions may be. We may have never experienced racial discrimination or gone through the strains of a transgender transition or been forced to seek asylum in another country because of troubles in our home country; but this does not stop us having opinions on those subjects. We may have never met somebody who has faced those experiences, or if we have, we may have never taken the time to talk to them, question them, and to build a much deeper understanding and empathy; but this does not stop us having opinions. Whilst we may not actively seek out the discussions; we can easily be drawn into a strong conversation if someone says something controversial or contradicts our gut reaction on a subject. As soon as we think someone is wrong, it is hard to keep quiet!

To make things worse, we also tend to pursue the small victories when it is completely pointless. Earlier in the chapter, I talked a great deal about taste, and how society defines trends, fashions and popularity in order to make some choices appear superior to others. The reality is that taste is personal. We have no reason to say one thing is better than another. Musical genres are not better than each other, they are just different. When we choose to highlight that our choice is better, we are basically just looking for that victory over someone else. We are trying to look superior. But in our desire to feel superior, we make others feel inferior. By saying there is a right way, we are suggesting there is a wrong way. By looking to win, we are making someone else lose. There is no reason for this, and it is effectively just playground bullying, which we should have grown out of long ago.

We don't need to win every single time. We need to win when there is a purpose, and we need to avoid the argument when there is not. Suppose somebody makes a mistake or a bad decision, and that has led to a bad situation for us. If they are already feeling bad or guilty, do we gain anything by highlighting this and making them feel worse? It may make us feel better as it somehow excuses us from responsibility, but we are just making someone else feel worse, by trying to turn a defeat into a mini-victory for us. How many times do we block progress because we are dwelling on the error that somebody else made to make ourselves feel better? In rugby, we are taught the concept of trying to turn a bad decision into a good decision, which feels so much more positive. If one of our teammates makes a shocking decision and goes running straight into trouble, when there was open space on the other side, we do not criticise for a second. Pausing to criticise will make their bad decision even worse. So, we immediately pile in behind them and try and make good! In the training session next week, the coach can try and guide them on their decision-making; but now is all about making the best of the situation and pulling together.

There is a time and a place for making our point and sounding superior and getting that personal victory; but we need to find that time and place. As per the rugby example:

a. It is not when we are in the heat of the moment and we need to deal with the situation we are facing;

b. It is not when somebody knows they got it wrong, are feeling bad about it, and we are just kicking them when they are down;

c. It is not when we are being wise after the event and just sounding smug as it is too late to influence things.

In addition, as with the discussion on trends and fashions:

d. It is not when something is purely a matter of taste and it really does not matter whether they like the same thing or not; and

e. It is not when someone is just different, and we cannot understand or relate to that difference.

Ultimately, we should only chase victories when they matter. We should only try to change a person's perspective if it we believe it is important for their own good or for the collective good of society.

And this is particularly pertinent in the world of politics. There is still a time and a place for our opinion, and we still need to have a purpose. If we are talking to a floating voter and we genuinely feel that we can influence that person into voting in a different way, then we should do our best to change their mind. If we are extreme left-wing and right-wing ideologists who could square off until the cows come home without either of us budging, is it worth it? What exactly are we trying to achieve by battering each other into submission? If neither side is prepared to compromise, we should just agree to disagree and accept our differences. If the only purpose of our contribution is to try and win or be better or say that our way is right, then we should just zip it; and bide our time until there is a purpose. In summary, using a phrase that I probably overuse to those around me, we need to pick our battles.

But even when the time is right, and we have chosen to take on this particular battle, there are ways of doing things. We can be inappropriately superior and try to just force our opinion across because we "know" that we are right. But whilst we may think we are justified, we are not creating the environment where anyone is going to listen to us. In Chapter 4 and Chapter 8, I highlighted how we have a natural tendency to become defensive in the face of criticism, and I encouraged us to avoid this reaction to gain the opportunity for learning. But we all know how hard that it is, so when we are on the other side, and we are that critic, we should be conscious of how our opinion is going to be received. We should be constructive to keep ourselves in a discussion rather than an argument. It is so important that we never lose sight of the purpose of the discussion and what we are trying to achieve, and if that involves trying to persuade someone, then we need to keep them engaged in what we are saying, rather than enraged by our approach.

When everybody is selfishly trying to achieve a personal victory, then the reality is that nobody wins. We end up like two horn-fighting antelope, squaring up to each other and trying to assert our superiority with neither side prepared to budge. That is what we see, day in, day out, in the world of politics where they just pointlessly argue rather than exchange ideas and interact. It is a different world, when both parties are focused on learning rather than proving they are right and are therefore prepared to retreat or admit they are wrong or compromise if that is the best thing to be done. This is a much harder route in a discussion, because it requires us to listen, understand, reflect, question and think; but as with most things in life we get a better reward if we are prepared to go the hard way!

And where there is no purpose at all, we just need to let things be. There will always be trends and styles and fads, and many people who want to follow them, and it doesn't matter if they do. But it also doesn't matter if they don't! Rather than pushing people to conform, we should give people the confidence in themselves to make their own decisions. If they choose a different path, then nobody should judge them for being different, even if we find their choices difficult to comprehend! There is no right or wrong in personal choice, and we should respect that. It is amazing how often people who are a bit different say "it was good to know there are other people like me". How about, "I am happy that I am unique!" What is so scary about being different? The greatest gift in the world is individuality, and that's what we should cherish.

It is so important that we remain true, honest and authentic. Whilst we should care about being liked, it is so much better when we can do this without acquiescing to others' desires or preferences. We can get there by just being good people! Whilst we may find people who are similar, none of us is the same, and we all have different tastes and opinions. This variety of people in the world should be protected, appreciated and celebrated, meaning that we should not ignore our differences, but neither should we try to suppress them. This means letting people be themselves, enjoying that they are different to us, and only trying to persuade them of a different path if we have an altruistic purpose and we understand them well enough to know it is best for them. This will allow us to realise the potential of our diversity, reap the benefits of conversation and avoid the consequences of arguments.

 EIGHTH PRINCIPLE

Don't be a playground bully! Only persuade with a purpose and good intentions

CHAPTER 10

Tell me I am Wrong to Prove that I am right!

Criticism may not be agreeable, but it is necessary. It fulfils the same function as pain in the human body. It calls attention to an unhealthy state of things.

WINSTON CHURCHILL

The impact of greenhouse gases on the environment and global warming, in particular, is something that we have been taught for many years. I remember it being a key theme from my school geography lessons back in the late-1980s, some 30 years ago. Without getting too technical, we were told how light and heat from the sun was reaching the earth's atmosphere, and while some of this was reflecting off the atmosphere or the earth's surface, some of it was being absorbed and providing a warming effect to both the earth and its atmosphere. Where heat is reflected or radiated from the earth's surface, some of this is trapped by what we call "greenhouse gases", including water vapour, carbon dioxide, methane and nitrous oxide. These gases not only trap or absorb the heat energy but then re-emit it in all directions meaning that some of this heat is pushed back downwards again. This has the effect of keeping the earth's surface and lower atmosphere warmer than they would have been if these gases were not present.

It is believed that this was key to the development of life on earth, as the surface of the earth would have been considerably cooler if these gases were not present, and the conditions for the development of life may not therefore have been so favourable. However, considering the role that these gases play, significant changes in the levels of these gases would impact on the performance of this greenhouse effect, and this is what we were starting to see when I was at school. The evidence was focused mainly on the increased levels of CO_2 in the atmosphere, which had been on a steady upward trend since the end of the 19th century and was reaching levels that had never been seen before. Moreover, this appeared to be having a consequential impact on temperature, with corresponding trends in growth as shown in the graph below.

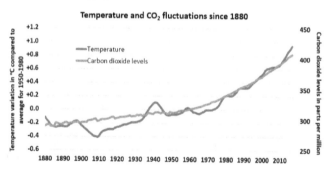

Temperature and CO_2 fluctuations since 1880

Now at the time of my school lessons, the unprecedented increase in CO_2 levels was observable and well understood. However, we can see that on the temperature graph, we were at the start of the trend of temperature growth. In the late 1980s, we had seen a steady rise in temperature growth since the start of the 20th century, but the temperature was probably only about 0.2°C above the long-term average. The presentation at the time was much more about a risk of that trend continuing, and some of the potential consequences, particularly around rising sea levels and the impact on low-lying parts of the country and the increased risk of flooding. The concept was being introduced to the public, but campaigning and support for action was limited, and focused with environmental groups such as Greenpeace, rather than being something that was more mainstream.

Since then, the trend of increasing temperatures has continued, and it is the continuation and acceleration of that trend that is really striking. The circulation of these "hockey-stick" graphs has therefore become much more prevalent, and the concern over the issue has broadened. All eighteen of the warmest years in the measured period have taken place since 1998. We are seeing the impact not only on global temperatures, but in the warming oceans, shrinking ice sheets, glacial retreat and the consequential rise in sea levels. These factors can all be inextricably linked to the rise in global temperatures and show that the possible risk that was highlighted in the 1980s, has now become a clear trend with consistent and accelerating temperature growth.

Less clearly linked to rising temperatures, is the other piece of evidence that is often cited as being evidence of global warming, and that is the increased prevalence of extreme weather events. Whilst the association may not be so obvious, from a meteorological perspective, there is a strong justification that this is indeed connected. A warmer atmosphere can hold more moisture, meaning that rainstorms and snowfall are likely to be heavier, and the resulting floods and avalanches may be more common or more severe. In addition, heat is a form of energy that contributes to the development of tropical storms, and it is therefore unsurprising if increased heat energy results in increasingly violent storms as the accumulated energy is released. Global warming does not cause these storms, but the fact that the risk is amplified is highly plausible.

This combination of evidence has gained attention of both politicians and the media, and the campaign for action is no longer just the preserve of the environmental groups but has become much more mainstream. The United Nations has created the Intergovernmental Panel on Climate Change (IPCC), which consolidates the research and views of climate scientists and produces regular reports on the risks of non-action. Climate change conferences involving the leaders from all over the world are frequently convened where the issues are acknowledged and countries make commitments as to the actions they plan to take. There is no doubt that since the time I was first taught about this issue, there has been quite a considerable shift in momentum.

However, even if this is the case, there is still not much progress being made. There still remains quite a significant minority who just don't believe it. But perhaps more importantly, there is an even bigger minority, probably even a majority, who are not sufficiently motivated to take action or make any real sacrifices. Considering the scale of change in the graph from the previous page and what appears to be an international political consensus, why is there not a more concerted call to action? Why are most people just too busy to do anything or so reluctant to make any sacrifices?

This may partly be driven by people feeling that their individual actions are pretty insignificant in isolation and can also appear very detached from the ultimate consequences. This is true and we genuinely need a collective effort, which is why the political solution is so important. But this is not the only reason. The way the evidence is presented comes across as preaching to the converted as whilst it is compelling to those who already believe, it often fails to resonate with disbelievers and fails to motivate the wider public to make sacrifices. There are particular elements of the communication style and the way this is received that contribute to this:

1. Selective presentation

Despite the huge amount of evidence associated with global warming, the presentation of temperature tends to focus on the last 150 years or so. There is a logic to showing these periods, as it not only coincides with the period when the CO_2 levels have escalated rapidly (from the time of the industrial revolution), but it is also largely the period when we have truly reliable measurements of global temperatures. Going back further requires analysis from things such as tree rings, corals, sediments and cave deposits, ice cores and glaciers, that can be used to provide a good estimation of the likely temperatures; but not with the same level of accuracy. However, the more extended analysis does present a very different picture, as shown from the below graph derived from ice core data, showing the estimated temperature fluctuations over the last 400,000 years.

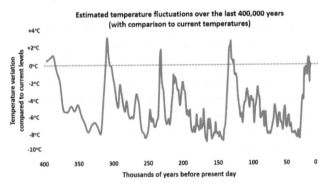

This longer-term analysis is clearly less reliable but does appear to indicate that whilst current temperatures are high, they are not unprecedented. As a result, sceptics would argue there is justification to suggest that there have continually been natural temperature fluctuations over the years, with deep ice ages and intervening warmer periods.

But so what? Even if we accept this theory and entertain the thought that we could just be on a natural temperature peak, then this does not disprove any of the climate change findings and the likely connection between increasing levels of CO_2 and the increasing temperatures. So why does this matter? The reason is that the avoidance of this in presentations suggests a lack of impartiality. Showing the most favourable graph and then avoiding discussion about other factors (not manmade) that must have contributed to the inflated temperatures of the past, encourages a sense of cynicism and scepticism amongst non-believers. The hockey stick graph becomes compelling and convincing to some, as it allows the conversation to focus on the impact since the Industrial Revolution and the central role of CO_2 on the problem. However, for others, the focus is just evidence of a conspiracy theory, with a desire to avoid the discussion about the uncertain explanations for the significant temperature variations of the past. Selective presentation allows opponents to question the findings and cast doubt.

2. Weariness at doom-mongers

Whilst the increases in CO_2 and temperatures can be factually evidenced over the last 150 years, the consequences of the rising temperatures remain largely in the future and also highly subjective. Is this merely a consequence that we can deal with or is it going to have the catastrophic consequences that we are led to believe? Predictions are difficult to prove in any instance, but when trying to predict something with as many variables as our climate, then difficult is an understatement!

This difficulty in proving things is quite a problem. If we're trying to encourage the world to take disruptive action that will cost money and massively impact people's lives, then we need certainty. This has caused two consequences in the way the conclusions are presented. Firstly, we put a huge focus on the issues we are seeing in the here and now, and particularly the frequency of extreme events. This is useful to shift the focus from "the world is warming up and this will impact us in the future" which doesn't get people worried, to "there will be a major increase in natural disasters and it's happening now". The hope is that immediate self-preservation is more motivational than prevention of a future risk. Secondly, we try to create certainty from the uncertainty, by presenting the output of climate models as the undoubted consequence of our current path. People are more likely to fight against something that WILL happen as opposed to something that MIGHT happen.

Yet again, this is an approach that manages to polarise opinion. For some, it is an important demonstration and reinforcement of the consequences of our current behaviour, and a call to action. It shows that we need to take immediate steps to avoid these disastrous outcomes. For others, who are tired of people predicting catastrophe, it feels like an exaggerated forecast of doom that is a cynical attempt to force us into action. We have seen too many predictions like the millennium bug, when all our electronics were going to break and planes would fall out of the sky; that we simply don't believe another one. This leaves an overwhelming feeling that there may be a problem, but it is just not as bad as they say!

3. Mistrust of experts

During the Brexit debate, Michael Gove who was one of the chief protagonists for leaving the European Union, stated that:

> The people of this country have had enough
> of experts from organisations with acronyms
> saying they know what is best and getting it
> consistently wrong.

There is little doubt that there is an element of truth in this. News presentations are shifting towards infotainment that want to entertain rather than purely inform, which places emphasis on people who can best communicate in a lively fashion, rather than necessarily those who know best. And moreover, the immediate access to facts via Google makes us all feel like experts, who do not need to listen to aloof individuals who profess to have all of the answers. This means that the knowledge of experts is valued less and questioned more.

Climate change scientists fall foul of this suspicion and the integrity of their opinions are therefore subject to challenge. And the media really doesn't help, by generally employing two types of expert. At one extreme, we get experts who are rolled out to talk technical and sound impressive but say things in a way that half of us do not understand. At the other end of the spectrum, the experts are asked to dumb things down and shift into oversimplified explanations and emotional hooks that rather undermine their status as experts. This is a problem in many fields, but on topics such as the environment where there is a presumption of what is "right", then this situation can become even worse. When experts and the media take the moral high-ground and dismiss counterstatements as nonsense and critics as stupid, then rather than being powerful and persuasive, it just alienates those that are not yet convinced. In the modern world where we can self-select the news and the views that we want to hear, we just look for a different source that will validate our thoughts and opinions. Rather than learn from the experts, we tend to just find other experts who agree with us!

These concerns focus around the way that the information is presented. They do not undermine the arguments of the climate scientists in any way, and yet they manage to open the door to scepticism and conspiracy theories. They do not cast doubt on whether the global temperature is rising, as this is clear-cut and that evidence is not questioned. But they are designed to cast doubt on whether it is caused primarily by the manmade increases in CO_2 and most importantly, to cast doubt that the consequences will be as severe as articulated. Suspicions can be further exacerbated if the impartiality of the scientists themselves is also doubted. Good research should always start with a "null hypothesis" suggesting that there is no relationship between two measured phenomena. In this case, it means the research assumption should always be that there is no connection between the increases in CO_2 and the increase in temperature. Even with the best will in the world, considering the way the research is currently discussed, it is hard to say it is conducted with complete impartiality. Again, this opens the door to the doubters.

The quality of the proof is all important and is also a passion of mine. In fact, this geekish "quality" means I still vividly remember the Maths lesson at school when I fell in love with probability. There were 30 of us in the room, and at the start of the lesson, the teacher turned to us and said that it was more than likely that two of us had the same birthday. We all looked round and everyone was thinking, "What a load of nonsense!" Just 30 of us in the class and 365 days in the year to choose from, so that could not possibly be true! However, he insisted that we go ahead and calculate the probability, and so I set into the problem determined to prove my teacher wrong. I worked through the calculations and concluded that the chances of two of us having the same birthday was about 70%. Still in a bit of disbelief, even though my teacher had said it was the case, I rechecked my workings numerous times, and sure enough, this was correct. Personally, I still found this very hard to believe, but as a mathematician, I was completely convinced by the calculation I had done, and knew it to be true. And just in case you were wondering, there were two boys with the same birthday!

Now this may seem like a random story from my schooldays, as I seem to be reminiscing in this chapter! However, there are two elements that are extremely relevant. Firstly, because I doubted the conclusion, I was extremely thorough in checking and rechecking my findings. GH Hardy, the great mathematician, was not a lover of probability or any applied mathematics for that matter, but he took joy purely in elegant mathematical proofs as if they were an artform. He once said to Bertrand Russell that:

> If I could prove by logic that you would die in five
> minutes, I should be sorry you were going to die,
> but my sorrow would be very much mitigated by
> the pleasure in the proof.

I may have been in a field of Mathematics that GH Hardy did not enjoy, but just like the great mathematician, I was motivated to prove the answer to myself.

We all do this, when we find something we genuinely do not expect. We show a thoroughness and depth of investigation to validate what we have found, something that it is hard to replicate when we find exactly what we were anticipating. When the result is expected, we tend to just move on to the next problem. Our natural inclination towards confirmation bias (as explained more fully in Chapter 8) means we are far more accepting of evidence that confirms our existing beliefs, even if it is just circumstantial. We simply do not place the same scrutiny on conclusions that reinforce our preconceptions, as we will for conclusions that are a surprise.

The second element of great relevance in this case, though, is that scientific or mathematical proofs can convince the individuals that do them, but they do not win over the hearts and minds of others. I had done the calculations myself, and yet I was still finding it hard to believe the evidence in front of me. Try explaining this to someone else, and they are just as incredulous as me and my classmates, when we started out to disprove our teacher. It is similar to some optical illusions, such as the one below.

Despite being told that both table tops are the same length and width, I could not accept it without drawing the shape, moving it from one to another and really convincing myself that it is true. Even having done this, I still find it hard to believe.

As a result, however impressive are the mathematical models that are determining the consequences of non-action, this is probably only going to convince people who have repeated the calculations themselves (i.e. fellow scientists) and/or those who already believe it.

These challenges to be impartial as our mind settles on an opinion become even more complicated when money and politics get involved. One aspect of research that can make people cynical is the source of funding for that research. An organisation may well be prepared to fund a one-off project with an open mind as to the outcome of its investigation, on the basis that it wants to establish the facts. But ongoing funding almost exclusively comes with the goal of advancing that organisation towards their objective. Not only are they therefore looking for research that is supportive of their beliefs and ambitions, they are also looking for results. They are looking for research that successfully proves their viewpoint or helps to undermine the opposite perspective. Whilst there are wonderful research institutes that place great emphasis on discovery research and the need for impartiality, it is hard to argue that climate change research is one of those. The enormous investment into research in this field is presumptive of the criticality of the situation – there simply would not be as much investment in climate change research without a belief in the problem and the underlying drivers. As a result, money wields great power in motivating both the topics that researchers may choose to investigate as well as the conclusions that they choose to present.

Politics wields a similar powerful influence over the direction of research. When there is almost unilateral support for a particular opinion, it can be hard to stand against the tide and to raise our voice against it. And this is no different in science. When there are possible repercussions for being "controversial" such as being discredited or side-lined, then it can appear like career suicide for a scientist to speak their mind. Even where support is not so unanimous, there can be consequences. For example, Donald Trump's well-known allegations of "fake news" against the green campaign might mean that anti-environmental perspectives may be more accepted in the United States. However, the danger is that scientific research can suddenly take on a party-political context. Suddenly, you are not just presenting your research, you are speaking for or against Donald Trump, irrespective of how you would vote in an election. Your conclusions are having a different impact than you may have intended.

Unfortunately, both money and politics are critical to the resolution of the environmental problems that we face. Success in stemming the rapid growth in CO_2 levels needs a combined political will across opposing parties and the various countries of the world to make the disruptive changes that are needed to really have an impact. Success in reducing the levels of greenhouse gas emissions also needs money to invest in new technologies and cleaner energy sources. But when politics and money come with such an agenda, it becomes hard to maintain a sense of impartiality, and even harder to retain the perception that information is not being skewed to support that agenda. This makes the sense of integrity and impartiality even more important.

With such a global issue, managing this sense of integrity unsurprisingly sits within the remit of the United Nations, and in particular, the IPCC. This organisation should be an independent coordinator of environmental research, combining the best research from across the broad spectrum of opinions to help us get the most honest and insightful perspective on this vital and critical issue. This is the goal of this group, producing periodic reports when they do exactly that. However, its impartiality is constantly questioned. There are allegations that it only approaches scientists that are aligned with their perspective, that they have amended, rewritten or cut the viewpoints of experts whose conclusions were not sufficiently forceful, and that they have discredited and blacklisted experts whose research is not compatible with their agenda. Who knows what is true, and what truly happens in these corridors of power, but either way, these allegations help to create suspicion that their claims of "unequivocal" evidence are not justified.

Now I have intentionally been playing devil's advocate in this chapter, as the presentation that we receive from all angles is a bit one-sided; and my questioning does not therefore mean that the impact of CO_2 should be ignored. Increased levels of CO_2 are clearly shifting the natural balance, and it is extremely likely that this is having a negative impact. Suggestions that we should try to clean up our act and proposals to try and reduce the levels of greenhouse gas emissions are wholly reasonable. But how do we know this is the only cause? How do we know there is not something else even more critical that we are missing? And how are we going to get the world to listen when all our warnings are falling on deaf ears? These questions are not easy ones to answer, but they are important questions that we need to keep asking.

Consider the world of invention and innovation. When somebody has a great idea, then it may be lovely to get all the plaudits from their colleagues who are keen to celebrate the genius of the idea. But ultimately, we need to keep asking questions! Imagine after the first sunglasses had been invented and we had just sat on our laurels? Then maybe we would be still using the basic concepts that were invented by the Eskimos to protect their eyes from the bright spring sunlight reflecting off the snow, as shown in the picture below.

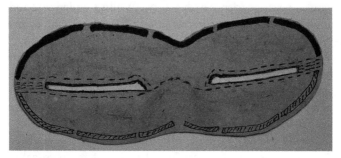

However, as we know, these have evolved into scientifically advanced fashion objects that are used across the globe, and we have glasses that can brighten the darkness as well as dimming sunlight. This has happened because we have never stopped to challenge and look for ways to improve. We have never stopped asking questions!

This openness to improvement is something that we would ideally employ in relation to opinions and ideas. We should openly accept that our current views, however informed, are not yet the finished article. We don't know everything! If we are open to the fact that our ideas still need to evolve and improve, then we should be keen to learn. Whilst we may like socialising with likeminded people and we may enjoy collaborating with likeminded colleagues, they suffer from the same biases as ourselves. They are not necessarily the best people to help us find the answers. Inventors need critics or competitors who think they can do better and will therefore challenge them to improve the idea. And we are no different. It is our arch-protagonists who are most likely to guide us to the right answer. Their questions and challenges and doubts may be uncomfortable, but they will make us think. The more we are questioned and challenged, and the more we are forced to think, the better answers we will find.

Unfortunately, there are many examples where people do the exact opposite, which is hugely frustrating and disappointing to observe. One of the most depressing examples I have seen was the discussion following Labour politicians saying that they would "never be friends with a Tory". Whilst I understand and appreciate their sentiment, this attitude is polarising and denies the opportunity to learn from those with a different perspective. We don't need to agree with everything that someone thinks to be civil with them and get on, or even to push this further and become friends. We should be able to argue and fight and disagree on a certain topic but really get along in every other facet of our relationship. And this is healthy.

Firstly, the way I vote, or my religion, or my taste in music do not define me. They are just elements of my personality that I can readily share with those that are interested. Secondly, the different perspectives of people I meet are a source of great insight and interest. Surround ourselves with friends and colleagues who think the same, and we learn nothing. Surround ourselves with people who will question and challenge, and we may have a heated discussion from time to time, but we have the chance to learn and evolve. We need to embrace that rugby mentality, where we are deadly rivals on the pitch, and maybe have a good fight, but once the match is done, we go for a drink and are all good friends again! A disagreement in one element of our beliefs should not consume the whole relationship.

In fact, these friendships are powerful as they provide a safe environment for challenging our understanding and they provide the opportunity to learn from the experience of others. Within the safe confines of a trusted relationship, we can share ideas and learn, but a diversity of thought is critical for this to happen. In line with the pursuit of diversity in the workplace, we need an eclectic mix of people with differing perspectives to create diversity of thought. If we successfully gather a group of people with diverse views and opinions, the collective output will be stronger than if we just collaborate with people who think the same. We all know and understand this as a point of principle in the workplace, but it is just as valid in our personal lives.

As I have been on some serious topics, let's consider a more light-hearted example of diversity, such as the film *Evolution*. This is a ridiculous sci-fi action comedy but is good entertainment if you have switched your brain off! My super-brief summary of the film is that a meteor crashes into earth with some alien microbes inside. Some scarily accelerated evolution means that within a matter of days, the single-cell organisms have developed into dinosaurs that are rampaging around a shopping mall, and the interesting science project quickly turns into a national emergency!!!! The US army arrives, and as you would expect, they are quickly arguing that the only solution is to blow the creatures to smithereens!

Now, once the army have decided and agreed that the only path is massive napalm-fuelled explosions, then you can probably imagine how difficult it would be to change their mind! When the scientists realise that the heat from the explosion will further accelerate the development, and that they need to find a more scientific solution, do you think the military are ready to listen? No, they have chosen their path and will ignore the opposition opinions and blindly push ahead! Fortunately, this is Hollywood, so although the army explode everything and cause the anticipated exacerbation of the disaster, a diverse group of heroes steps up and rescues the day. However, in the real world, the band of heroes and the guaranteed happy ending is not always around the corner.

I accept this is a fictional and pretty random set of circumstances in a crazy movie, but the reality is that on our chosen subjects, we all tend to act a bit like the US Army. At certain times, we all have our equivalent of the nuclear option, where we have convinced ourselves that it is the way to go and won't let anything get in our way. In some respects, this is a good quality – that determination and perseverance to see something through to a conclusion is vital for us to achieve success and to reach our goals. We need that sense of purpose, the real focus on the task in hand, and the unrelenting determination to do what's needed to get things done. Constant questioning and re-evaluation would be a distraction, and probably stop progress in its tracks. However, if we never reconsider and if we close our mind, then we will not realise if we are on the wrong path.

Now Hollywood loves the rogue army general, who is either corrupt or stupid so that we can create the right environment for the underdog hero. Whilst I hope and believe that our real-world military do not share this characteristic, there is one major similarity to the movie portrayal, which is that most military units are trained to follow orders. Discipline and unquestioning loyalty are paramount. If they are told that that the agreed solution is to use napalm to blow up all the creatures, then that is the solution they need to implement.

They are not questioning whether it's best, and neither are their leaders. They accept that "higher authorities" have considered the alternatives and agreed the best course of action. They concentrate on delivering that task, and are totally focused on their role in successfully delivering that mission.

However, there is also an important difference in the real world, and that is that there would be a separate Intelligence team, who would be looking at the situation with an open mind. They would be looking for risks, events, information that present a new set of circumstances that may change the previous decision. They are constantly evaluating the alternatives, maybe pursuing an alternative strategy in parallel, or preparing the Plan B or Plan C that may need to be initiated at any moment. If any of this Intelligence suggests a possible change in course, then it will be listened to, questioned, challenged and evaluated; knowing the disruptive impact of changing plan, but accepting that sometimes this is needed. And if this review reinforces that a different strategy is appropriate, then the message will go down to the leaders and troops on the ground, and they will accept that decision to change plan without question, delay or hesitation. They respect the decision-making from above; trusting and relying on those with "superior" knowledge to have evaluated all alternatives and made the best choice.

Now this is great. By separating everything into different teams, we can get the best of both worlds. We have one team that are absolutely focused on successfully implementing the current agreed solution. They have no distractions and are concentrating all their efforts on the task in hand. Then we have the other team with the open mind; with no responsibilities to deliver things and a pure responsibility for looking at the big picture, assessing if there is anything that we have missed, looking for things that might make us change our mind. This is the ideal situation.

In the context of the environment, this means that we should have teams of people who do focus on addressing the issues with the escalating levels of CO_2. This is currently the most plausible and likely cause of the increasing temperatures and is also something that we can influence and should therefore get real attention. Most of our researchers and scientists and inventors and engineers should therefore be focused in that direction; exploring ideas that may help us to reduce and control the level of CO_2 emissions, and therefore, the level of CO_2 in our atmosphere. But another team should be exploring the alternatives. What else may have caused it? Is there some completely unrelated activity that may help to reduce temperatures, which is maybe more palatable to people who are not taking action? I'm no insider, so maybe this does happen. However, everything produced publicly would suggest that this alternative research and this intelligence on the wider topic is being led by the disbelievers who are trying to prove their suspicions. Is there genuinely collaborative and open research between believers and doubters, who align on the single goal of trying to find the real answer? Or do we just have two sides operating separately with neither of them ready or willing to learn and benefit from the intelligent challenges from the other side?

They appear to be struggling in a big international organisation to make this work, so imagine how hard it is for us individually! When we are considering our own opinions, we are just one person. We cannot separate ourselves into two teams, with a bigger team remaining loyal on our core view and belief, taking the decisions and actions that align with this; while another smaller team keeps its eye open looking for information that may make us change our mind. We need to do all that ourselves. And this is where our critics can be invaluable. We can spend most of our time acting in line with our current views. But every now and again, our critics can give us a short intense burst of questioning or counterarguments or an insight that gives us the chance to question ourselves for a short while. We don't need to spend ages doing general research on the topic to try and find out if there is any new information that may possibly have an impact on what we think. We let our critics do that!

People who believe the opposite to us are going to quickly find the new knowledge or information or insight that supports their argument. They may blindly repeat what they have said before, and if we listened last time, then we know and can rest comfortable in our opinion. However, if there is a new argument or perspective, then it gives us the chance to think and question and evaluate as to whether this changes anything. All we need to do is be prepared to take them seriously and listen to them properly with the open mind that genuinely believes it may have something to learn. And even if they start with some spurious nonsense that we believe is inaccurate or misleading or irrelevant or is just a repetition of arguments that we have heard before and do not agree with, we just keep listening in case they have something else that is new or interesting to say.

Even if they don't change our mind, the other valuable thing we can learn from people who disagree with us, is the reasons that they disagree. On a subject where we are completely convinced, but the message is not landing (as with the environment), then this is priceless information. Who should the experts be turning towards to get hold of this insight? Again, it is the opposition. Those who criticise and express no interest in making changes to their way of life, are the people who can explain the reasons why they are not prepared to budge. In the Third World, it may be because of the cost, the barriers to their development, or the perceived "white privilege" hypocrisy of First World countries which reaped all the benefits from the industrial revolution and are blocking developing countries from doing the same. In the developed world, it may be the time and hassle that makes individuals resistant to action, or a refusal to give up the luxuries that they have grown accustomed to, or simply a belief that the risk is over-stated and we will find a way to cope. There are many potential reasons, and we should strive to understand them, because reinforcing the proof or the ideological mantra is worthless if people are not prepared to take action. Finding the way to undermine or eliminate their resistance is more likely to reap success.

Once we engage in open-minded questioning, and generally seek to learn from our rivals, then that will increase our chance of success in any subsequent discussion. First and foremost, we will create a better atmosphere for the conversation. There is nothing more annoying in a discussion than someone who presumes to know what we think, when they have never bothered to ask! By showing them that we are considering their opinion, then we will get the chance to build a bit of rapport. This is important, as it will also make them more receptive to hearing our arguments. If we want someone to listen, then we need to get them engaged in the conversation. Listening to them is an effective way to do this. As soon as we sound like a steamroller who is just going to impose our opinion on someone, then the defences will come up!

However, we can go beyond this. Showing that we are listening will do nothing more than develop a connection. Actually listening will give us useful information for the subsequent discussion. When I am going to a second interview for a job, I want to know the perceptions they took from the first round. I want to know where they may have concerns about my ability, or where they think there may be gaps in my knowledge. If I know, this gives me the chance to prepare for the next time. Any discussion is the same. The more we know and understand about what the others are thinking, why they are thinking that way, and the gaps they see in our argument; the more we can prepare for a discussion with them.

If they have concerns or questions for which we don't currently have the answer, then we have the chance to go and find the answer, through a bit of self-examination or further research. Alternatively, if the challenges relate to areas that we know and understand, then it gives us the chance to approach the discussion in the right way. After all, having powerful arguments on what matters to the opposition is much better than sharing evidence they consider unimportant or irrelevant. This insight into the thoughts of our protagonists can help us in two specific ways:

Developing a negotiation strategy: Discussing a topic with someone who is uninformed is very different to a discussion with an expert who has reached a contrary opinion. Talking to someone who has drifted with the crowd or has been given a biased perspective is very different to a conversation with someone who has intensely personal reasons for thinking the way they do. We need to know this, before we start getting into a conversation. Different people with different perspectives need different treatment to be persuaded.

Structuring our arguments: Building on this, once we understand what motivates their opinion, we can develop an approach and identify the arguments that maximise the chance of success. Emotional tirades are only likely to persuade those who already agree with us and will not resonate those we need to convert. A respectful, well structured, thoughtful approach with facts and emotion in the right place is likely to have more impact. Different people with different perspectives need different arguments to be persuaded.

In addition, by listening, there is one other important thing that we will learn, and that is when it is not worth even trying. We are all different, and we will never convince everyone to our way of thinking. As discussed in the last chapter, getting drawn into a conversation with people who will never change their mind is futile. And the reality is that these are not the important people. I have talked before about the importance of floating voters (i.e. the ones who might change their mind) as they are the ones that influence the election. We should walk away from the avid zealots, as it will probably be a draining experience, and go and focus our attention on those floating voters.

This last point is probably the most critical. Those on the campaign trail, whether in politics or on a subject such as the environment, will usually be those with strong and passionate views. These are the people who are ready to put in the effort and commitment to campaign. The non-committal floating voters just do not care enough. As the campaigners talk with colourful, emotive language, sharing the ideological reasons that make them believe, they are generally appealing to people with equally strong views. Their supporters may shout and cheer and make a lot of noise, or congratulate them and feed their egos, but this is immensely unproductive. It's getting the supporters even more excited about the cause but having no impact on those who are not yet convinced. They have heard that story so many times, and it still isn't working!

If we want to get more people on our side, we need to talk in the language of the middle-ground. We need to appeal to the doubters that are ripe to be persuaded. During the Brexit debate, the Remainers lost their way, because they were convinced that leaving the EU would be a complete catastrophe, and so they launched into Project Fear painting Brexiteers as xenophobic isolationists. Unsurprisingly, that wasn't a great message to those in the middle who wanted links with Europe but were disillusioned with the European Union. These were the people who needed convincing, and they failed to talk to them. The environment is much the same, with the same predictions of doom that leave so many unconvinced. However accurate the predictions, the message is not landing with the "silent majority" in the middle and repeating the mantra is not going to encourage them to make the sacrifices that are needed. By identifying the "floating voters", concentrating the message on these individuals and communicating in a language that will appeal to them and motivate them is the key to driving change.

Reverting to the product analogy from earlier, then this is similar to the marketing approach in selling sunglasses. Different styles of sunglasses will appeal to very different demographics, and so for any individual model or brand, there is a specific group of people who are most likely to be tempted to buy the product. Marketeers need to use their understanding of this target market to ensure any advertising or campaign will appeal to those who are likely to be tempted. Attracting people who will have no interest in buying the product is a waste of money and effort, so the approach, style and messaging all need to be tailored to that target market. The skill of good marketing is therefore not focusing on what the designers, producers, or manufacturers think is the unique selling point, but what is likely to attract customers. Have the environmental scientists and campaigners thought in doing this? Are they focusing on what will influence the people who they are trying to persuade? Or are they purely repeating the arguments that convinced themselves and expecting this to have the same impact on everyone else? We must never forget we are not all the same!

If our arguments are strong and our evidence is compelling, then there is no need to shy away from the critics and the difficult questions. We should have the confidence to engage our opposition, knowing that our arguments will stand up to scrutiny, because we have truly thought them through. We should be open about any weaknesses in our arguments, avoid any suggestion of a cover-up and demonstrate that we were aware of these as we developed our own point of view. We should share facts and knowledge and information and true expertise but do this in an engaging way. If our opponents react badly, we should not blame it all on their stupidity or bias or ignorance; but realise our responsibility to be more aware of their perspective and the need to structure our own argument differently. By doing this, we will keep our cool and continue to share a thoughtful and well-constructed argument, rather than get dragged into an aimless confrontation.

Ultimately, there is so much to gain by truly engaging with our counterparts and capturing the heart and soul of their argument. We can learn so much if we really listen to their views and research their perspective as if we genuinely believe it might be true. All of this is lost if we just nod along and pretend, without entertaining the possibility that we could be persuaded. We should avoid this at all costs, testing out the theories of others with an open mind, retaining the curiosity of a child, the joy of research and the excitement of being surprised. By taking the risk of discovering we are wrong or misdirected, we empower ourselves with new knowledge and insight that will hugely strengthen our own argument. At the same time, by gaining a better understanding of the contrary perspectives, we have a better chance of constructing our arguments in a way that will resonate strongly with the people we want to persuade. These are things that we can only learn from people we disagree with, and therefore failing to constructively engage with such people is an opportunity that should not be wasted.

NINTH PRINCIPLE

Enjoy challenge as the ultimate chance to strengthen your own argument

CHAPTER 11

We're Both to Blame!

*Never argue with stupid people, they will drag you down to
their level and then beat you with experience.*

MARK TWAIN

Back in 2015, there was great publicity around the story of a young Oxford student who had been indecently assaulted walking from the Tube station to her London home. What was remarkable about Ione Wells was that she chose to waive her right to anonymity, writing an open letter in a university newspaper to get across the victim's perspective and to confront the attacker, asking him what he was thinking when he committed the heinous act. When so many live in fear after an attack, it was bold and brave. But it was also heart-warming, strong and poignant because she was effusive in her praise of the community support that she received during and after her attack.

> I am a daughter. I am a friend. I am a girlfriend.
> I am a pupil. I am a cousin. I am a niece. I am a
> neighbour. I am the employee who served everyone
> down the road coffee in the café under the railway.

> All the people who form those relations to me
> make up my community and you assaulted every
> single one of them. You violated the truth that I
> will never cease to fight for and which all of those
> people represent: that there are infinitely more
> good people in the world than bad.

She was also upliftingly defiant in the way that she was responding to the attack, making clear how she would not change her everyday life to stay safer, because she had an unwavering belief in the goodness of the world and particularly her local community. And this came with an inspiring and heart-felt belief that the bad guys would not win:

> I'm sure you remember the 7/7 bombings. I'm also
> sure you'll remember how the terrorists did not
> win, because the whole community of London got
> back on the Tube the next day. You've carried out
> your attack, but now I'm getting back on my Tube.

> My community will not feel we are unsafe walking
> back home after dark. We will get on the last
> train home and we will walk up our streets alone,
> because we will not submit to the idea that we are
> putting ourselves in danger in doing so.

> We will continue to come together, like an
> army, when any member of our community is
> threatened. This is a fight you will not win.

I am sure there are many reasons why Ione chose to write her wonderful letter, but one of the influences was the social media #notguilty campaign that launched at that time. This movement was partly launched to give victims of sexual violence and assault a platform to speak anonymously and also in order to provide a support network that empowered victims with a sense of solidarity. But it was also launched in response to the concept of victim-blaming – "the idea that a victim's actions, body, or choices are to blame for sexual assault". The campaign asserted that blame and guilt rest fully with the attacker and they are 100% right in what they say.

Ione was a normal girl, walking home down the street where she lived, and was just unlucky to be tracked and attacked. Had she been drunk or provocatively dressed, would that have changed things? No, of course not. After being interrupted by the victim's neighbours in this first attack, he returned to the Tube station to target another victim, just emphasising that he was a bad or troubled person, and she was just unlucky to be targeted. But even if he had not done this, there is still no fault with the victim. The guilt is always 100% with the aggressor. In cases like this, we all know the difference between right and wrong, and there should be no debate. Whatever the motive, reason, temptation or provocation, the attacker is completely responsible. They can't blame anything in their life, and they can't blame anything the victim has done. They must shoulder the blame themselves and accept full responsibility for their actions.

The only time I have been a victim of a violent crime was when I was on holiday in South Africa. I was fully aware of the high crime rate in the city and was warned of the need to be careful. I was therefore particularly conscious of this when I first arrived. Get away from the affluent and safe tourist areas and you do feel very wary, and I therefore followed all the good advice about wearing no valuables, taking as little money as possible and the best guidance of all, which was to have a second wallet with little inside. If anyone approached me and demanded money, I could give them the second wallet and would lose nothing more than a small amount of cash. My cards and anything that would be more challenging to replace would be kept safe. Little did I think this advice would be so valuable!

One day, my partner went shopping and I decided to get on the open-air tour bus which snaked its way around the centre of Cape Town and then headed out to some of the nicest beaches. It all started wonderfully, and I popped around some of the tourist locations before getting off at the Parliament buildings and walking through The Company's Garden just next door. This was a lovely area with beautiful buildings and pretty gardens, and it all felt very touristy and safe. When ready to go, I could have walked back to the bus stop I had disembarked, but as I would do in any other city, I realised I could exit the park on the other side and walk just a couple of blocks up to one of the next stops. Just two blocks, what could possibly go wrong? Well… quite a lot, unfortunately! I hadn't made it more than about ten metres outside the park, when I realised that I had made a mistake, as I could see men loitering all around. Before I had the chance to turn and head back into the park, one of them was beside me, holding a knife just below my neck and demanding money. Fortunately, the second wallet trick seemed to work; and he lowered the knife and I just ran to safety, still shaking, but obviously immensely relieved.

In relation to the story about Ione, I reflected on the issue of victim blaming, and categorically reiterated that no blame should reside with her. But what about my mugging in Cape Town? Who was responsible for this attack? Well, once again, it was totally the fault of the attacker. There may be real poverty in South Africa that provides some sense of a motive or explanation, but this goes nowhere to justifying the action of threatening someone at knifepoint. The attacker must have known what he was doing was wrong, and yet still went ahead with it. However desperate he was for some money, whether it was just for him or whether it was to feed a starving family, this was wrong, and he should take full responsibility for his terrible actions. I do not doubt this or ascribe any semblance of guilt to myself. But in a dangerous city, had my stroll through some luxurious government areas left me rather more relaxed and laid back about my security than was appropriate? Absolutely! Was I a bit naïve to take a route (even if it was just two blocks) through an area that I did not know was safe? Probably yes – I certainly wouldn't have done it on the first day! To be more direct and to the point, had I taken an unnecessary risk that I probably should have avoided? In hindsight, absolutely yes. I shoulder no guilt for what happened, but I genuinely believe I should have been more careful.

There are plenty of similar situations we could imagine:

1. Suppose you are visiting a city with a lot of poverty and a high crime rate, would you go out showing off expensive jewellery or a Rolex watch, or brandishing your expensive camera or your flashy mobile phone? Not if you want to keep them until the end of the holiday!

2. Suppose you leave a bar and become aware of a shifty-looking hooded man who starts following you. Would you turn down an unlit side-street as this is the quickest way to get home? Not if you want to get home safely!

3. Suppose you went to a peaceful protest and became aware of a group of activists who were planning to get violent and started taunting the police. Would you stay around to carry on your peaceful protest? Not if you wanted to avoid being at the centre of a riot!

In an ideal world, we could give a different answer to these questions. In an ideal world, we would not need to hide our possessions, or take the long route home or leave the protest early when things started to get a bit "lively". But unfortunately, we don't live in an ideal world. We live in a world where there are people who do bad things and we need to take precautions to keep ourselves safe. Some crimes will happen just because we're in the wrong place at the wrong time. They are bad luck and there was nothing we could have done. But sometimes, we know there is a risk. If we take the risk and become a victim, then we are still not to blame. However, that should not stop us from admonishing ourselves for putting ourselves in danger.

And if we are lucky enough to escape unscathed (as I was in Cape Town), then we can take away the valuable lessons for next time.

A BBC drama called *The Last Train* went a step further than this in questioning not only the responsibility to keep ourselves safe, but also our role in keeping other people safe. The scenario involved some people on a late-night train home from London, gradually emptying as it approached the end of the line. Everything focused on a young woman travelling alone, an unknown stranger who was being aggressively flirtatious with her and then a third man who was observing the situation. We reached a point when these were the only three people left on the carriage. The woman felt extremely unsafe and was making plenty of eye contact with the observer who was fully aware of the danger. Despite them not knowing each other and not even talking to each other, the woman was taking a lot of comfort from another person being present, and the man knew that he probably had a key role in keeping the woman safe.

At this point, we arrive at the penultimate stop, which is where the observer is getting off the train. The woman looks at him pleadingly as he leaves the train, he looks a bit hesitant and guilty about leaving her on her own. However, despite both of their reservations, he leaves the train and she stays on, alone with the aggressive male. He feels guilty for a short while, but once back home and after a good night's sleep, he thinks nothing of it, until he hears on the news that a woman was assaulted on the way home from the station and then finds out that it was the woman that he had seen on the train. Would circumstances have been different if he had stayed an extra stop?

I have to be honest that I found the tone of the drama a little bit irritating in the sense that they appeared to place a lot of blame on the third party. Why did he not stay on the train for an extra stop and make sure she got home safely? Any of us would feel a bit guilty if we were in his shoes, but was it really his responsibility to intervene? I would ask a completely different question, based on my earlier questions about personal responsibility. Why did the woman not choose to leave the train a stop early? As soon as she realised that she was going to be all alone with the aggressive man, why didn't she take steps to make herself safe? I have been on trains, including late night ones, where there have been aggressive individuals or groups, and on more than one occasion, I have either moved carriages or exited the train and got a bus or taxi the rest of the way. It is not her fault that she was attacked, but why didn't she take the simple actions that would have avoided an obvious risk? Ultimately, even though we may disagree as to who should have acted, we had a situation where two people knew that there was a very high chance of a crime being committed, and neither of them took the responsibility to eliminate the risk. Why did neither of them feel that personal accountability?

Hindsight is a wonderful thing, but in instances like this, we should not need it, as we can see the dangers that are likely to unfold. When this is the case, simple actions to avoid the inevitable consequences are just common sense. Whilst premeditated crimes that are planned (such as the assault on the Oxford student) may be impossible to avoid, other crimes are more opportunist in nature, and these are much more preventable. Imagine the following examples:

1. Suppose you leave your iPhone and wallet on the table in the pub when you go to the toilet because everyone seems friendly. Would you be surprised if it's gone when you come back?

2. Suppose you take out £500 from the cashpoint and you walk down the street counting the money. Would you feel you had been careless if someone grabbed it out of your hands?

3. Suppose you leave your laptop on the back seat of your car in full view of people walking past. Would you regret that if you came back to find a smashed window and no laptop?

Just as in the examples before, none of these actions remove any of the blame from the culprit. It is not acceptable to steal something just because it is on public display! We shouldn't need to hide and protect our valuables, and within reason, we should be able to dress, behave and do what we like, benefiting from a sense of respectful freedom. But whilst that freedom is a very simple principle, the world is sadly not that simple! People get drunk, they need the money, they're addicted to drugs and desperate, they're being egged on by a gang who think it's hard or cool, or they're just plain bad – and they will do bad things. Nobody can ever remove responsibility from the person who commits the crime. We know what is right and wrong, and there's no dispute on this. But whilst we may reminisce about the trusted world of yesteryear, we all know that in modern times we should lock our house, car or bicycle, and that we should keep our valuables concealed. This is just common sense. There are bad people out there and provoking them, or tempting them with easy prizes, is unwise in the extreme. We would never offer a drink to an alcoholic, so why would we "tempt" the bad guys to commit a crime? We can never guarantee our safety, but taking personal responsibility to try and minimise the risks by way of common-sense precautions will go a long way to keeping us safe.

This sense of personal responsibility to look after ourselves extends well beyond crime into many other areas of our life. We are applying the same common sense if we choose to put money away in "rainy day" savings or a pension fund; or if we live a healthy lifestyle to keep ourselves fit and well. We don't have to do these things, and many choose not to. These sensible measures do not guarantee a comfortable retirement and a long, healthy life; and the failure to take them does not ensure the opposite. All that happens is fluctuations in the level of risk, and this therefore depends greatly on our appetite to risk and to what extent we want to manage the ups and downs.

One great example where we all choose to take different levels of risk is cycling. Some people are happy to cycle down busy roads, bustling with traffic including big lorries and buses; whilst others simply think that is too dangerous and are not prepared to take the risk. Some people will always cycle in a helmet, even if they are in quiet surroundings; while others will take to that busy road, and still consider that any form of head protection is a completely unnecessary precaution. Our attitude to risk means that we see the level of danger in completely different ways. Whilst the risk-averse see hazards everywhere, the risk-taker is a bit blasé and will happily race through red lights or slide up the inside of traffic. They are either blind to the hazards, totally comfortable with their ability to deal with them or relaxed about the potential consequences. And whilst it is possible for these risk-takers to be completely unaware of the risks, they are usually conscious of the risks, they just do not take them that seriously. You just need to see the parent who tells their child to wear a helmet but doesn't bother themselves, to know that people can be aware of risks without feeling the need to take any personal precautions. Bizarrely, we often have more concern for those that we love than we do for ourselves!

Now, cycling is a particularly good example of this personal responsibility, not only because we all need to decide how much risk to take, but because there are two parties involved. Cyclists have the dubious pleasure of sharing the roads with vehicles; and the high number of accidents sadly tells us that this is sometimes not a good combination! When these accidents do occur, the victim is likely to be the cyclist – whatever protection they are wearing, they are far more vulnerable than the motorist sitting inside his protective metal box! However, unlike the crime examples from earlier, being the victim does not necessarily mean being the innocent party. Take a walk down any London street and we will probably see numerous examples of bad driving and bad cycling. As a result, whilst some collisions are caused by drivers being careless or not paying sufficient attention to their fellow law-abiding road-users, others are caused by the reckless manoeuvres of brave or brainless cyclists who seem to know no fear. The cause of the accident will vary on a case-by-case basis, and ultimately, we need both sides to be acting responsibility if everyone is to stay safe.

In situations like this where we are needing a sense of personal accountability from two sides, then we normally need a bit of mutual respect, something that is often lacking in the turf-war between motorists and cyclists. When we have high opinions of each other, we tend to behave in a positive and constructive manner towards each other, something that can rapidly degenerate into the blame game we see on the roads when this respect is taken away. Sadly, this does not just apply to cycling!

Looking at ourselves, we may think we generally rise above this sort of behaviour; but if we honestly self-reflect, we may be surprised by just how often we display an unconscious lack of respect for those around us. Have you ever been standing in a lift when you have seen someone rushing to get in, and you have just allowed the doors to close so that you get the lift to yourself? I certainly have! Immediately after we have done this, we feel a little bit guilty and therefore tend to self-justify our actions. We may reassure ourselves that we are running late, or that we need to get to a meeting on time, but we do not actually know if the other person is in the same position. The reality is that we are placing our needs above the needs of the other person.

This may be a trivial example, but we do these sorts of things all the time. There is a wonderful book by The Arbinger Institute called *Leadership and Self-Deception* which calls these actions "self-betrayal". These are actions we do, where we act contrary to what we feel we should do for another person. We are fully aware of what the right and kind thing to do is in this instance, but for whatever reason, we choose not to do it. This makes us feel a bit guilty, and we don't like that feeling of guilt, so we look to justify our actions. By doing this, we successfully manage to make ourselves feel justified and innocent, but is this really the case? Although on a less serious charge, isn't this the same principle as my mugger justifying his actions because he was languishing in poverty? Ultimately, we are both doing wrong, and then exacerbating this by making excuses for our actions,

The book has a definition for this as well and calls it "self-deception". For each individual case, this is simply just deceiving ourselves into feeling that we haven't done anything wrong. However, whilst it is possible that this was an isolated instance, it is more likely that we do these things more frequently than that. This does not mean we let the lift shut every time, or that we queue jump in our car every time we are behind the wheel. But we may do it when we're late or stressed or in a rush. It is effectively a characteristic that we do these self-betrayals under a certain set of circumstances. We approach other people with a belief that our needs are more important than theirs and use the reassuring "self-deception" to shield us from any guilt and to stop us from feeling we are doing anything wrong. We may not want to admit it, but we are acting as if we are superior to those around us.

And this sense of superiority is just as prevalent in conversations, normally because one or both of us think we know better! When this happens, we are putting ourselves in a position of superiority and as a result, we usually fail to give the other person and their views the respect they deserve. In effect, we are standing in the lift and pushing the "door close" button as the other person is approaching. We are entering the conversation with a biased perspective where we are sure that we are right and equally sure that the other person is wrong, and this should never be the case. We should be open to listening and learning, just as much as explaining! In fact, even if we are genuinely "superior", as a subject matter expert or teacher, then we still should enter the conversation with this goal. If I reflect on the best lessons at school, this was where the teachers appreciated the good questions that made them think and where they were happy and prepared to get into a good dialogue. They were clearly in a superior position with much greater knowledge that they needed to impart and share, but they still respected our intelligence and our ability to engage with the subject. These teachers showed how we should approach every interaction, but the truth is that few of us can successfully replicate this respectful approach when we are already convinced the opposition is wrong!

When we have this predetermined view of right and wrong, it is not just our lack of desire to engage that becomes a problem. When we truly believe that our opinion or perspective is superior to those around us, we get in a dangerous cycle of confirmation bias. We exaggerate the strength of our own argument and severely underestimate the strength of the opposing view. This leads us to becoming increasingly confident in our own opinion. Rather than self-reflect when someone disagrees, we just see our opponent as a dumb-ass for their failure to see the truth. As we lose respect and start to blame their stupidity, we start to display the behaviours that we shouldn't, talking to our adversary in a way that we know is inappropriate. But we are so deep in our self-deception, that our behaviour is excusable because of the manifest stupidity of our counterpart. It is all their fault!!!! The problem is that whilst we believe this, and are stuck in that mindset, we would not know the truth if it hit us in the face!

The Arbinger Institute gives a simply fantastic example of this, and I will probably fail to do it full justice by trying to paraphrase. However, I will try my best!!! They use an example of a mother and her son (Kate and Bryan), where Bryan has been an irresponsible teenager over many years. Even though Kate loves her son very much, the frustration at his track record means that she keeps a very close eye on him, disciplines him harshly and tends to be overcritical of his actions and behaviour. Bryan, being on the receiving end of this parenting, sees a nosey and interfering mother, who is a bit dictatorial and does not have a good word to say about him. Any love that his mother has for him is buried under some unfriendly and confrontational parenting, and so Bryan simply does not see it. Whilst the intention behind the firm messaging from his mother is to get him to toe the line, do what he is told and to be more responsible; it is more likely to have the opposite effect because once he sees the lack of love, Bryan fails to see the good intentions.

This is a classic example of self-deception and self-betrayal. Kate is behaving poorly towards her son – someone she really loves (self-betrayal). However, she feels that it is justified because she is seeing it as a reaction to the way her son is behaving and is blind to just how badly she is talking to her son and the impact that it is having (self-deception). Similarly, Bryan is behaving poorly and irresponsibly when he knows that this is massively upsetting his mother – someone he deeply loves (self-betrayal). However, he feels that it is justified because he sees it as a reaction to the antagonistic and unloving parenting he is receiving and is blind to just how hurtful his behaviour is (self-deception). Both of them are blaming each other, and in doing so are inflating the faults of the guilty party and exaggerating their innocence in proceedings.

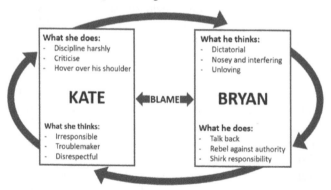

The above diagram hopefully helps to highlight the vicious circle that results from this blame culture. When we are blaming somebody, then we tend to react negatively to their behaviour, and do not therefore respond in the most constructive manner. In addition, we apply the oversimplistic crime mentality that says there is only one guilty party, and we therefore excuse our negative responses and excuse ourselves from any responsibility. As a result, it keeps going around and can quite easily start to spiral as our reactions becoming increasingly dysfunctional.

This is exactly what happened in the Kate and Bryan situation. The book describes a specific situation as an example of this, where Bryan asks if he could borrow his parents' car to go out one evening. Kate's strategy was to try and look like the "good" person by saying yes, but imposing a very early curfew as a condition, something that she thought Bryan would refuse to accept. However, Bryan said that was fine, took the keys and headed out. Kate then had an appalling evening stressing about why she had let him go, as he would be as irresponsible as usual and come home late. Five minutes before the curfew and no sign of her son, you can just imagine the intensity of her irritation. However, much to her surprise, with about a minute to the deadline, she hears the car rushing into the driveway, and her son appears back at home just in time!

Put yourself in Kate's situation, and have a guess what you think she said to her son. Obviously, she should have said "thank you", appreciated his efforts and given him the credit for his responsibility. That would be the correct, rational action. However, as she had been raging all evening about her son's irresponsibility and was completely convinced that he was going to demonstrate this again, she was not thinking rationally. As a result, what she actually said was something along the lines of "You cut that a bit fine, didn't you?" Her son had done exactly what she asked. He had respected her wishes, even though she had intentionally imposed a curfew that she knew was a bit unreasonable. He had been responsible, the thing that she most wanted. And yet she had rewarded him with a snide remark! Effectively, she had got what she most wanted (i.e. a responsible son) but was quite irritated that he had proved her wrong. Once we are in this cycle of blame, then we would often prefer to be proved right, rather than get what we want!

The battle between cyclists and motorists and the squabbles between a mother and her teenage son may seem very different things, but they both show the dire consequences of the blame culture that arises when we start to lose respect for each other. To rise above this, despite any provocation that we may perceive, we need to take personal accountability for our own role in the discussion or interaction, ensuring it is as respectful, constructive and blame-free as is humanly possible. If we can do this, we have more chance of encouraging the other person to behave in a similarly positive way, and we have a better chance of a productive discussion.

I would love to claim that I manage to avoid getting into these vicious circles, but that would not be honest! Although I am still guilty at times, the worst patch for me in this respect, was when I first met my husband. Being two completely different people, the first few months were quite an experience as we tried to work each other out; and unfortunately, these spiralling self-betrayals became a rather regular occurrence! In fact, I don't think it is an underestimate to say that we had considerably more arguments in the first six months than we have had in the subsequent 20 years. Even though I did not think so at the time, many of these arguments were caused by me, and there was one that became especially toxic. Everything all tracked back to one very simple and innocent comment he made: "Oh... you're not playing tennis again this Sunday, are you?"

Had I been in a positive mindset at the time, away from the arguments we had been having, I would have interpreted this correctly as a desire to spend time with me! And his comment was valid. As I did not live near the tennis club I played at, a tennis match was a bit of a day-killer, even if I enjoyed it. Considering as well that I worked during the days in the week, and he worked during the evenings, then the weekend was important for us to get some quality time together. Sadly, that was not the rational way I interpreted it. I took it as a rather unsubtle dig from my unsporty boyfriend and started to resent the fact that he was stopping me from doing things that I loved and had always done before we met. He never stopped me once, but once I had interpreted his message in that way, I genuinely believed he had. Each time there was an opportunity to play tennis, I did one of two things. Either I would make some sarcastic remark to him and just go off to play tennis anyway, or I would make the "sacrifice" but just spend the whole afternoon whingeing and moaning. Unsurprisingly, he interpreted this as me not wanting to spend time with him and therefore started to make snide remarks and to genuinely complain about my love for sports and my avoidance of the opportunity to spend time together. It may have been a reaction to me, but in my head, I now had real reason to be annoyed at his comments. Round and round we would therefore go, with the topics broadening and the frustration intensifying.

The irony is that we both wanted to spend loads of time together. Despite our arguments, we were in the exciting early days of our relationship and completely smitten with each other. However, our self-deception and the resulting self-betrayal meant that just like Kate and her son, we achieved the exact opposite of this. When we were together, we were sulking, sniping at each other and arguing – basically just annoying the hell out of each other. As a result, we started to spend less time together – going to play a tennis match was even more desirable when the alternative was moping my way around a shopping centre on a Saturday afternoon! As in the previous examples, once we both started to blame each other, we were completely blind to our own failings and pinned everything on the dysfunctional behaviour of our partner. We got ourselves in the cycle and it suddenly became very hard to see the way out. And what was the outcome of this? As is always the case once we are blaming each other, both of us thought we were right, but neither of us got what we wanted.

It is probably very easy for you all to picture similar instances to these, where anger or frustration propel us into our mindset where we cease to be constructive, and we rapidly descend into these spirals. We get ourselves trapped in situations where just like Kate, we behave in a way that exacerbates the other person's behaviour, even though that is the opposite of we want. This may be most common in the case of family rows where emotions are running high. However, the reality is that the same happens in more formal debates and discussions, and this is what causes them to rapidly spiral into arguments. Once this has happened:

1. We cease to believe that we are two people with different perspectives and start to fundamentally believe there is right and wrong. And obviously, we are the ones that are right! As a result, we assume a sense of superiority as we are completely convinced that our arguments have more merit. We start to overestimate the quality of our own argument and understate the quality of our opponent's views, and we therefore find it impossible to consider that we are any part of the problem;

2. If our opponent does not budge as we think they should, we believe they are uninformed, stubborn or stupid. We therefore start to get irritated, frustrated and irrational. Rather than stopping to think clearly how we may influence things, we tend to respond in a way that reflects our frustration. This just helps to exacerbate the spiralling situation. Because we think the opponent is stupid, we find it impossible to consider that we are any part of the problem;

3. Now that we are sinking into an argument, we are getting emotional and blaming the other side. We often cannot remember exactly how the argument started, but we know it wasn't us! If the other party made the first confrontational remark, then it's their fault. If we made the first confrontational remark, it's because they annoyed us or were stupid, so it's still their fault. We think we are the victim and our opponent is the guilty one, and yet again, we find it impossible to consider that we are any part of the problem.

To avoid these pitfalls, we both need to enter the discussion as equals, and we both need to be acting responsibly. It is not enough for just one of us to think this way, as we tend to get the reaction we deserve. If we are negative, sniping or condescending, we will induce the same reaction from our counterpart. If they are very confrontational towards us, then we would need to be a saint to maintain a calm demeanour and will probably get pulled down to their level. Ultimately, we both need to apply the same sense of responsibility if we are to have any chance of a good conversation.

This sense of personal responsibility is needed as we enter a discussion, but it becomes even more important once we have started the slide into an argument. Once this has happened, we are probably both frustrated with the other party and convinced that they started it. But by blaming them, however justified that may be, we are doing nothing but adding fire to the situation. As a result, one of us needs to be big enough to acknowledge our accountability and change our perspective. We often have a reluctance to do this, feeling that we are taking the blame and exonerating the other person of their responsibility, but one of us needs to take the lead and as John Maxwell once said:

> A good leader is a person who takes a little more
> than his share of the blame, and a little less than
> his share of the credit.

In any case, this is not a crime-like situation where there is a simplistic allocation of blame and innocence, based on the principles of right and wrong. In this instance, we probably have at least some element of blame, even if it is purely the way we reacted to something that was said. In addition, accepting some accountability is by no means excusing the other party of blame. After all, it takes two to tango!

This admission of accountability is all about someone taking the lead in extracting ourselves from the malignant situation. But just as it needs two people to take responsibility for a good conversation, we need two people to take responsibility for saving us from a bad one. If the other party does a Bryan and surprises us by offering an olive branch with their actions or their words and we just throw it back in their face in the way that Kate did, then we will just drag everything back down into the negative spiral. Bryan stepped out of his self-betrayal, gave her an opportunity to do the same, but she was unable to take it. It is best of all if we can take the lead in resurrecting the discussion, but if we are beaten to it, it is crucial that we react and respond in the right way. This is our opportunity to lift us out of the hole.

Now it sounds incredibly easy to say that we should take personal responsibility to rescue ourselves from an argument, but we all know that it is not quite as easy as it sounds. This is mainly because when we are arguing, we are not seeing things clearly and thinking rationally. It is therefore incredibly difficult to take this backward step. It needs us to self-reflect, acknowledge that we are not helping the situation and work out the appropriate shift in behaviour and language that will best bring us back from argument do discussion. We can sit and wait for the other person to take that lead, but it is much better for us to follow the guidance of Michael Jackson in his beautiful song, 'Man in the Mirror', and to take the lead ourselves.

We need to take the lead, but it also needs to be convincing! Sincerity is important, and this is not easy when we are angry or blaming the other person. This means that we cannot just apply some course-learned "skills" to pretend we are taking responsibility. It means we really need to care as it will be perfectly obviously if we don't. In fact, a bit of fake management talk could make matters even worse. As outlined in The Arbinger Institute book:

> The point is we can sense how others are feeling toward us. Given a little time, we can always tell when we're being coped with, manipulated, or outsmarted. We can always detect the hypocrisy. We can always feel the blame concealed beneath veneers of niceness. And we typically resent it. It

won't matter if the other person tries managing by walking around, sitting on the edge of the chair to practice active listening, inquiring about family members to show interest, or using any other skill learned in order to be effective. What we'll know and respond to is how that person is regarding us when doing those things.

Putting it more simply, we need to "walk the walk" as well as "talk the talk". The importance of showing a genuine desire to properly engage in discussion cannot be overstated. This is not about tricks or techniques or pretences, but a genuine effort to invest ourselves into the process of exchanging ideas, caring about what the other person is saying and sharing the responsibility to make it a success. We also need the ability to share the blame when things go wrong. Whilst a clear allocation of blame to a single culprit may be appropriate in a criminal trial, with a clear definition of right and wrong, there are other circumstances where shared blame is much more appropriate. Conversation is one of these circumstances, because it needs two people working together to be successful, and as soon as one person blames the other, then the engagement and collaboration completely falls apart.

We can only really engage in a productive discussion when we approach it with honesty and sincerity and give the other person the respect they deserve, continuing to treat people fairly, even when we feel there is justification to do otherwise. We should always strive to intellectually challenge people when they wrong or offend us, and never get tempted by revenge in either word or action. However right we believe we are, we should enter the conversation as equals and share the responsibility for maintaining that balance throughout. This will allow us to avoid the destructive outcomes of an argument and reap the benefits of a great discussion, with a true meeting of minds, exchanging ideas and establishing the truth, whatever that may be.

TENTH PRINCIPLE

Share the blame for the argument and take the lead to save the discussion

CHAPTER 12

The Ingredients of the Perfect Discussion

As we have meandered through the chapters of this book, we have scraped the surface of some incredibly complex subjects. Many of us have strong opinions or emotional reactions around these topics, and that should absolutely be the case. They are critically important as they influence the way we live our lives, the way that society is constructed and the way our future will develop. However, whilst these subjects are incredibly important, and the viewpoints from many are deep-rooted, passionate and informed, the quality of discussion that results simply does not reflect this. The book has shown how many of these discussions descend into confrontational jousting from polarised and inflexible protagonists, which is more reminiscent of pantomime slapstick than intellectual debate. This serves nobody and we could make so much more progress on these complex issues if we could combine the insight, knowledge and perspectives from all sides. This diversity of thought and idea will always give us the best answer, but we will only realise its true value when there is a true meeting of the minds within a proper discussion.

In response to this, this book has used a mix of facts, observations, personal experience and psychology to allow us all, for a short while at least, to think about these subjects in a different way. It has tried to suspend any focus on what is right and wrong and allow us to reflect on how we approach the discussion and why this contributes to the declining quality of debate. Having done so, I would like to think it has made us all a bit more aware that we are all contributing to this escalating problem, and it is not always someone else's fault! In fact, I have been on this journey of self-realisation as I have been writing, having started thinking I had so much to share and having finished thinking that I have so much to learn! As a result, hopefully the principles and themes from the book will help all of us to improve the way we engage with each other and enable us to reap the benefits.

As we reflect on the multitude of themes covered in the book and pull together the guiding principles of a good discussion, we should start by remembering the Korean girl who spent 30 minutes asking me questions about homosexuality with a deep curiosity and an innocent fascination. If we truly stand back and reflect on our daily lives, how often do we really do that? How often do we look at someone and genuinely think that they must have great insight from which we would like to learn? How often do we ask these people open questions and encourage them to talk and share that knowledge? How often do we listen with a great hunger and desire to gain that new information?

I think these questions are best answered by the quote from Simon Sinek, when he said that:

> We may believe that we are good listeners, but
> listening is more than waiting for your turn
> to interrupt.

Not only are our listening skills worse than we often think, but they tend to become even worse when we have strong opinions as this just inflates our desire to get our point across. It is so important to remember that a good discussion requires more than one person, and that we therefore need to get the right balance of talking and listening. This doesn't just mean that we give them time to say their piece at the start before we take the floor! This means listening throughout such that our verbal exchanges are not preprepared speeches but are actively evolving to take account of what we have just heard. True active listening requires us to think but it makes the discussion and conversation so much more powerful.

FIRST PRINCIPLE

Maintain an open mind and a preparedness to listen all the way to the finish line

Listening is a good start, but going beyond this, how often are we prepared to use that knowledge to challenge and evolve and unravel our current perspectives? As adults, we have allegedly become older and wiser, but somehow many of us seem to have lost that ability to learn. We seem to think that we can't "teach an old dog new tricks", but is that really the case? As a child we think we need to learn from adults who know better and we therefore go about the world with that natural curiosity. As soon as we grow up, it is as if we think we are the finished article and we suddenly seem more motivated about sharing our knowledge than learning something new. In addition, when we look at our children, we give them credit for learning and the extra knowledge and insight they have taken on. As adults, our long memories tend to focus on reminding people of the way they used to think, rather than celebrating that their thinking has evolved. Maybe if we approached the world with childlike curiosity and appreciated people's efforts to change, we would find we are just as capable in our old age?

The reality is that the greatest people never seem to stop learning. During the book I discussed Richard the Lionheart's great curiosity to learn from his enemies, and Roger Federer's tireless and ageless focus on self-improvement. However, as far as I am concerned, the ultimate role model for timeless learning was Gandhi. We see him as a man of incredible wisdom, but he got there and stayed there by learning from everything that he saw and heard. As per the wonderful exchange with one of his followers who asked:

> Gandhi ji, I don't understand you. How can you say one thing last week, and something quite different this week?

We need to all think like Gandhi, when he replied:

> Ah… because I have learned something since last week.

That readiness to learn from our surroundings and the courage to withstand the criticism about being weak or indecisive if we change our mind are great lessons for us all.

SECOND PRINCIPLE

Never stop learning and have the courage to change your mind

Whilst the ability to listen and the open mind to absorb counter-opinions are both important to learning, another key factor is our ability to self-reflect. As discussed throughout the book, the experiences of our life shape so much about what we believe, and whilst this adds positively to our knowledge and insight, it also fills us with assumptions, biases and prejudices. Our gut reaction will be heavily influenced by the beliefs and mindsets that we have created for ourselves, and through confirmation bias, we are likely to reinforce whatever we currently think. If we act like the parents in *The House of Tiny Tearaways* who believe the problems are all with their children, then we will never get to the right answer. As we gain new insight, we should start by looking at ourselves to understand how we are contributing, before we transfer our attention elsewhere.

And whilst this is very relevant to our behaviours, it is equally important to our opinions on major topics. They are hugely shaped by our surroundings, the people we interact with and the newspapers we read, and none of this is as impartial as we may think. Every bit of news or history or information, however factual it may appear, is actually the perspective of the person who recorded it. Moreover, our interpretation of that information, however objective it may appear, is just our perspective on that information. This means that information we consider as facts are not always quite as factual as we believe. It is invaluable to realise this, so that when new information comes along that contradicts what we thought or believed, we don't dismiss it as nonsense, but we process it and think about it. Only through this process of self-reflection will we get the chance to re-evaluate our prior knowledge, and to see if the foundations of our beliefs are as firm as we thought.

THIRD PRINCIPLE

Cherish new insight and use it to self-reflect and challenge your entrenched beliefs

Having developed our self-awareness, and really got to know ourselves, there is one other thing we need to think about before we start boldly sharing our opinions. With the risk of stating the obvious, we must realise that we are not all the same! Whilst we may think we know this; our behaviour tends to suggest that we don't as we are incredibly adept in believing that two people who are given the same information will reach the same conclusion. And if they don't? Well... they are either stupid or wrong! Bizarrely, we think that everyone does this except us, which is why we love to criticise our politicians for being "out of touch" without realising we are probably equally (if not more) unaware.

We have a natural desire to try and blend in with the crowd, but the world is richer when we appreciate our individual differences and celebrate diversity rather than just tolerate it. The differences between us are the world's greatest gift, even if we often don't treat them that way. By avoiding the temptation of assuming we are right or that we know better, we start to appreciate that other people's experiences are different, their knowledge is different and as a result, quite validly, their opinions might be different. In addition, when we show that openness, we are repaid in kind. When we presume knowledge or show our prejudice, we encourage behaviour such as the young girl in the short film *Balcony* who said:

I tell them what they're already thinking.

But when we show our warmth and appreciation, we get to the truth and we learn so much. All that is needed is our ability to bite our tongue and let them talk, even when we are getting overexcited and are desperate to throw our opinions into the melting pot! When we let people talk and ask them purposeful questions, we can learn so much from the incredible diversity in the world.

--- FOURTH PRINCIPLE ---

Explore the perspective of others with curiosity and a desire to understand

Once we gain this appreciation that other people are different with contrasting views that are completely valid, this raises another interesting realisation that was the title of Chapter 6 – right for me is not necessarily right for you. Again, this sounds like something obvious that we all should know, but do we? Do we act in conversation like we understand this simple truth? In reality, we have a great tendency to impart our own perspective with the blinkered view that it will automatically apply to our audience. For example, we may share what makes us happy or successful, but do it with the expectation that it will work for everyone else like some magic pill. Moreover, we sometimes then wonder why we are not getting any gratitude for our amazing suggestions that should have fixed everything! Once we truly appreciate our differences, we hopefully start to realise that the world is not that simple.

At least if we have taken the time to get a bit of insight on their personality, perspective and circumstance, we may have a chance of knowing how our suggestion may fit with them, and we can start to evaluate whether it may be appropriate or if it needs to be adapted. We can then start to understand the potential impact on them, and therefore get some sense of whether we will be impacting them for the better or the worse. Without this, we are shooting in the dark. Moreover, as we share our guidance and advice, although we may not be forcing the other person to make a change, we should never underestimate our influence. Whilst it is true that:

> A wise man makes his own decisions. An ignorant
> man follows public opinion.

.... nobody can be wise about everything, and we all know things where we have drifted with the crowd when it was not in our best interests. As a result, we should take a bit more responsibility to ensure our views will be helpful to the recipient before we start sharing. With a bit more thought, we may be able to see whether our view is just an opinion or something that would benefit others, and only then do we know if and how we should share that information.

--------------------- FIFTH PRINCIPLE ---------------------

Appreciate our individual differences before you share your views

But this concept of different versions of the truth is one of the main things that makes some of these topics so horribly complicated. Our natural tendency is to try and simplify things to make them more manageable and easier to process. When we study physics in school, we might solve a problem about a falling rock by assuming it was a sphere with even density all the way through and to ignore any friction or air resistance. But we do that with everything, trying to eliminate all the insignificant factors that overcomplicate things so that we can focus on what is relevant. This is highly effective in physics but is also highly effective in the way we make decisions and therefore hugely influential in the way we form our opinions. To a certain extent, that is exactly what we should do in discussions as well. Drowning in irrelevant details or immaterial exceptions is unhelpful and can also be an adept tactic of people who are trying to stall or prevent a decision.

But as effective as simplification may be, it only works when we simplify in the right way. Eliminate the wrong "complexities" or focus on confounding factors and we lose all the important insight, will have a misguided conversation, and if there is a decision to be made, quite possibly make the wrong one! Erroneous simplification can be completely intentional, such as "playing the race card" or throwing in an insult to derail the discussion, but as Jean-Jacques Rousseau pointed out:

> Insults are the arguments employed by those who are in the wrong.

But it can also be our unconscious bias, with our one-dimensional perspective leading us to jump to an immediate conclusion without seeing the full story. Either way, a preparedness to explore the necessary complexity is hugely valuable, as is the persistence and capability to calmly process and evaluate this detail and reach a decision when the going gets tough!

---------------- SIXTH PRINCIPLE ----------------

Don't oversimplify with assumptions. Dare to face the complexity!

In order to face this complexity successfully, one of the true challenges is to properly see both sides of the story and to assess them equally. One of the reasons we struggle to do this is "labels", wonderfully helpful tools of simplification that can be empowering and harmful in equal measure. Labels can be particularly problematic when they create a black and white perspective on right and wrong, as we lose the sense of the grey in between. This is particularly problematic as the label is driven by our opinion, as highlighted by the famous quote, which says that:

> One man's terrorist is another man's freedom fighter.

The reality is as soon as we put a label of good or bad on something, then we generalise. We start to think that good people are universally good, failing to notice their bad points or giving them the benefit of the doubt. Similarly, we start to think that bad people are universally bad, ignoring any of their nicer qualities, or working on the assumption that they must have an ulterior motive.

As jokily portrayed in the cartoon, which said that:

> You are not a murderer; you are just a person who murdered someone!

… we should see past the labels if we are going to get to the truth. And whilst this is important in people, it is just as important in our opinions. Undoubtedly, we tend to look at our own arguments and opinions with rose-tinted glasses and think we have got everything right. At the same time, we can look down on those who disagree with the oversimplified presumption that they have got it all wrong! This seriously hampers the discussion. Approaching a conversation with an open mind and being prepared to see the bad in our own argument and the good in theirs is really enlightening, and is the best way to allow us to combine our perspectives in a way that helps us get to the truth.

SEVENTH PRINCIPLE

See the good and bad in everything and always aim to find the truth

Whilst our attitude and mindset towards a conversation are important, if it is more than just an exchange of information and we are actively seeking to persuade someone, it is also very important that there is a purpose to this. Pushing our thoughts, opinions or guidance onto other people is wonderful if we are trying to influence the way they may vote or an action they may take, or if we care for them and we genuinely think it is in their best interests. But if this is not the case, what are we doing it for? Why are we pushing people to do things that we like, rather than encouraging them to do what they like? Why are we pretending we are an expert and shouting an opinion when we don't have much information? Why are we trying to win arguments that are not very important? Whilst we may love those small victories as we journey through our daily lives, they are short-lived and meaningless to us, but can be demotivating and demoralising for the person on the receiving end.

Even if we may start out with a purpose, it is amazing how often we can get distracted on the way. Pushing our thoughts on to someone in the wrong way will just lead them to put up the barricades and defensively block anything we may say, so we need to be thoughtful and constructive in the way we challenge people. And even when we share a purpose with someone, we can be quick to lose sight of that when we do not like the way they are approaching things or if they make a mistake. As soon as we start to criticise, it is easy to get distracted from the purpose by an internal dispute, and both of us shift into a mindset where we are defending what we have done, rather than seeking the path forward. Maintaining the rugby mentality where we charge in behind our teammates in support, even when they make a shockingly bad decision, creates a much more positive environment. But more importantly, it keeps us all focused on the purpose with a more constructive, collaborative mindset and it gives us the very best chance of success.

EIGHTH PRINCIPLE

Don't be a playground bully! Only persuade with a purpose and good intentions

Whilst we may have a purpose, the conversation is going to be quick if we are the only person with one! It requires two people with conflicting purposes for things to get a bit more interesting. In many cases, the challenge from someone who forcefully disagrees is perceived as a risk and can quickly send us on to the defensive. There is an element of truth in this, as an incredibly slick, informed and compelling argument from an opponent may be a threat. But actually, this is a good thing. If we truly have confidence in our own argument, which hopefully is now the case following the previous eight principles, then we should not get distracted by the threat, but excited by the opportunity that the challenge will provide.

If we are prepared to properly listen and engage, our opponents can tell us some crucial things that our supporters simply cannot provide. Firstly, even if we have the best argument in the world, they will pinpoint the weaknesses. We can "put ourselves in their shoes", empathise with their point of view and try to pre-empt what they may be thinking or how they will challenge, but none of this is as effective as letting our enemies do it. They are best placed to pinpoint any weaknesses, because they are focused on finding them! We should therefore listen and learn from that insight so that we can strengthen our own argument for the next round! Secondly, and probably even more importantly, the opposition can tell us why they think what they do! Only by analysing why people disagree can we devise a line of communication that may help them to change their mind, and this is the route to the floating voters that are key to success. We simply cannot get this knowledge from our supporters and need to realise how powerful our rivals are as a source of insight, even if they are completely wrong!

--------------------- NINTH PRINCIPLE ---------------------

Enjoy challenge as the ultimate chance to strengthen your own argument

Whilst we can do all the above to try and maintain a good quality, intellectual discussion, then with strong and passionate views on both sides, we are not always going to be successful in keeping things cool! At times, it is going to spiral into an argument, and whilst it can sometimes be fun to have a bit of verbal jousting, it will rarely if ever lead to a constructive outcome. Once the red mist has enveloped us, rational thinking quickly disappears, we lose any sense of a coherent discussion, we start to blame the other person for everything and quite probably say things we will later regret. As soon as this happens, we effectively have two options. If it has descended into a slanging match, then we should probably just walk away and then resume proceedings when we have both had the chance to calm down a bit! But assuming it hasn't quite reached that stage, we should placate the situation and guide each other back to the discussion.

Once we are in an argument, and the blame game has started, then it can be hard to take that first step, but it is important that we both take the responsibility for that. Just as with Kate and Bryan in the last chapter, if one person tries to guide us back to a more harmonious and rational discussion, and we just slap that down, then we will be quickly back into a dogfight! Rather than look for someone to blame, we should take the personal responsibility to admit that it takes two people to have an argument and take the lead on guiding us back to a positive and productive discussion.

--------------------- TENTH PRINCIPLE ---------------------

Share the blame for the argument and take the lead to save the discussion

In our personal lives, we all know how invigorating a great conversation can be, when we really learn and have the chance to exchange ideas with someone who has an intelligent but different perspective. When this happens, we both feel we have had an equal chance to learn and educate, and as a result, both of us leave the discussion feeling better than before. The goal of these guiding principles is to help us to have mutually rewarding interactions much more frequently.

I acknowledge that there will be circumstances when applying such guidelines is not easy. In politics, for example, the need to win votes encourages competitive squabbling and a focus on making the opposition look bad! But in truth, while politics may reflect an exaggerated caricature of schoolground behaviour with pantomime arguments, soundbites and cheap shots, the same behaviours are endemic across most discussions we have on a daily basis. When others are talking, we don't listen enough, and we lack the open-minded empathy to properly relate to their views. When we are talking, we resort much too quickly to cheap tactics and distractions as we know that is the easiest way to win. That should stop. We should reframe the boundaries of good conversation, with an emphasis on honest debate, understanding of truth, exchanging of facts and ideas and a desire to achieve the "best" solution for all, whatever that may be. We should open ourselves to the idea, that these values in a discussion need to be cherished and protected. In sport, we expect people to play by the rules and we discredit those who cheat, and we should think the same in conversation. Whilst we may hold a passionate opinion and want to do everything in our powers to influence things in a certain way, we should still believe that winning is only winning if we win fair!

And before we start to attribute these poor behaviours to others and pick out people like Donald Trump as the real culprits, we need to accept that we are equally guilty. We all constantly abuse conversations, just like he does, and the real difference is that he is much more visible and much more successful! As is seen from the polarised views of him, we don't like such behaviours when we don't like the person or their opinions, but we view it very differently if we think the person is on the "right side". The problem is that in our biased minds, we are always on the "right side" and once we have put ourselves there, we don't perceive our behaviours in the same critical way. But we must. Our failure to maintain the values of a good discussion contributes to the problem, and ultimately, this fails everybody as we don't hear the real perspectives, we don't discover the truth and we don't find the best solution.

But all is not lost. If we all apply the principles outlined in this book, then I genuinely believe things can change for the better and we can get the true value from the wonderful diversity of opinion that exists in this amazing world. Moreover, if we each commit to entering every conversation with an appreciation of these values and an agreement to play by the rules, then we increase the chance that the other participants in the discussion will respond in the same intelligent and respectful fashion. So, let's start listening, embracing the truth and taking our turn to give opinions. Let's share our thoughts and ideas with passion and insight but without ever losing the emphasis on honesty and openness. Let's be brave enough to take the risk of losing to the better argument, rather than winning at all costs in a deceitful world of half-truths. Let's aspire to be the best, rather than the least bad! Maybe if we do this, others will follow, and we will start to rid ourselves of the lazy, negative and low-quality discussions that are far too frequent in the modern world. Maybe this book will be the first step by guiding us to a better path, where we demand high standards in our discussions and do not accept anything less. Time will tell, and it is certainly time for a change.